START-TO-FINISH
DECKS

ORTHO

Meredith® Books
Des Moines, Iowa

Ortho Start-to-Finish Decks
Writer: Martin Miller
Contributing Graphic Designer: Tim Abramowitz
Senior Associate Design Director: Tom Wegner
Assistant Editor: Harijs Priekulis
Copy Chief: Terri Fredrickson
Copy and Production Editor: Victoria Forlini
Editorial Operations Manager: Karen Schirm
Managers, Book Production: Pam Kvitne,
    Marjorie J. Schenkelberg, Rick von Holdt
Contributing Copy Editor: Barbara Feller-Roth
Contributing Proofreaders: Kathi DiNicola,
    Sara Henderson, David Krause, Catherine Staub
Indexer: Donald Glassman
Editorial and Design Assistants: Renee E. McAtee,
    Karen McFadden

**Additional Editorial Contributions from
    Art Rep Services**
Director: Chip Nadeau
Designer: Ik Design
Illustrator: Dave Brandon

Meredith® Books
Editor in Chief: Linda Raglan Cunningham
Design Director: Matt Strelecki
Executive Editor, Gardening and Home Improvement:
    Benjamin W. Allen
Executive Editor, Home Improvement: Larry Erickson

Publisher: James D. Blume
Executive Director, Marketing: Jeffrey Myers
Executive Director, New Business Development:
    Todd M. Davis
Executive Director, Sales: Ken Zagor
Director, Operations: George A. Susral
Director, Production: Douglas M. Johnston
Business Director: Jim Leonard

Vice President and General Manager: Douglas J. Guendel

Meredith Publishing Group
President, Publishing Group: Stephen M. Lacy
Vice President-Publishing Director: Bob Mate

Meredith Corporation
Chairman and Chief Executive Officer: William T. Kerr

In Memoriam: E.T. Meredith III (1933-2003)

Photographers
(Photographers credited may retain copyright ©
    to the listed photographs.)
L = Left, R = Right, C = Center, B = Bottom, T = Top
Gary Branson: 23B
Ernest Braun: 22T, 26B, 28TR, 54BR, 57TR
Kim Brien: 53B
Crandall & Crandall: 8BR, 9BL, 10TL, 16CR, 17CL, 30BL,
    37TR, 42CL, 52BL
Stephen Cridland: 7B, 16BL, 36TR
Catriona Tudor Erler: 27TL, 34TL
John Fulker: 23T, 24T, 39T, 40BL, 65TR, 81TR
Gjersvik and Associates: 114TR
Saxon Holt: 34BL
Bill Johnson: 51T, 54T
Michael Landis: 21BL, 26TL, 38B
George Lyons: 15T, 15C, 15B
Michael McKinley: 6B, 42BL, 42BR
C. Nilsen: 25TR
Geoffrey Nilsen: 73T
Robert Perron/Positive Images: 10BL, 60BL
Ken Rice: 17TL, 71CR
Susan Roth: 25BL
Marvin Sloben: 20TL, 68T, 69TL
Pam Spalding/Positive Images: 58TL
Southern Pine Council: 31T
Michael Thompson: 30TR, 37BL, 60TR
Unicorn Stock Photos: 9T
Deidre Walpole: 7T
Western Wood Products Association: 66TL
Wholman Wood Products: 6T

All of us at Meredith® Books are dedicated to providing
you with the information and ideas you need to enhance
your home and garden. We welcome your comments and
suggestions about this book. Write to us at:
    Meredith Books
    1716 Locust St.
    Des Moines, IA 50309–3023

If you would like to purchase any of our home improvement,
gardening, cooking, crafts, or home decorating and design
books, check wherever quality books are sold. Or visit us at:
meredithbooks.com

If you would like more information on other Ortho
products, call 800/225-2883 or visit us at: www.ortho.com

Note to the Readers: Due to differing conditions, tools,
and individual skills, Meredith Corporation assumes no
responsibility for any damages, injuries suffered, or losses
incurred as a result of following the information published
in this book. Before beginning any project, review the
instructions carefully, and if any doubts or questions remain,
consult local experts or authorities. Because codes and
regulations vary greatly, you always should check with
authorities to ensure that your project complies with all
applicable local codes and regulations. Always read and
observe all of the safety precautions provided by
manufacturers of any tools, equipment, or supplies,
and follow all accepted safety procedures.

Decks provide the perfect spot for private getaways. Use natural surroundings, like the branches of these mature trees, to enhance the space.

When designing your deck, consider more than its basic function. You'll enjoy it more if you enhance your deck's appearance with colorful furnishings, built-in planters, and other decorative accents.

ADD VALUE TO YOUR HOME

A well-designed deck can increase the value of your home because you're actually adding to its livable area. And the more work you do yourself, the more of your investment you'll recoup. According to the National Association of Home Builders, you can recover an average of about 75 percent of the cost of deck construction when you sell your home.

How much you get back will vary, depending on two factors:

■ The area of the country in which you live.

■ The average resale value of homes in your neighborhood.

One of the key considerations is deciding how long you'll remain in your home. If you plan to stay in your home for some time, how much you get back on your investment may not be important. But if you plan to sell your home in the foreseeable future, do a little research before building your deck. Ask a local realtor if decks are an improvement that potential buyers want and will pay for. Then add the cost of the deck to the average resale value of homes in your neighborhood.

As a general rule, the total costs plus the current market value of your house should not exceed the value of any home in your neighborhood by more than 20 percent. Selling a house priced well above neighboring homes will be difficult.

PLANNING AND DESIGN BASICS

Decks are among the most popular home improvements—and with good reason. They can make your home more spacious, comfortable, and valuable. If you've been thinking about building a deck, you probably have an idea of some of the additional benefits it can offer:

■ More outdoor living space for your family.

■ A relaxing place for casual entertaining.

■ A more attractive yard.

When you get down to actually planning a deck, however, numerous questions arise.

■ Where exactly should you locate it?

■ How big should it be?

■ What special features do you want to include?

■ How will it tie in with the overall landscape?

■ What will it look like?

■ Will it include other structures?

■ What materials should you use?

■ And finally—how do you build it?

Finding answers to these questions will prove much easier if you create your deck with your lifestyle in mind. All deck plans start with the answer to one question: "How will you use your deck?" Whether you plan to use your deck for family dining, entertainment, recreation, quiet contemplation—or all of these activities— you'll enjoy it even more when you create it with these specific purposes in mind.

Building a deck is a good do-it-yourself project. Most decks involve simple materials and straightforward construction techniques. With common sense, basic carpentry skills, the right tools, and a good plan, you can build a deck that will become a beautiful addition to your home.

This elegant covered deck proves that "casual" and "contemporary" aren't the only architectural styles that a deck can complement. This one features classic style and extends the living area of it's traditional home outside, to views of the river and surrounding mountains.

HOW WILL YOU USE YOUR DECK?

When planning your deck, consider what size groups you will entertain. This octagonal extension, with its perimeter seating, provides a forum for conversation. Notice how its surface is set two steps below to separate this area from the main deck.

A special place to relax with your morning coffee or catch up on your favorite book; a spot to unwind after a hard day's work; a front-row seat to outdoor vistas; an area for festive parties: Your deck can serve any one—or all—of these purposes. How you design it will depend largely on how you want to use it. In short, deck design begins with a look at your lifestyle.

A GETAWAY

If your needs are simple—for example, adding an outdoor space for getting away from it all—a small, unused side yard might be the perfect spot for a ground-level deck. Keep it private with a few screening plants. Add accents and some built-in or movable seating and you've transformed an area you used to mow into a low-maintenance private room.

Remember that even small areas require comfortable seating. And if the space will double as a spot for family gatherings, you'll want enough seating and table space to accommodate everyone.

ENTERTAINING

Deck space for parties is like guacamole dip—there never seems to be enough of it. So if

Minimal plantings, a little shade, comfortable seating, and natural vistas are all that's necessary to lure you out into the landscape.

you entertain—even infrequently—
that narrow side yard just won't do.

Consider guests in your decks plans. Decks
are an ideal way to relieve a cramped kitchen
and can quickly turn an overflow crowd into
a festive occasion.

Small groups may not require much more
space or furnishings than your family would
need. But large gatherings need seating,
cooking, and dining areas. If you have
teenagers—a deck can offer them privacy
and at the same time reward you with some
peace and solitude.

PLAY SPACE FOR CHILDREN

Decks can be perfect for children's play, but
your plans need to account for both the ages
of the kids and their number. Sandboxes are
good adjuncts for toddlers, but when the kids
grow older, they'll need tree forts, swings, and
things to climb. Plan your space so you can
phase in these activities in the future.

PLANNING CHECKLIST

Good planning means taking a thorough
look at both your lifestyle and various
aspects of the landscape. Here are some
factors to keep in mind.

■ **TRAFFIC FLOW:** If your deck lies
between the house and other destinations
in the yard—a utility shed, for example—
add space for 3-foot walkways to your plans.

■ **VIEWS:** Keep natural views in your
vision of your landscape. Orient the deck to
make the most of a pleasing view. Arrange
furnishings so you and your guests face the
landscape. Don't hide the yard behind
planters and decorative elements.

■ **SUN, SHADE, AND WIND:** Nature's
forces can turn an otherwise perfect deck
into an unusable spot. Note the patterns
of the sun and wind. Shade is a movable
feast—use lightweight, portable furniture
to take advantage of it, or create shade
with an overhead structure. Plan attractive
windbreaks to thwart prevailing winds.
A tall hedge or lattice fence will knock
the wind down and muffle street noise,
increase privacy, and hide unsightly views.

■ **STORAGE:** Make a list of implements
and equipment you need to stow away, and
plan storage that's easy to get to. Attach a
small "backpack" shed to the wall of the
house if you don't have room for a separate
structure.

A fully-equipped outdoor kitchen lets the cook mingle with guests while preparing the meal. A high counter offers serving or dining space and helps keep children safely away from a hot grill.

Even small spaces can be comfortable. The right choice of furnishings oriented to direct the view to the open garden makes this space seem larger than it really is.

HOW WILL YOU USE YOUR DECK?

continued

This deck was designed for small groups and quiet brunches. Note how the painted design on the decking calls attention to itself and creates an attractive area that is continually inviting.

GOOD NEWS FOR OLD DECKS

Even a deck in the most beautiful location won't be used much if it isn't convenient and attractive. If cooking space is cramped, guests are sitting sideways, or its surface is fraught with splinters, your deck probably won't attract activity. If you've inherited a deck that doesn't invite you out of the house, don't dismay. Enhance it strategically.

Often, adding just a small addition, constructed from the same lumber and finished like the existing deck, can not only increase your comfort, it can also improve the looks of your landscape.

Be adventurous and mix materials. A ground-level flagstone or brick surface will go well with an existing redwood platform deck. And if there's no room adjacent to the deck, build a detached area and unify the two spaces with a river-rock path.

Whatever the nature of the improvement, build on what you have if possible. Could you extend the deck into the yard, creating room for a fire pit or a water garden? Wouldn't new paving stones—or even decking on sleepers—do nicely on top of the old slab? How about recycling the concrete by breaking it up and using the pieces for a garden wall?

OUTDOOR ROOMS

Think of your landscape as an outdoor room and approach its design as you would the rooms inside your home. Planning a deck is really not much different from planning a family room. Though it might not be apparent at first, your outdoor room will have a floor, ceiling, and walls.

The floor, of course, is the decking. It defines the purpose of a room and blends it with the overall style of your house.

An outdoor ceiling can protect you from the elements and provide a sense of enclosure. Ceilings can also increase privacy on a deck, blocking the view from second-story windows—either your own or your neighbor's. What's an outdoor ceiling? Well, you might already have one and not realize it. That old oak tree might be the outdoor ceiling you're looking for. It not only can cast some welcome shade on your backyard retreat, it can give you a sense of protection. If nature hasn't provided your deck site with such a ceiling, make your own by building a pergola or arbor overhead.

Outdoor walls do the same thing that indoor walls do—they separate one kind of space from another. But their function extends beyond marking boundaries. Walls also create a sense of enclosure, increase privacy, act as a backdrop for decorative elements, screen out unsightly views, and mollify harsh winds. You can do all these things with solid walls or fences, of course, but let your imagination go and you'll see that shrubs, hedges, even plants set out in containers on the deck surface can function as outdoor walls.

Decks are often called upon to do double duty. Spaces designed for dining can also provide supervised children's play areas while parents are engaged in other tasks.

Comfortable seating is a must for good deck design. Consider the possibilities that built-in seating offers. Here, a long planter doubles as a permanent bench that conforms to the curve of the deck. Bright blue furnishings offer a pleasant contrast to the brick hearth and wood tones.

Design your outdoor space to include areas for children's play. If the kids aren't old enough for elevated playhouses or tree houses, design your deck so it can accommodate them later.

GETTING THE FAMILY TOGETHER

Lifestyle is a family matter, and so is planning a deck. Get the whole family together for a freewheeling discussion so everyone can propose ways to use this new outdoor space. Make a wish list and be prepared to compromise.

■ Start with things you absolutely must have, then add elements that are desirable but not required.

■ Cooking and eating areas are primary. Parties will need extra seating and conversation areas.

■ Plan for use first, then incorporate your deck aesthetically with the rest of the landscape.

HOW WILL YOU USE YOUR DECK?
continued

One of the outstanding features of this design is the way it unifies space to meet needs. The entire combination of basketball court and deck seems to spring out of the landscape as a single unit. Such harmony can be achieved only with careful planning, a process that includes a thorough assessment of the needs of all family members.

Multipurpose storage saves space. This deep cabinet also functions as a potting bench and outdoor buffet, hiding the portable barbecue from view.

Responding to an uneven site and a variety of recreational needs, this multilevel deck conforms to the terrain and includes a generous pool surround and a separate area reserved for sunning and relaxation.

BE FLEXIBLE

Although you hope your deck project will sail smoothly along until it's done, climate and cost can often interfere with the best intentions. Flexible plans will keep you on course.

If your summers are short, add an enclosure to your landscape plans. A summerhouse or gazebo will let you entertain when the weather turns chilly.

Contain your costs by using materials that are local to your area. For example, where native stone is abundant, a stone retaining wall may end up being less expensive than natural timber.

Avoid basing your plans on budget alone, however. Balance budget, structures, and materials to meet your needs.

A JUGGLING ACT

Getting the maximum enjoyment out of building and using your deck may require you to juggle a variety of factors: how you intend to use the space, the complexity of any structures you include, your skill level, how much time you have, your materials, and your budget.

The photographs above and below offer an excellent example of how these factors can come together to produce dramatically different yet perfectly appropriate designs.

In the design shown above, two levels of pressure-treated decking can easily handle the entertainment and leisure requirements of the family's lifestyle. The space is large enough for groups and includes a shelter for inclement weather. Even with the enclosed space, the design, material costs, and skill levels of such a project are within the means of most homeowners.

In the deck shown below, the tile-lined spa makes an unusual focal point. Mitered cypress decking is water resistant and provides subtle distinctions between areas designed for different uses. The entire space is open to the sky and is designed for large groups. This deck was planned with an eye toward comfort and visual impact and less concern for economy. The space bears the stamp of professional design and execution.

Both decks will serve their intended purposes, both are attractive and useful additions to their respective homes, and both have been planned by homeowners who paid careful attention to their needs, abilities, and budgets.

SIZE AND SHAPE

How much space will you need? Some designers say any outdoor living space should be about the same size as the interior room it adjoins. Others suggest it should be one-third the size of the main floor of the house. For many installations, both of these "rules of thumb" might result in about the same amount of space. "Rules" aside, the primary guideline is to make your deck large enough to accommodate all of the functions it will need to serve.

FUNCTION FIRST

How many functions will your deck serve? You can answer that by listing the activities you want to carry out on your deck. Assign each activity to a different part of the deck, allowing ample space for:
■ the activity itself;
■ traffic flow through and around the proposed area; and
■ outdoor furniture (which tends to be larger than indoor furniture).

Perhaps you'd just like a place for family dining. In that case, you might get by with an area as small as 6×10 feet. But a hot tub will call for a substantial addition. Personal relaxation may not be possible in the same space where children play, and a basketball hoop could be disastrous near a dining area.

Where incompatible functions must occur close to one another, keep them visually separated with planters, trellises, benches, or even a change in decking patterns. Or employ structural solutions to separate one area from the others. Build a T-shape deck or tiers and connect them with stairs or ramps.

PLANNING TO SCALE

Once you've estimated the size of your deck based on its intended uses, step back and consider its scale. The deck should complement the house and grounds. A small deck can appear overwhelmed by a huge house, and a lavish site will likely seem out of proportion to a modest home. Your budget and lot size may provide the most help in solving this problem. Start with a design that fits the uses you envision, then scale back to fit the limits of your budget and terrain.

TESTING THE SITE

The best way to find out if the size of your proposed deck will meet your needs is to rope off the area and move in the furniture and equipment you will use—tables and chairs, barbecue grill, lounges and recliners.

If you haven't purchased the furniture yet, use interior furnishings and add about a foot more space for each item. You can generally figure about 2 feet square for each outdoor chair, plus about a foot or do to push it back from a table. Tie helium balloon in places where new trees and shrubs will go.

Adjust the size of the space until you get it right for your needs and then draw the plan on paper.

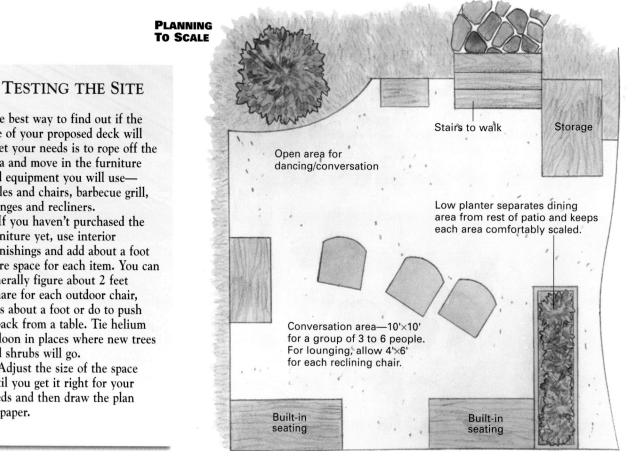

PLANNING TO SCALE

Stairs to walk

Storage

Open area for dancing/conversation

Low planter separates dining area from rest of patio and keeps each area comfortably scaled.

Conversation area—10'×10' for a group of 3 to 6 people. For lounging, allow 4'×6' for each reclining chair.

Built-in seating

Built-in seating

LEGALITIES

Your deck design will, of course, be affected by your lifestyle and budget—things you can control. Certain legalities outside your control—building codes, zoning ordinances, deed restrictions, and easements—may also have something to do with how and where you build.

These regulations, enacted by your community, can have a major effect on where you put your deck and how you build it. Some preliminary research will save you time, effort, and frustration later.

■ **BUILDING CODES:** Almost all communities enact building codes to ensure the safety and uniformity of building quality. Some communities consider decks as permanent additions and have regulations that define footing depths, material choices, and fence heights. Check with your local building department before you develop your plans.

■ **ZONING ORDINANCES:** These provisions govern the use of property and the placement of structures on it.

They can establish minimum setbacks from property lines, easements, and the size of your deck. In recent years, many communities have become strict about the size of decks because large hard-surfaced areas can increase rainwater runoff into storm sewers.

■ **DEED RESTRICTIONS:** Some communities have adopted deed restrictions to maintain control over local property values or architectural style. You may find restraints on the kind of deck you want to build, its style, and the materials you want to use.

■ **EASEMENTS AND RIGHT OF WAY:** These rules guarantee access by local utilities to their service lines and may restrict your ability to build a deck exactly where you want to. If, for example, a utility company has a line running through your yard, you might not be able to build any part of a deck lying above that line.

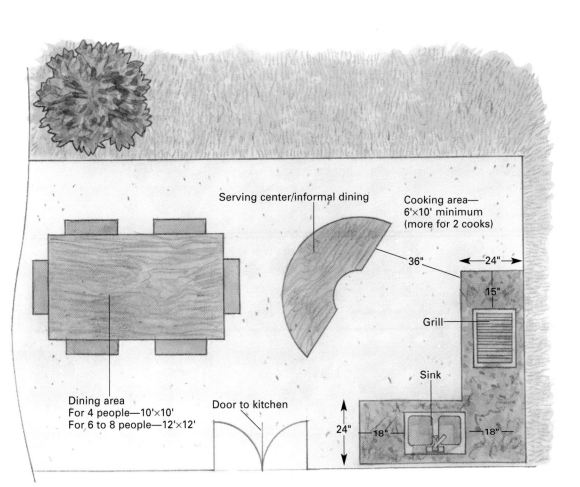

Serving center/informal dining

Cooking area—
6'×10' minimum
(more for 2 cooks)

36"

24"

15"

Grill

Sink

Dining area
For 4 people—10'×10'
For 6 to 8 people—12'×12'

Door to kitchen

24"

18"

18"

SIZE AND SHAPE
continued

THE SHAPE OF YOUR DECK

Decks can assume a limitless number of shapes and forms. Your design will depend on the terrain and landscaping of your property, your proximity to neighbors, and how you plan to use your deck.

GROUND-LEVEL DECKS: Typically associated with flat yards and single-story homes, ground-level decks present fewer design and construction challenges than raised or multi-level decks.

Ground-level decks make pleasant entryways, breakfast spots, and outdoor mudrooms. Construction is uncomplicated and, because these decks are low to the ground, they may not require railings (but check your local codes to make sure). Bring together multiple ground-level decks and experiment with decking patterns to create a cascading effect down a slope, or form a pattern to define a garden space.

Ground-level decks can be supported by traditional post-and-pier foundations, by continuous footings, or by an existing concrete slab. For a design that seems to float, cantilever the edges so they extend beyond the posts or footings. Be sure to check with your building department to see what your local codes have to say about how far the cantilevered section can extend.

RAISED DECKS: Raised decks provide access to upper-level rooms and also can solve landscape problems caused by steep terrain. Making tall supports look graceful can be an exciting challenge.

Slopes that fall away sharply from a house present special design and deck-building challenges. The easiest solution is to build a single-level deck that's attached to the house and supported by piers and posts. Perched on

Although the design of this redwood deck is simplicity itself, it took careful planning. The forward platform spills easily into the surrounding yard, but the rear section, which vaults over a slope, has required railings for safety. Note the comfortable cushions—an innovative approach to seating that can be permanent or temporary, depending on the family's needs and budget.

a sloped lot, even a simple deck can offer good views and increase your living space.

Safety concerns increase with elevated decks. Be sure the height of the railing and the space between balusters comply with local building codes.

MULTILEVEL DECKS: These deck designs avoid problems caused by rolling terrain or naturally terraced landscapes. Sections can be different sizes and shapes, connected with stairs or walkways.

Multilevel decks built to follow the landscape are ideal for sloping lots. They cascade down a hill in stages, providing different views along the way. Multilevel decks are complex, however, and require precise planning. Stairs, railings, and all of the structural components must come together correctly.

You don't need a sloped lot to build a multilevel deck, however. This design can create an easy, smooth transition from the ground to an upper level of your house. Instead of one long stairway, build a series of platforms to lead up the elevation.

WRAPAROUND DECKS: These are built along more than one side of a house and often feature multiple entries to the home. Wraparound decks are the perfect solution for lots that receive varying amounts of strong sunlight at different times of the day. They also provide an easy answer for families that need spots for private gathering and parties on the same structure.

This multilevel deck contains several small areas, each designed to accommodate its own function. All of the areas provide distinct views of the rest of the property.

Not all decks cling to houses. This freestanding redwood deck takes advantage of a setting with views into a wooded glade.

A landing breaks up this long stairway ascending to a raised, second-story deck. Landings make the climb less tedious and the design more attractive.

SINISTER SHADOWS

An upper-level deck can plunge interior rooms beneath it into a darkened gloom. If you're designing a second-story deck, and your site and sun pattern allow it, slim down your design. Narrow structures can offer plenty of room for seating and enjoying the view while casting a smaller amount of shade. A deck no wider than 8 feet can strike a good compromise, offering ample floor space without darkening any of the rooms below.

SOLUTIONS FOR SMALL SPACES

If your proposed deck seems as though it will look cramped in your small yard, don't dismay. There are a number of steps you can take to make small decks seem larger and more comfortable. The key to small-space design is simplicity.

■ Create the appearance of one large area from two smaller spaces. If, for example, your deck is bordered by the lawn, let the deck spill out into the open space and it will seem larger.

■ Dig garden beds on one or more sides of a detached deck so it doesn't seem to float like an island in the lawn.

■ Draw attention to the deck, not the property line. Instead of letting the lawn end undramatically at the property line, sculpt the perimeter of the lawn with planting beds. That will turn attention inward where you want it—on the deck.

■ Use plants with interesting textures to focus attention on the surrounding landscape rather than on the limits of your property.

■ Concentrate color in a patch instead of scattering flowers throughout the landscape. Groups of flowers create more impact than scattered blooms. If you use color in more than one location, repeat two or three colors to tie the areas together.

■ Whenever possible, borrow neighboring views. For example, if you're lucky enough to live next to an attractive pond or rolling lawn, leave that view open to make the most of what the surrounding scenery has to offer.

■ Instead of walling off the deck entirely, place screening strategically to enhance privacy and block only those sights that are distracting.

■ Put up wind chimes or install a fountain. Their soothing sounds will subdue noises that remind you how close you are to the neighbors or the street.

■ Install built-in seating—it takes up less space than freestanding furniture. This same goes for round tables—they'll leave you more room than rectangular ones.

■ Keep decking patterns scaled to the size of your deck. A lot of small patterns and contrasting textures will leave you feeling dizzy and hemmed in. Besides, they're expensive.

DECKING WITH PAVING

Is your existing deck too small but you can't afford to enlarge it? Expand it with a patio. Paving offers a more affordable solution, especially if you do the work yourself.

This tranquil garden is made for relaxation—the perfect marriage of space and purpose.

Large, natural stones adjacent to this deck expand the useful floor area. The large planters with their colorful contents provide a cheery and fragrant wall to define the space.

This small deck looks big. Moving furnishings to the sides opens up the central space. Outdoor curtains help define the space but still leave the view open to the outdoors.

This rough-textured house provides an interesting backdrop for a small deck. Simple, compact furnishings and container plantings complement the scene.

Even small lots can meet a variety of needs. This side-yard deck makes good use of limited space, providing a play area and container-gardening opportunities. It allows parents to supervise young children and a small herb garden within a few steps of the kitchen.

DETAILS, DETAILS...

Details—those special decorative touches—must work extra hard in small spaces because there's no room for clutter. Finishing touches—artwork, found objects, or architectural salvage—give small spaces personality. And your small deck might just be perfect for an object that would get lost in a larger setting.

Too much of a good thing, however, can ruin an otherwise artful design. To avoid overwhelming the space, step back and view your deck in its entirety. Look for noticeable bare spots. Do they function better as empty areas that draw attention to your decorating scheme, or would a potted plant, artwork, or other accent improve the setting? Leave room for each detail or collection to "breathe."

If you line a wall shelf with shells, don't put a lot of small items on the table below it. And if you have more things to display than you have space, store the surplus for a while and use it to rotate your decorative stock every two to three months.

FORCING PERSPECTIVE

Forcing perspective is one way to make a small area seem larger. Narrowing the line of sight through a small space, as shown above, is a technique that goes hand in hand with this optical "space saver."

The stepping-stones that curve around the house make this space look larger by seeming to connect it to a hidden area. Small plants in the background and large ones in the foreground enhance the effect, as do the placement of coarse textures in front, fine textures to the rear. In this way, an empty side-yard space becomes a cozy garden getaway.

ACCESS AND COMPATIBILITY

No matter how complete you make your landscape design, you won't use even the most luxurious deck if you can't see it from the inside, if you don't provide an easy way to get to it, and if its uses conflict with the uses of the adjacent interior room. These factors—visual access, actual access, and compatibility—can spell the difference between successful and unsuccessful designs.

VISUAL ACCESS

At its most basic level, *visual access* means that you can see the deck—or a portion of it—from the inside. Ideally, however, visual access should also extend a palpable invitation into the space.

Windows and see-through doors provide visual access, but you don't need to see the entire deck to want to get out and enjoy it. In fact, just a glimpse of the space can actually draw you in more effectively than a complete view. When landscaping your deck, try to include ways to entice guests outdoors by providing visual hints of the destination. At least some of the area should be visible from more than one interior room. The most complete view of your deck should be from the room that adjoins it.

ACTUAL ACCESS

Actual access refers to the physical method by which you get from inside your home to the deck outside.

Actual access should be easy. Whenever possible, avoid having to step too far up or down to move from the interior to the

DESIGN TIP

To improve the visual flow between an outdoor living area and an interior room, select decking and accents whose colors and patterns resemble the decor of the interior room. The similarity establishes the indoor-outdoor connection at a glance.

Wide doorways create an inviting transition between the house and deck, making the deck actually feel like part of the room. Glass and screen doors maintain this feeling even when they are closed. Plants and furniture groupings also create a feeling of transition between the spaces.

exterior of your home. That means that the level of your deck should be as close as possible to the level of the interior floor. (From the doorway to the edges, however, the surface should slope slightly for proper drainage.)

If the deck is significantly lower than the doorway from the house, add a landing or an entry deck to avoid having to step down immediately as you go outside. Such a threshold gives you the opportunity to get your bearings as you move from indoors to outdoors. If a landing is out of the question, build steps—and make them wider than the doorway to create an illusion of spaciousness. Each tread (the part you step on) should be no less than 12 inches deep so the stairs don't appear too steep.

Create safe access by having interior and exterior floors as close as possible to the same level.

REVISITING ACCESS

If you don't use your deck as much as you thought you would, perhaps it's because the design doesn't allow sufficient visual or actual access.

For example, if you feel you're on display while meditating on the deck, the site probably allows too much visual access. Look for ways to shield the area by adding a fence, shrubs, or an overhead structure. Areas for private use require limited visual access. Areas for public use can afford to be more open to outside views.

Inconvenient actual access from interior rooms can also reduce the use of your deck. If you feel that getting to your deck from inside is a journey full of obstacles or is circuitous, rearrange the furniture. Add a landing to even out the levels of the deck surface and interior floor. Improving access is often all it takes to turn an underused outdoor room into a popular destination.

Broad doorways offer visual and actual access to a private deck outside a bedroom. The deck gets lots of use because it's easy to see and to enter. In your situation, consider whether so much use is acceptable.

EASY AND INVITING

A deck that's difficult to get to probably won't be used. So make it easy. Start by making sure the main door to the deck is wide enough to permit an easy in-and-out traffic flow as well as provide an inviting view from inside the house. French doors, atrium doors, and sliding doors work especially well because they give a sense of continuity between the indoors and outdoors. If your house does not already have such openings, consider including them in your deck plan and budget.

Decks adjacent to the house should be as close to the level of the house floor as possible. If winter brings snow, set the deck 3 inches lower than the floor to keep snow out of the house. If rain is your primary concern, build the deck about 1 inch lower than the floor. If the drop to the deck level is greater than 3 to 4 inches, build steps.

ACCESS AND COMPATIBILITY
continued

Cut stone arranged in a formal pattern and edged with ground cover connects this deck to the rest of the yard, providing easy and attractive access.

DESTINATIONS

You'll spend a lot more time on your deck if you furnish it with features that turn it into an inviting destination.

Consider what you'd like to do on your deck and design it to accommodate your needs. You can add something as elaborate as a spa or as simple as a comfortable spot to sit and have a snack.

Although most people like to engage in some kind of activity, they will also look for places to sit, so you'll probably rarely use an area that is designed for standing only.

THE ART OF REARRANGING

When actual or visual access seems confined and unwelcoming, it may be the furniture, not the amount of access itself, that's the culprit.

Examine the placement of both interior and exterior furnishings. Can you see at least a portion of the deck from indoors? Is there a welcoming path from indoors to outdoors, or do furnishings impede the progress of guests on their way outside?

On the inside, rearrange the furnishings so you can see some of the deck from the family-room table or your favorite chair. Rearrange furniture inside your home to improve both visual and actual access from within.

Outdoors, if a large table limits movement around your deck, think about replacing it with smaller tables that you can scatter among chairs in less dominating locations.
An objective eye and simple rearranging transformed the deck below from crowded to inviting. Finding a new site for the grill and picnic table reduced clutter. Opening up floor space improved access.

Use accessories in moderation. Too much of a good thing becomes overwhelming, especially in a small area. If your love of collecting exceeds your display space, alternate what you exhibit. This keeps the outdoor space from becoming crowded and gives it a fresh look from time to time as well.

COMPATIBILITY

Even when all of the other design elements are complete, the success of your deck may depend on how you use the nearest indoor room. That's because you'll most likely use your deck more often when the general purpose of both the indoor and outdoor spaces is similar. If the primary purpose of the outdoor area differs substantially from its connecting indoor room, you're less likely to make full use of the space.

A small deck for coffee and the morning paper, for example, will feel just right if it's adjacent to your bedroom. But the same site would not work for party space. For frequent dining, put the deck close to the kitchen, even if you plan a completely self-contained outdoor kitchen. And remember to build in storage for the trash. That way you avoid carrying it inside, only to have to carry it outside on collection day. For entertaining, plan a location that's close to the public rooms of the house. Decks that serve more than one function should be large enough

Build steps wider than their entrance so they can double as casual seating areas.

to be accessible from several rooms.

For private areas, look for ways to limit access, such as shielding your deck behind hedges or fencing. For entertaining, look for ways to increase access. For example, consider adding doorways from rooms where you would entertain. Also think about exterior walkways that allow guests to move to and from your deck without traipsing through the house.

WHICH WAY DOES THE TRAFFIC GO?

You may find that changes to the interior of your home will improve its indoor/outdoor connection. Sketch the floor plan of your house, and label each room. Show the location of doors and windows. Examine the flow of family traffic and how people move into and out of your house. Mark these routes with arrows. Then rearrange the furniture to open views and paths to the outdoors, or consider converting existing windows to French doors.

Sliding doors provide both an open invitation to the outdoors and a wide passageway that makes access easy.

EVALUATING COMPATIBILITY

To evaluate the compatibility of your indoor and outdoor rooms, consider how they relate to each other. Take a careful look at your floor plans and list how you use each room. Then label each use as active (such as entertaining) or passive (such as reading). Although each room may be home to both passive and active uses, one type of use probably dominates.

Where an active area meets a passive area, you can either change the use of the indoor room to better suit the nature of the outdoor area or change the outdoor room so it complements the interior use. For example, a deck favored by the kids riding tricycles will see lots of active use. This deck would be compatible with an active playroom, family room, den, hobby room, or kitchen. It would not be compatible outside a quiet area such as a bedroom, study, bath, or formal living room.

Potential solutions include converting the bedroom into a playroom until the children are older, finding another place for tricycle riding, or limiting outdoor access to the deck by adding a gate, blocking off the route with planters, or replacing a paved walkway with stepping-stones to discourage the use of riding toys.

CREATING A STYLE

The choice of flooring materials helps set the style of an outdoor area. Here, tile contrasts nicely with the decking and steps up to a built-in bench. Repeating the zigzag edge ties the two areas together and adds shape to the lawn.

Your deck needs to be practical, of course, but your deck-design process should go beyond the merely functional. You'll enjoy your outdoor living space more when its style appeals to you and reflects your personality. One of the quickest ways to develop an understanding of style—and to get you going in a direction that reflects your taste—is to split the subject into two categories: formal and informal.

FORMAL AND INFORMAL

The chief difference between formal and informal styles lies in how lines, shapes, angles, and materials are used.

■ Formal designs employ straight lines, right angles, regular geometric shapes, and decorative objects arranged in even numbers. For example, a formal layout might feature a rectangular ground-level deck surface surrounded by rectangular planting beds. Pairs of classic urns or columns might enhance a deck in this style because formal designs tend toward symmetry. In many formal designs, if you imagine a line down the center, you'll find that one side mirrors the other exactly.

■ Curved lines, irregular and often free-flowing shapes, and odd-numbered groupings characterize informal decks. The goal is a casual and comfortable balance rather than symmetry. A typical informal landscape might even employ loose material—small stones, or wood chips—on a path from the garage to the deck, but many successful informal designs employ brick and cut stone in curved layouts. Informal designs often use garden beds to enhance their casual feeling and appearance.

HERITAGE

Style can be further categorized as traditional or contemporary.

■ A traditional deck can evoke a feeling of a formal courtyard using decorative items such as urns, fountains, columns, and lush foliage to help achieve its effect. Think "Greek" or "Roman" and you'll conjure up an approximate image of what "traditional" means.
A traditional deck usually comes dressed in formal lines, but informal styles can be set traditionally as well. For example, in a formal garden, you might find steps built with brick set with clean, orderly edges. In an informal traditional setting, the same steps might be made of dry-stacked stone.

■ Contemporary decks are cool, serene, and comfortable. A contemporary deck would be more likely to include bold shapes and colors, sleek lines, and unusual combinations of materials. Decorative items in a contemporary design tend toward the abstract—emphasizing color, texture, and light instead of representational forms.

FINDING YOUR STYLE

The best way to discover your own personal style is to take a tour of the neighborhood and make mental notes of things you like. Jot down your impressions when you get home and file them in a manila folder. Clipping photos and diagrams from magazines also is helpful. Put them in the folder too.

When you are ready to make your final design decisions, take your notes and clippings out of the folder and spread them on a table so you can see everything at once. Discard what doesn't appeal to you and keep the rest. You'll notice a general consistency in the images left on the table. Use the elements of that style in your decking patterns, fences, and overall landscape plan.

This abstract contemporary overhead isn't designed to provide shade; it defines the edge of the deck with a dramatic flair and adds a focal point to what might otherwise be an uneventful surface. The owners addressed the need for shade by including the umbrella and the shaded arbor in their plans for this eclectic design that combines elements of a variety of styles.

BLEND WITH THE ENVIRONMENT

Although the structures and other elements of your deck plans will be determined largely by how you want to use your landscape, they should blend with the architecture of your house and the configuration of the land.

Style and scale are the links that unify your deck and your house. For example, the architecture of a 1920s four-square home might be better complemented by a deck with massive framing members and substantial railings. A delightful bungalow might seem to shrink away from an elaborate series of decks linked by walkways. Scalloped trim is most at home with the gingerbread of Victorian homes.

Also consider the lay of the land, the climate, and the natural vegetation. Then create a style that reflects what is natural. Uneven terrain lends itself to simple and informal lines; a large lot will let you use bolder strokes.

Choose materials that are native to your area. You'll save on shipping costs, and the additions to your landscape will appear as though nature helped you put them there. Redwood, for example, is less expensive in the western states, cypress in the south, and cedar in the north from west to east.

CREATING A STYLE
continued

The repetition of a decking pattern can break up large, continuous spaces and in many cases can help simplify construction.

REGIONAL FLAVORS

Some deck styles transcend the categories of formality and informality, having evolved with the local climate, culture, and native plants and materials. Such regional styles can provide a handsome solution to design problems because they "fit" their surroundings so well. A regional design can also make good budget sense: Local plants and building materials are easier to find and less expensive, and native plants require less care and maintenance than imports.

Regional elements can also add interest to a deck design or help make your deck a world of its own. Bring in unusual accents from distant places, especially items that won't require extra cost and maintenance. A single bonsai tree won't transform your deck into a Japanese garden, but it will provide a harmonious contrast to a Southwest theme. Adobe pavers and cacti are inexpensive and easy to care for and will add a touch of the Southwest to a Midwest design scheme.

CREATING HARMONY

A successful deck design combines all its various elements into a unified whole. Achieving that harmony requires an artful blending of many diverse elements, primarily the shape of the deck, the decking pattern, and the style of railings and balusters. All of these elements give the deck its form, mass, and texture, and define its relationship with the house and yard.

To achieve a sense of unity, shape the contour of the deck so it repeats or blends with the dominant forms of its surroundings. These often are the rectangles of the house but may also include curves, angles, and free-form shapes suggested by property lines, a swimming pool, garden beds, or sloping lawns.

Select accessories and furnishings that are in harmony with the deck and tie together the house and yard. Fortunately, there is a style of deck furniture to fit almost every taste and budget, from sleek, contemporary pieces to classic cedar or charming, old-fashioned wicker.

GUIDELINES FOR DESIGN

You need not feel constrained by rigid rules of style. Combine classic and modern styles to create a deck with old-style charm and modern convenience. Mix in different regional accents to spice up the outdoor space with surprises.

UNITY AND CONTRAST: Create a sense of continuity between your house and deck by using similar materials, colors, shapes, and patterns in both areas. Use small, carefully placed elements to contrast color, shape, or texture. Gardens, edgings, walls, colored concrete, stone, tiles, bricks, logs, gates, furnishings, lights, and decorative pieces all add pleasing and lively accents.

Interweave trees and plants in your deck design, or contain them on the perimeter of the yard with edging, fences, hedges, or planters. Don't crowd the paved areas leading to your deck—paving is for people.

Repeated patterns and finishes can help unify a design theme. Here, the unstained but treated pine doors on the service island blend with the rear privacy fence and the furnishings.

A second-story deck can take advantage of wasted space over rugged terrain. Raised decks, however, can create unattractive spaces below them, a problem solved here by the lattice skirting and plantings.

This deck is so harmoniously melded into the overall landscape that you may not notice it at first, an effect enhanced by finishing the deck in a hue similar to that of the painted shingles.

As you consider various plants, think about how their textures, shapes, colors, and mature size will complement your structural materials.

CENTER STAGE: Arrange walls, plants, and walkways so that they lead to a focal point, a destination—any object or view you want to call attention to. Place your main deck furniture around focal points to give them greater definition.

If your deck is large or is made up of many smaller areas, position smaller groupings of furnishings and decorative elements in ways that won't clutter the central area.

How will you know when the design you've created is harmonious? It will look soothing rather than jarring. It will present a cohesive blend more than a jumbled clutter of parts, and its general impression will be inviting and comfortable.

CREATING STYLE WITH DECKING

Dress up a deck by painting a pattern to designate a sitting area. Paint eventually wears underfoot, but the partially exposed wood grain lends charm.

Stain camouflages deck additions, hiding the transition from old material to the new.

The lion's share of any deck is its surface—the decking itself. But just because it's flat doesn't mean the surface has to be humdrum. Decking patterns offer countless options for design that can improve the style of your landscape and make the deck more attractive. Even the simplest platform deck can get a big dose of style with an unusual decking pattern. Choosing patterns should be an essential part of your planning, and your choice should be indicated in the sketches you'll make as your plans evolve (see pages 100–101).

STYLE

Like other design elements, decking patterns bring either a formal or an informal sense of style to an outdoor living space. The style depends on the patterns in which the planks are laid, the finish of the wood, and auxiliary features of the deck, such as the railings and baluster configurations.

■ The more geometric and highly finished the wood, the more formal the impact.
■ Allowed to weather to a soft gray, parallel cedar decking will generally look casual.
■ Well-sanded and oiled (or stained) decking will result in a more formal appearance.
■ You'll get an even fancier look with planks laid diagonally or with their ends mitered to create a box pattern. Short boards can be set in sections that resemble parquet flooring.

Decking laid in modular squares adds interest to a deck design and creates a focal point for conversation areas. Repeat smaller versions of this pattern over the surface of a large deck to designate areas of use.

Who says that parallel decking has to look boring? This tread decking is a good example of how texture can create an unusual amount of interest. The deck ties the tiers together and complements a dazzling array of plant colors.

SELECTING A PATTERN

The possibilities for creating decking patterns are almost endless. Any one of several might fit your overall landscape design adequately. A few general principles will help you choose a pattern.

■ On long, rectangular installations, decking set perpendicular to the length of the deck will tend to minimize the length and make the surface seem wider than it is.

■ Borders lend a finished look to the deck.

■ On small decks, simple patterns work better than intricate ones. Complexity can result in a pattern that looks "busy."

■ Diagonal patterns look best if they reflect a similar line elsewhere in the landscape—an angle of the house or an outdoor structure, for example, or the lines and angles made by planting beds.

■ Complex or intricate patterns accentuate rather than hide defects in lumber. Use premium-grade lumber for such patterns. Otherwise, consider simply painting the surface.

FRAMING FOR DECK PATTERNS

Unusual decking patterns require careful planning for both the surface and the framing that supports it. The ends of the decking must always rest directly on a joist or blocking. For simple patterns, install the decking perpendicular to the joists and scatter the butted ends at random throughout the deck. Support modular units with framing that holds up both the ends and the interior of each section. Typically, this means that blocking—short sections cut to fit between the joists—must be installed at regular interval. (See page 126 for more information on installing decking patterns.)

DECKING PATTERNS

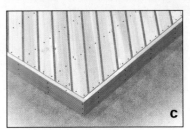

Laying planks to form a pattern dresses up an outdoor room. Build the simplest and least expensive pattern with parallel planks (A). Trim them with a border to hide cut ends (B), or lay planks on the diagonal for a dressier look (C).

A more complicated, basket-weave pattern requires more cuts. To "weave" the decking, lay alternating panels of perpendicular (D) or diagonal planks (E).

CREATING STYLE WITH RAILINGS

Railings express a deck's personality. The style of the balusters—straight-cut, fluted, turned, or hewn roughly out of timber—can have more of an impact on the style of your deck than any other element. It's important, therefore, that you design the railings so they appear as a harmonious aspect of your overall landscape theme.

Planning your railings at the same time you design the rest of the deck will prevent construction errors. Railing design can influence where you place the posts as well as how you fasten them.

Start by considering the character of your house and its trim. Is it formal or casual? Are its lines primarily horizontal or vertical? What kind of shapes are featured? Such questions will help you determine which railing designs fit best. If you are not sure, simplicity is almost always goof proof.

Consider also the practicality of your design. Will you want to set food and drinks on the railing? Will you need to space balusters closely to increase privacy? Get further direction by looking through landscaping magazines for design ideas.

Here's a novel—and sturdy—approach that alters the normal baluster orientation and provides support for built-in seating.

This redwood deck and railing were stained to enhance the beauty of the wood. The 4×4 "through-posts" carry all the way to the ground, so they support the structure as well as the railing. The top and bottom rails are 2×4s, and the balusters are alternating 2×2s and 1×6s.

Log railings were a natural choice for this house. Building a railing like this involves a special carpentry technique: Large mortises—conforming to the shape of the logs—are bored into the supports to hold the ends of logs or tenons cut from the ends. The railing is assembled on the ground, then raised and attached.

This railing combines several unusual but complementary elements. Posts are massive 6×6s with 2×4 rails and 2×3 balusters. The newels (the wooden globes on top of the posts) are commercial products available at a deck supply yard. The top rails are 4×4s wrapped with corrugated plastic drainpipe. To be sure they fit exactly, the curved purple metal rod partitions were custom made and anodized by a metal fabricator after the rest of the railing was built.

The bottom half of this railing is a solid wall, covered with grooved T1-11 siding and trimmed with rough-textured 2×4s and 2×6s. The top portion is made of 4×4s ripped to 3×3s. All parts are covered with opaque stain, which is nearly paintlike in its coverage but emphasizes the grain of the wood.

This railing uses lengths of standard metal fencing hung between 4×4 posts—distinctive and less expensive than custom-made components. The dadoes on the posts were cut with a table saw, as were the chamfered tops.

FURNISHING YOUR DECK

Every deck, no matter how beautiful, needs some kind of furnishings to look complete. Furnishings give outdoor living space its style and make it feel homey and inviting. They have a remarkable influence on how you feel about the space, as well as how often you use it.

FURNISHINGS AND LIFESTYLE

Furnishings should reflect the purposes of the deck. For example, chairs for a deck that adjoins an intimate dining area will likely be different from furnishings on which children play. Take time to think about the relationships between seating and lighting, cooking facilities, and accessories.

UPKEEP AND PORTABILITY

Outdoor furniture represents an investment, so choose durable materials that can be used year-round. If you can answer "yes" to the

An outdoor room isn't truly inviting without good seating. Choose outdoor furniture for durability as well as comfort and style.

following questions, it will help you narrow your choices.
- Is it weatherproof?
- Are the pieces sturdy, but light enough to be moved around easily?
- Are cushions removable?
- Can the furniture you're considering be stored outdoors over the winter?

JUST RIGHT...

Outdoor furnishings should be proportionate to their space. If your outdoor room is small, use round tables—they take up less space than square or rectangular ones. In larger spaces, set up conversation areas with groupings of tables and chairs or lounges and side tables. Include a serving cart and leave plenty of room to walk around the furniture.

A trellised garden bench makes an attractive resting spot that you can build as part of your deck or virtually anywhere in your landscape.

STAIRS

Stairs offer another opportunity for casual seating. In crowded settings where seating is limited, people will eventually sit on stairs. But your guests will feel more comfortable if they don't block the up-and-down traffic flow. Plan ahead and build wide steps.

For steps to be comfortable for sitting, the tread (the part you step on) should be at least 18 inches deep, and riser height (the vertical part of the step) should be no more than 4½ inches. Finally, be sure to install a sturdy handrail.

By combining permanent built-in seating with a portable table and chairs, the owners of this sunken deck can have a cozy brunch with a small group, or use the space for a party.

MOVABLE SEATING

Movable seating comes in many forms—from hammock chairs and lounges to dining sets with cushioned chairs. Freestanding units also increase the flexibility of your deck. You can shift them around or out of the way to change the nature of the space.

You probably need little encouragement to set out enough lounge chairs for everyday seating. But go beyond that and consider what the space will need when you entertain. Keep a stack of folding canvas chairs handy for impromptu parties.

BUILT-IN SEATING

Built-in seating may not be portable, but it has several advantages over freestanding furniture:
■ It takes up less floor space than freestanding chairs.
■ It can also serve as storage. Attached benches might be the first form of built-in seating that comes to mind, but good deck designs will include additional choices. Raised planters and retaining walls can fill in as benches when built wide enough.

So can freestanding walls, constructed to define the perimeter or areas of use.

Choose flat stones for the final course of a wall that will double as seating. Top the wall with pillows or finished bench slats for extra comfort. If the wall borders a raised planter, install low-growing, soft-textured ground covers, perennials, or shrubs next to the sitting area. Put taller, stiffer plants farther back in the bed so they don't discourage people from sitting on the wall.

DIMENSIONS FOR BUILT-IN SEATING

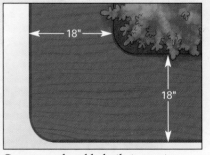

Side view — 18"
Top view — 18", 18"

Create comfortable built-in seating with the 18-inch rule: The top should be 18 inches above the finished surface of the decking, and at least 18 inches deep.

DECORATING WITH PERSONAL TOUCHES

When displaying collections, vary the color of objects, such as these watering cans, if the forms are similar. If the shapes are different, the colors should be the same or similar.

Spending time on your deck will be more enjoyable if you're surrounded by a few of your favorite things. But, as with any good design, decorating a deck can profit from planning.

SURVEY THE SCENE

Relax in a comfortable chair and survey your space. Let yourself go, and without consciously trying to plan the space, notice where your gaze rests. Those are the places that need details.

■ Choose one good-size item per seating area for emphasis. For example, a smooth, round granite or concrete ball or a colorful bowling ball perched beside a bench adds a focal point by creating an unusual juxtaposition.

■ If floor space is limited, mount your largest object on the wall.

COLLECTIONS

Grouping related objects, such as birdhouses, folk art, or finials, invites comparison and draws attention. All those small pieces take on greater importance when displayed together.

A collection creates one focal point out of several objects, so choose its setting carefully.

■ Walls, ledges, windowsills, empty corners, —even flower beds—are good places for displaying collections.

■ Avoid placing one collection close to another collection or other accents that compete for attention.

■ Neutral backgrounds, such as walls, fences, and green plants, show off collections to their best advantage.

INDIVIDUAL PIECES

When setting out decorations, it helps to establish a theme—for example, using star-shaped objects, rabbits, or things that are blue—so the space maintains a unified look. Avoid clutter. Allow enough room between items so each one gets its chance to be showcased. Displaying accessories at various heights also helps avoid clutter.

A dull corner becomes a lively little scene when dressed with outdoor art, a few old tools, and a potting bench.

ADD PERSONALITY

There is no right or wrong way to display personal details in your outdoor living space—only suggestions. Try these ideas:

■ Mount driftwood on a wall and slip orchid plants into its crevices during warm months.

■ Tuck seashells on top of rafters where they're visible only if you're looking up from your hammock or chaise lounge. Sometimes the discovery is half the fun.

■ Prop a shell-shaped fossil or other salvaged artifact against a pot of flowers at floor level.

■ Nail or glue old bottle caps across the foot of the screen door.

■ Paint a prominent fence post a different color from the rest. Fill in a face, if you like, and attach arms, wings, or a hat to create your own garden sculpture.

■ Spike a weather vane in a pot of flowers to draw attention to the seasonal color.

■ Open air serves as a gallery itself. Hang mobiles or wind chimes to catch the breeze.

■ Suspend unexpected objects such as old silverware or prisms.

Above all, look for ways to make your outdoor room more comfortable. Soften furniture with plump cushions. Keep a small stack of books handy. Add an ottoman. Then put your feet up and enjoy!

OBJECTS D'ART

Beauty is in the eye of the collector. Whatever catches your fancy and can withstand the elements has potential as a decoration for your outdoor room. Set out objects, such as old window shutters, where you need something special to fill a dull spot. Consider these items or have fun thinking up other possibilities:

■ pottery
■ keys
■ old tools
■ canoe paddles
■ shells
■ fossils
■ birdhouses

■ marbles
■ antique signs
■ folk art
■ architectural salvage
■ watering cans
■ sun motifs
■ fishing gear

A little paint magically transforms ho-hum decking into a pretty and durable outdoor rug. Repeating the paint colors in outdoor fabrics and furniture completes the setting.

PLANTING

Plants can bring your deck to life. What's more, they can solve design problems in a way no other element can. Containers with brightly colored blossoms create a pretty view from the house. A nearby hedge screens an unattractive view. Potted trees provide shade and privacy, as well as fruit. Large planters help establish traffic patterns. Well-placed planting beds, trees, shrubs, perennials, and ground covers blend your deck right into the landscape, making the entire scene a single, attractive composition.

When you're ready to integrate plants into your landscape design, first decide where they should go. Use your design concept (see page 104) to tell you where you need shade, privacy, and shelter. Then select plants that do the job in style.

MAKING GARDEN BEDS

Before you decide what to plant in a bed, first decide on the right shape for the bed. Remember that the perimeters of a garden bed also shape adjoining lawn areas.

If you don't yet have your plans on paper, experiment with a garden hose in the general area of the bed, creating outlines that are in keeping with your overall style choices. Most homeowners find that curved lines—even bordering the square corners of a deck—

Lines of flower beds shape both lawn and garden, creating plantings that snuggle up to this deck.

ROOM FOR VINES

It takes only a small opening cut into paving to grow plants within a deck. Vines thrive in openings as small as 8 inches across. A single vine can cover the face of a wall with a cloak of leaves. Or plant one at the foot of an arbor to twine up a post and grow overhead.

Fill a window box as though it were a miniature garden, complete with plants that grow upright and others that trail down.

give their landscape a more expertly designed look than straight lines.

Once you're happy with the contour, mark it on the lawn with spray paint. Then remove the hose and cut the contour and the bed from the soil. Plant beds in tiers, placing the shortest species toward the front and gradually increasing the height of the planting toward the rear of the bed. Plants right next to the deck should be no more than eye level when you're seated, unless you're using them to screen out a view or increase your privacy.

TREES

Trees make shade, reduce erosion, keep homes cooler in the summer, and help clean the air. If you expect your trees to do all these jobs and more, research your choices and plant trees that will adapt to the extremes of your climate as well as to the soil and drainage characteristics of your yard. When selecting new trees, use the following as a guide:

■ Choose first between deciduous trees, which lose their leaves in the winter, and evergreen species.

■ Consider the growth rate and mature size of the tree. The 6-foot sapling brought home from the nursery may root into your foundation if placed too close to the house.

■ Check out the "personality" of the tree. What might seem to be the perfect botanical addition to your landscape could be messy, dropping seed pods, foliage, and blossoms that might demand constant cleanup.

SHRUBS

The midsize stature of shrubs makes them good plants for transitions between larger

Bright flowers lead the way up the stairs, where the brightest accent hangs at eye level.

Group together various potted plants with the same blossom color for big impact.

For a tasteful, expertly designed appearance, aim for a unified color scheme in flowers and containers (right). Mixing lots of different plants and containers (far right) is disharmonious because it lacks unity.

PLANTING
continued

elements—other trees, sheds, or decks, for example. Shrubs fill in nicely for trees in places where trees won't fit.

Purchase shrubs that meet the needs outlined in your plans. Be sure to consider these factors in your decision:
■ How much care they require
■ Their mature height and width. A full-grown shrub encroaching on your deck will prove to be an unwelcome guest
■ How well they take to pruning, if needed.

GROUNDCOVERS

These "lowly" plants are perfect for covering broad areas or reducing erosion. Plant wide, sweeping beds that curve around a deck, and complement adjacent lawn space with a single variety of ground cover. This simple strategy defines areas without dividing a large space into smaller parts. You can also fill shaded areas where grass won't thrive or cover slopes you don't want to mow.

CONTAINER GARDENS

Container gardens allow you to make quick changes when you tire of the current scene. With containers, you can grow just about any

Container-grown plants clustered at the foot of steps lend color, texture, and importance to the entrance of a raised deck without blocking the way.

Plants growing in containers need a bit more care than those growing in the ground. But they'll reward your effort when you provide as much water as they need, control pests diligently, and fertilize regularly.

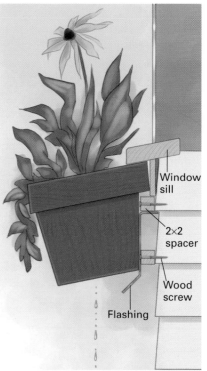

Window sill

2×2 spacer

Wood screw

Flashing

To protect siding from stains and water damage, install a 2×2 spacer and flashing behind the window box. Pitch the box forward for drainage.

kind of plant, even when you're faced with hot, dry weather or lack of space. Before you decide what plants to grow, figure out where you'll put them. Here's how:

■ Sit on all of the benches, hammocks, chairs, walls, and steps of your deck and look at the views. Go inside and check the view from the adjoining room.

■ Take note of any distractions in the background—utility wires, heating and cooling units, meters, outlets, and tools. Then use the containers to block these views.

■ Pay attention to any areas that seem to need more privacy. Plants can add height to a wall without creating a walled-off feeling.

■ Look for empty corners, blank walls, and signs of shabbiness. Liven up these areas with container-grown plants.

BOXES AND BASKETS

Window boxes and hanging baskets offer an opportunity to create a self-contained composition on a small scale. A window box or basket filled with formally clipped topiaries or tumbles of bright flowers always adds cheer to your deck.

Generally, plants in a box or basket should have the same requirements for sun, water, and fertilizer. For reliable results, combine plants of similar colors or contrasting textures. Billows of fine-textured plants, such as baby's breath, make fine companions for plants with spiky foliage, such as rosemary. Upright forms accent compositions when surrounded by trailing flowers.

BASKET TIPS

Before hanging a basket, make sure it's in a spot where no one will bonk their head as they pass by. Then use the following "recipe" for sure-fire success.

■ Start with a 12-inch or larger basket.

■ Purchase three trailing plants (in 3-inch pots or six to a pony pack).

■ Position the trailers in the basket of soil at the points of a triangle, spaced equally apart and a few inches from the edge.

■ Place the upright plants similarly in the center of the basket.

■ Tuck in a few filler plants randomly.

The style of a window box planting should match the mood of adjacent rooms, indoors and out. Here, a multitude of flowers gives this window box a cottage-garden look that works.

Because they're so accessible, window boxes and baskets offer a perfect place for tiny edible gardens too. Include lettuces, a few herbs, and edible flowers in your planting scheme. Finally, remember fragrance, which enhances any window garden's appeal.

WINDOW BOX TIPS

■ The deeper the window box, the healthier your plants will be. Boxes at least 10 to 12 inches deep hold more soil and allow room for adequate root growth.

■ Be sure your window boxes have at least two drainage holes in the bottom.

■ Slide a sheet of plastic foam inside the front of your window box before filling it with soil for planting. The foam insulates roots from heat and reduces evaporation of soil moisture.

■ Before planting, mix water-retaining polymers in the soil at rates specified on the package. These tiny pellets swell when wet and hold moisture in the soil.

■ Water window boxes daily (sometimes twice a day) during hot weather. If the soil is dry to the touch, it's time to water.

A limited color palette and tidy dracaena give this window box a formal flair. Such a composition would complement a deck or balcony that featured a symmetrical arrangement and formal furnishings.

PRIVACY AND ENCLOSURE

Decks need definition. Without it—both above and at the edges—your deck can leave you feeling exposed and uncomfortable. If your site lacks natural attributes that enhance your privacy and sense of enclosure, you can create these qualities with your plans.

Consider privacy first. Is your deck effectively screened from the street and from the neighbors' view? If your proposed site is on the least exposed side of the house, at a corner where the main body of the house meets a wing, or tucked behind a retaining wall or hedge, privacy may not be an issue. And if your site is isolated from the house or on a hillside above the surrounding views, you may not need to alter your design at all. But if you need to increase your privacy, add a fence, a wall, or trees and shrubs to your plans.

These same elements will also produce a sense of enclosure, of course. But so will benches, garden beds, and other features. And remember to look up. Overhead space will affect your comfort too. Consider including an outdoor "ceiling"—an overhead, such as an arbor or a pergola, or tree limbs.

DON'T BUILD A FORTRESS

To avoid turning your yard into "Fort Redwood," avoid barrier-style screens—solid walls, high fences, and dense, straight hedges. Use these only in areas that require the absolute maximum screening.

A deck shouldn't put you on display. A living barrier can screen you from the neighbors. Here, a standard entrance to a deck mimics a hallway and creates an intimate sitting nook in the surrounding vegetation.

"UP" SCALE

Overhead space, both indoors and out, has a psychological impact. For example, grand, vaulted indoor ceilings feel awe-inspiring and even a bit overwhelming, and low ceilings can feel confining. The same holds true outdoors, but the rules of scale are different.

Indoors we feel most comfortable in rooms with 8- to 10-foot ceilings. Outdoors we're accustomed to higher "ceilings," but feel more comfortable when the outdoor space is somewhat closer to the indoor standard. Your lowest tree branches, for example, may be 15 to 20 feet off the ground, but even that height above an intimate dining table might feel excessive.

In general, make sure deck space that's reserved for intimate activities has some suggestion of cover over it—from 10 to 12 feet high. Areas for more public activities, such as parties, will feel more comfortable with "ceilings" up to 20 feet high.

A general guideline for "covering" your deck from above is to shelter at least a third of the surface area.

The walls of this house create a protected alcove, an ideal location for a deck that offers privacy without confinement.

Colorful climbers and plants in baskets create both privacy and style.

Even the suggestion of something overhead adds intimacy. Try fast-growing tropical vines, such as mandevilla.

WALLS AND FENCES

Walls and fences make beautiful additions to an outdoor design, connecting your deck to the larger landscape and adding a vertical contrast to the horizontal expanse of lawn.

Walls and fences can solve problems too:
■ They define space, giving it an identity that suits its purpose.
■ They can tame slopes, create privacy, block annoying winds, form backdrops for decorative accents, and hide utility areas.
■ They can make large areas seem less imposing by dividing them into smaller ones.

DEFINING SPACE

More than any other design element, walls and fences delineate space. For example, without a clearly defined perimeter, a ground-level deck may seem just an extension of the lawn. Without something to set your family dining space apart from entertainment areas, your weekend brunch area can feel exposed. Both on your deck and beyond it, you need something that visually separates one area from the others.

There are obvious walls, such as fences, hedges, and the sides of the house. Then there are walls that are not so obvious—perceived walls:
■ Ankle-high hedges
■ Built-in seating
■ Planters, posts that support an overhead
■ A change in decking pattern
■ Plants and small trees
Anything that separates your deck from the

This fence is a design feature in itself. It hides a utility area and offers a garden seat plus a cozy nook with a table for two.

rest of the world—or separates one area of the deck from another—is behaving like a wall.

A low shrub hedge, for example, becomes a living wall that divides the deck from the rest of the lawn. A row of trees can do this, too. Their trunks become the surface of the wall or fence, filtering the views but not blocking them.

Built-in benches and raised planters can keep your party space from encroaching on the private areas of your deck. Freestanding benches create the suggestion of a wall or fence and divide areas without completely enclosing them. They're especially useful when you need to separate two spaces that have closely related purposes.

Erecting solid walls, fences, or closely knit hedges to divide your property into bits of space can result in separate but isolated areas. Perceived walls, on the other hand, imply the separation without isolating areas from one another. They interrupt both visual and actual movement but don't block views, so they direct traffic effectively and define space without creating a claustrophobic feeling.

Subtle "walls" in this space define the seating area. The simple redwood planter, the terraced planting beds, and the open-topped fence all create a sense of intimate enclosure.

CONSIDER THE VIEW

Open up your landscape by removing trees or shrubbery that block pleasant views. Remove or repair unsound and unsightly sheds and other structures instead of building fences to make them invisible. Weed out anything that's overgrown or looks messy. Replace out-of-control shrubs with low-growing varieties.

LOCATION AND PRIVACY

Defining space and creating privacy often go hand in hand. How much separation you need between your deck and the lawn may actually depend on your location, the size of your yard, and how much privacy you need.

Where lots of foot and vehicle traffic passes nearby, it might take a solid barrier, such as a brick wall or board fence, to provide enough privacy. Where the deck is visible from only a few exterior vantage points, a couple of ornamental trees or a latticework fence might be all that's required to stop prying eyes.

Simple built-in benches and lattice panels form a practical perimeter for this deck, clearly separating the space from the lawn. Colorful flowers unify the elements in this design.

A high, solid fence can turn your private retreat into a stockade. Here, the owners have softened the potential isolation with painted lattice panels.

Even a change in level, such as the single step at the edge of the house, can act as a subtle wall, separating this comfortable seating area from the dining space at the rear of the deck.

Vary the fence height to meet different needs. The panels on this deck offer privacy and safety. Those at the rear of the yard define the property without blocking the view.

WALLS AND FENCES
continued

SCREENING

"Screening" means strategically placing plants, fences, walls, trellises, and other structures to block views and provide privacy.

To determine the amount of privacy screening you need, take a moment to go outside and sit in the proposed location of your deck (or the present deck, if you have one already).

■ Take notes about the levels of privacy and exposure from different vantage points. Trust your instincts; if you feel on display in any given spot, it's not private enough.

■ Then sit in the same locations and make a list of any unsightly or unattractive elements you want to screen out.

Fences create privacy and security, but with a little thought, they can also contribute beauty to the landscape. Fast-growing vines, or planters full of blooms and cascading foliage, can add color and texture to perimeter fencing for little expense and effort.

SCREENING FOR PRIVACY: The amount of privacy you need will depend on how you plan to use each of the areas on your deck.

■ Cozy, intimate spots for reading, conversation, sunbathing, or meditation should provide plenty of privacy. Screen these areas with walls, high fences, or dense evergreen plantings.

■ Active areas, such as rooms for parties, family gatherings, or children's play, require less privacy. For these areas, partial screening—latticework fences, airy trees, or seat walls—should do the trick.

Where you put privacy screens matters, too. The closer to the deck area, the more privacy you'll get. The farther from the surface, the less privacy.

Few decks require screening around the entire perimeter. Before you plant a hedge all the way around your deck, figure out the angle from which other people can see you. Then plan the screening to block the most revealing views first. Remember your goal: Enhance privacy without barricading your outdoor space. Lattice, picket, and ornamental iron fencing form a friendly, see-through screen.

BLOCKING UNSIGHTLY VIEWS: When you're enjoying your outdoor room, you won't want to be looking at the garbage cans, the dog run, a heat pump, your neighbor's open garage, or parked cars. Consider the angles from which you see these items, then strategically place screens to hide them from view.

SOLID-WALL SCREENING: For maximum privacy and security, consider installing a

This vine-covered lattice screen turns an air conditioner into a thing of beauty and lets the air circulate around it. Lattice is also excellent for concealing utility areas and creating private outdoor garden rooms, or screening views from the outside of your home.

Lattice panels can be used as baffles to control views and still allow easy access. This side-door entry maintains comfortable access while screening the rear yard from view.

solid wall, a high fence, or a dense hedge. These structures bring a number of advantages. They can function as effective boundaries that keep children and pets in the yard and unwanted visitors out of it. They can also make an ideal backdrop for your garden beds and create a nurturing microclimate.

A wall of any sort provides an instant visual backdrop for an outdoor setting—whether it defines the boundary along all sides of an area or simply encloses part of a deck. Flower borders, ponds, and sculpture show off nicely against both walls and screens. If your yard has an old wall or fence that you'd rather hide than boast about, use climbing plants to form a verdant disguise for it.

MATERIALS: Choosing materials for outdoor walls and fences offers yet another design opportunity. You'll find vast choices, but your main goal should remain the same: Select materials that suit the style of your home and landscape.

A solid brick or stone wall can look classic and imposing. Interlocking concrete blocks, designed for retaining walls, suit most home styles. Another possibility combines a simple fence with an evergreen hedge or roses for an effect that's decorative and almost impenetrable. Or you may live in an area where adobe offers the most appropriate building option.

See-through structures, such as this spindle deck rail, create separation and screening without forgoing friendliness.

HOW HIGH?

The purpose of a wall or fence should dictate its height. A structure for security, a windbreak, or total screening can be 6 to 8 feet high. Walls built solely to separate spaces can be as low as 6 inches or as high as 3 feet. In general, any wall or fence should be either well above or well below eye level to avoid cutting your view in half.

SCREENING WITH SOIL

Berms, or mounds of soil, form small hillocks in a landscape. Heavily planted, they block views and deflect traffic noise.

To keep a berm from resembling an awkward bump or a pile of leftover soil, build it at least several feet wide and no less than 30 inches higher than the existing grade. The berm should slope gently upward, instead of abruptly rising from the yard, in order to minimize erosion. As the roots of plants on the berm grow, they'll help stabilize the soil and prevent erosion.

Shape the berm into a rounded form with a nearly flat top and wide sides. You may want to curve the mound of soil so that it hugs your deck.

Plants on the berm offer privacy because they appear taller. Located next to a hard surface, the berm forms a swale along its length at the foot of its slope. (A swale is a shallow indention that collects runoff water and moves it to another part of your yard where it can be dispersed.)

Like any raised bed, the soil in a berm drains readily and dries out quickly. So choose plants that tolerate dry conditions, and water them as often as necessary. Mulch plants with materials that won't wash away easily. Lay a 2-inch-deep layer of chopped leaves and shredded bark for a long-lasting mulch that's likely to stay where you place it.

OVERHEADS AND SHADE STRUCTURES

Whether you call it an arbor, a pergola, a lanai, or a canopy, an overhead will enhance your deck with a minimum of materials and work.

FUNCTION FIRST

Let the use of your deck determine whether it needs an overhead. The sky might be considered the ultimate ceiling for all of the outdoors, but many times it's a ceiling that's simply too high for a deck. Active areas, such as those designated for entertaining large numbers of guests or for children's play, can, of course, function well if left open. But more intimate areas, such as those planned for dining, talking, or relaxing, will feel more inviting and cozy with an overhead.

Shelter from the elements is also reason to plan for an overhead structure. If your site analysis (see pages 104–105) indicates a need to provide relief from the sun and rain or to cool a room, an overhead is the answer.

An otherwise blank side of a house becomes lively with this simple overhead. The beefy 2×8 rafters, spanning only about 4 feet, are strong enough to support the swing. The overall effect is reminiscent of an old-fashioned front porch.

STYLE

Whatever your reason for building an overhead, make sure its design reflects and complements the overall architecture of your home. An overhead structure should appear

Even a simple, prefabricated arch makes a statement. A well-marked entrance, such as this arbor, lets everyone know they're entering a special place.

to be an integral part of the design, not an add-on. By repeating some detail of your house, such as a molding or post style, pitch of the roof, accent color, or building material, you can link the overhead to your home.

Curved overheads lend a romantic, cottage style to an outdoor space. Dressed and painted lumber suggest formality. Rough cedar or bentwood lend a rustic air to an archway. A modern, metal framework or masonry arch adds a touch of Old-World charm.

COMING TO TERMS WITH OVERHEADS

Technically, an *arbor* is a freestanding structure, and a *pergola* is attached to something, such as the side of the house. Both have columns that support an overhead network of beams and rafters. A *lanai* is a porch or veranda, which can be uncovered or covered, and *canopy* is a term used to describe both a solid roof or the roof of any such structure.

RAFTER ANGLES

If you want an overhead to provide shade, take the time to experiment to find the maximum amount of shade in the heat of a summer day and the minimum amount when it's cooler.

Monitor your proposed deck area to see when the sun makes the deck site too hot and bright to use. Note the season, the time of day, and the angle at which the sun shines on the area. Then position the overhead and design it to block the sun's rays from that angle by shading the areas where it's most needed.

Control the amount of sunlight reaching a sheltered area by varying the size, spacing, and orientation of framing members. Build the structure, then experiment with different slat configurations before attaching them to the roof.

Lattice slats oriented east to west will shade the area underneath for most of the day. Oriented north to south, they will provide the same amount of shade as east-to-west slats in the morning and evening, but allow some sun through to the area below at

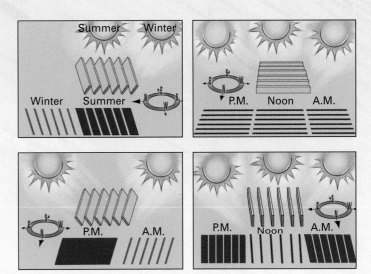

midday. Setting rafters at a 30-degree angle blocks more sun. Spacing slats close together will also provide more shade.

Attach louvers or lattice to the sides of the structure to filter low-angle rays on late summer afternoons, or plant vines to sprawl across the top and the sides.

Thanks to a careful analysis of sun and shade patterns, this design offers shady comfort with open, airy views.

ROOFED STRUCTURES

Structures with a solid roof—corrugated metal or plastic, cedar shakes, asphalt shingles, or slate tiles— offer more physical protection than open roofs. They keep you dry when it rains, and they totally block out the sunlight. They're especially helpful above outdoor cooking areas.

Solid-roofed structures create miniature environments underneath them. Shadows cast by the roof may cool nearby paving but may also darken the interior of your home. If possible, locate solid roofs away from the main portion of your deck so that the space can be used in both fair and inclement weather.

GROWING PRIVACY AND ENCLOSURE

Should you build a wall or fence to increase your privacy, or let plants do the job? The answer depends on your budget, your patience, and the look you desire.

Plants grow. Fences and walls don't. For that reason, privacy plantings make good economic sense. If you have the patience, you can start with small plants and wait for them to grow. Or you can invest in a few large plants to block critical areas and set out smaller plants to fill in where you don't mind waiting for a living screen to mature.

Trees offer a sense of overhead enclosure and shelter. But you may need to augment such lofty canopies with an umbrella or other lower "ceiling" over intimate dining areas.

Then there's the neighbors. A substantial fence can create sore feelings next door. Trees, shrubs, and other plants create a softer look than fences or walls so it might not be as evident to the neighbors that you're putting up a privacy screen. Plantings also remove the possibility that your neighbors (or you) won't like looking at the back side of a fence. If your yard already has a lot of paving or decking, using plants instead of fencing keeps the hardscape from overwhelming the space.

Privacy planting doesn't mean you have to enclose your deck completely. Tree trunks, branches, and foliage can filter views for natural privacy.

SELECTING PLANTS

If you've decided to plant a screen but aren't sure how to choose the plants, consider the amount of privacy you need on your deck.

■ If you need year-round and total privacy, evergreens yield the best results. These species shed their foliage discreetly throughout the year instead of dropping the leaves all at once. You may have to put up with a small trade-off, however: Many evergreens grow at a slower pace than deciduous plants.

■ If seasonal privacy will suffice, plant deciduous species. Their screening ability increases in spring and summer when they bear leaves, and decreases in autumn and winter when foliage falls. Even without leaves, the structure of the plant forms a visible barrier that defines space.

Some tree species, such as serviceberry, feature multiple trunks that lend themselves beautifully to separating areas and creating a sense of enclosure. They offer a measure of privacy too. Deciduous trees permit winter rays to warm your deck and allow sunlight to reach inside your home. Mixing evergreen and deciduous trees and shrubs together gives you the best of both worlds.

The fronds of a potted palm serve as a perceived wall. This simple barrier turns attention inward toward the outdoor room.

EVERGREEN SCREENS

Common Name	Botanical Name	Zones
TREES		
Canadian hemlock	*Tsuga canadensis*	3–7
Colorado blue spruce	*Picea pungens glauca*	3–7
Douglas fir	*Pseudotsuga menziesii*	4–6
Eastern red cedar	*Juniperus virginiana*	3–9
Eastern white pine	*Pinus strobus*	3–8
Leyland cypress	× *Cupressocyparis leylandi*	6–10
Loquat	*Eriobotrya japonica*	8–10
Norway spruce	*Picea abies*	3–8
SHRUBS		
American arborvitae	*Thuja occidentalis*	3–7
Hick's yew	*Taxus × media* 'Hicksii'	5–7
Inkberry	*Ilex glabra*	3–10
Leatherleaf viburnum	*Viburnum rhytidophyllum*	6–8
Lusterleaf holly	*Ilex latifolia*	7–9
Nelly R. Stevens holly	*Ilex* 'Nellie R. Stevens'	6–9
Oleander	*Nerium oleander*	8–10
Yew pine	*Podocarpus macrophyllus*	8–10

PLANTING STRATEGICALLY

BEFORE

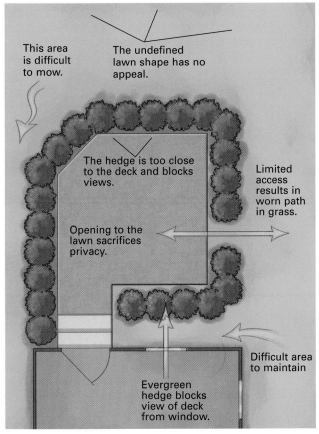

AFTER

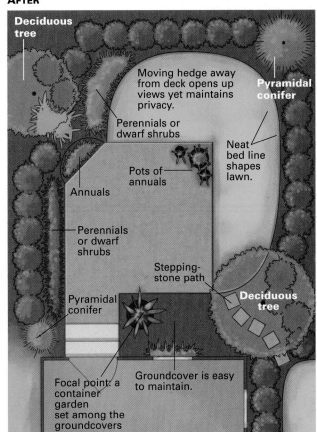

Ringing an outdoor room with shrubs provides privacy but closes in the area, turning it into an uninviting, difficult-to- maintain space (left). A better, more inviting way to achieve privacy is to block views strategically (right).

GROWING PRIVACY AND ENCLOSURE
continued

TREES

You'll find many species of trees to fill the role of sentry beside or within your deck. Even a small tree, one that matures at 10 to 20 feet, makes a spot feel people-sized and offers shade. Keep in mind that deciduous trees shade outdoor rooms in summer, and lose their leaves in fall. In winter, they allow sunlight to reach the interior of your home, brightening and warming it.

When planting new trees near your deck, select a species that matures between 30 and 35 feet tall or less. Trim the lowest branches of mature trees, allowing a minimum 6-foot clearance so you can walk under them without getting poked in the eye.

Look for hardwood species that don't drop messy fruit or twigs. Avoid planting too close to pavement; tree roots can buckle it.

Fast-growing shrubs screen unwanted views, such as the foundation of the neighbor's house, letting prettier features stand out.

GOOD DECK TREES

No tree is completely mess-free, but these trees come pretty close. They mature at 30 to 35 feet tall or less and adapt to confined conditions.

Common Name	Botanical Name	Features	Zones
American yellowwood	*Cladrastis lutea*	Fragrant flowers	5–8
Amur maple	*Acer tataricum ginnala*	Shade, fall color	3–8
Apple serviceberry	*Amelanchier × grandiflora*	Spring flowers, fall color	3–8
Chinese elm	*Ulmus parvifolia*	Interesting bark	4–9
Crape myrtle	*Lagerstroemia indica*	Summer flowers, sculptural form	7–9
Eastern redbud	*Cercis canadensis*	Spring flowers	4–9
European mountain ash	*Sorbus aucuparia*	Fall color	3–6
Japanese maple	*Acer palmatum*	Fall color, sculptural form	5–8
Sargent cherry	*Prunus sargentii*	Spring flowers	5–8
Sweet bay magnolia	*Magnolia virginiana*	Fragrant summer flowers	5–9
Washington hawthorn	*Crataegus phaenopyrum*	Winter berries	4–9
Wax myrtle	*Myrica cerifera*	Fine-textured, evergreen foliage; prune into tree form	8–10
Wax-leaf privet	*Ligustrum lucidum*	Glossy evergreen foliage; prune into tree form	7–9
Yaupon holly	*Ilex vomitoria*	Winter berries; prune into tree form	7–9
Yoshino cherry	*Prunus × yedoensis*	Spring flowers	5–9

Position trees where they'll frame (not block) views and protect your home from winter winds as well as summer sun. Good deck species feature neat and trim silhouettes that suit confined spaces.

Be sure to include a variety of trees and create a landscape that offers beauty and a haven for wildlife year-round. Choose trees that thrive in your area. Look around your neighborhood to see which trees appear to be thriving in the climate. Then visit a local nursery and consult the experts; verify the hardiness of your favorite trees before you make final selections. A little homework goes a long way toward avoiding costly mistakes.

VINES

Vines add leafy layers and colorful blossoms to posts, arbors, and trellises. Plant vines at the base of posts and let them grow up and over your deck. Plant them in ample containers, taking care that their roots have plenty of room to grow. Use fast-growing varieties, such as trumpet vine and clematis, to provide a quick umbrella. Some vines offer greenery year-round; others lose their leaves in autumn, letting the warming sun reach the interior of your home during the colder winter months.

MORE FOR THE MONEY

When you use plants to increase your privacy or help create a sense of enclosure, you're making a practical investment and a design statement.

Plants can help soften the hard edge of an overhead structure. Leafy canopies offer pleasant, dappled shade, whether you opt for a vine-covered pergola or the stately shelter of large trees.

Mature shade trees in the yard spread a generous, high-domed canopy over an outdoor room. They define the upper limit of the outdoor ceiling, filter sunlight, and offer a sense of protection. Their size creates a sense of stability.

Plants of a smaller scale work too. Look for smaller trees to set beside your deck or vines that will scramble over the top of an arbor. Small trees will grow in pots, and you can train potted shrubs into the shape of small trees. Be sure to select dwarf-type plants that will grow slowly and remain smaller than standard varieties. These plants shouldn't outgrow the space you allot for them.

Multi-trunked trees provide quick screening by blocking upper views with their canopies and filtering lower views with their trunks. Use evergreens for year-round privacy.

VINES FOR ARBORS AND PERGOLAS

Common Name	Botanical Name	Features	Zones
Armand clematis	*Clematis armandii*	Fragrant flowers, evergreen foliage	7–9
Bougainvillea	*Bougainvillea glabra*	Winter flowers	9–10
Carolina jessamine	*Gelsemium sempervirens*	Spring flowers	8–10
Clematis	*Clematis* hybrids	Spring flowers	4–8
Climbing roses	*Rosa* hybrids	Showy flowers	Varies
Confederate jasmine	*Trachelospermum jasminoides*	Fragrant flowers	8–10
Coral vine	*Antigonon leptopus*	Summer flowers	8–10
European hop	*Humulus lupulus*	Bright foliage	5–8
Hyacinth bean	*Lablab purpureus*	Purple fruit; rapid-growing annual	7–10
Moonflower vine	*Ipomoea alba*	Summer flowers; rapid-growing annual	8–10
Morning glory	*Ipomoea tricolor*	Summer flowers; rapid-growing annual	4–10
Silver lace vine	*Polygonum aubertii*	Summer flowers	4–8
Sweet autumn clematis	*Clematis terniflora*	Fall flowers	6–9
Trumpet honeysuckle	*Lonicera sempervirens*	Summer flowers	4–9

SMALL TREES FOR PLANTERS

Many of these trees can grow for years in a container on a deck, if you give them adequate water, fertilizer, and drainage.

Common Name	Botanical Name	Features	Zones
Australian tree fern	*Cyathea cooperi*	Fine-textured foliage	9–10
Japanese maple	*Acer palmatum*	Fall color	5–8
'Little Gem' magnolia	*Magnolia* 'Little Gem'	Summer flowers, evergreen foliage	7–9
Rose of Sharon	*Hibiscus syriacus*	Summer flowers	5–9
Tree-form wax myrtle	*Myrica cerifera*	Fine-textured, evergreen foliage; prune into tree form	8–10
Wax-leaf privet	*Ligustrum lucidum*	Glossy evergreen foliage, multiple trunks; prune into tree form	7–9
Windmill palm	*Trachycarpus fortunei*	Fanlike fronds, hairy trunk	8–10
Yapon holly	*Ilex vomitoria*	Winter berries; prune into tree form	7–9

ADDING AMENITIES

Amenities bring many of the comforts of the indoors into the beauty and spaciousness of the outdoors. Which ones you choose depend on how you want to use the space.

Outdoor cooking areas get the heat out of the kitchen and allow the cook to enjoy more time with the guests. An outdoor kitchen with a propane grill and cabinetry will be nearly as easy to use as the one indoors. With a working sink outdoors, you can cook entire meals without dashing in and out of the house.

Outdoor lighting adds decorative beauty as well as extra hours to the enjoyment of a deck. Easily installed low-voltage systems can provide just the right mood.

A fireplace warms up an interior room and becomes a cozy focal point for family gatherings and guests. Firelight outside has the same effect, and you can install a fireplace,

chiminea, or fire pit easily—especially if you plan the installation from the start.

Just off the deck, a small pool with a fountain adds charm. So will a container fountain, which you can pick up at your local home center or from an Internet outlet. Research a water feature first, however, to find plants and fish suitable to your climate—species that require a minimum of maintenance.

If your plans include any of these amenities but your budget doesn't, plan for them now and add them later. At a minimum, you'll probably want outdoor electrical receptacles and running water.

PLANNING FOR AMENITIES

Many outdoor amenities require plumbing, electrical, or natural gas lines. You should include all of them in your plans before you start building your outdoor living space.

For example, a spa requires running water and a drainpipe. Spas, ponds, fountains, and waterfall pumps require electrical outlets with ground fault circuit interrupters (GFCIs). Lighting systems require electrical lines. A permanent natural gas line for a gas grill might be preferable to a propane tank. An exterior phone jack is useful for households that don't want to go portable. If outdoor activities include watching TV, you'll need an electrical outlet and perhaps an exterior cable connection.

Utilities are best run underground to the site—both for safety and to avoid visual clutter. Plot the utility run so that it does not interfere with anything else in the area. Rough in the systems after excavation but before you lay any of the foundation.

An outdoor kitchen lets the cook prepare food and mingle with guests instead of being confined indoors.

Outdoor lighting extends the use of your deck into the evening hours. It creates its own special ambience, giving your deck an entirely different character at night than during the day.

A deck with a heavy-duty hot tub needs support, outdoor wiring, and plumbing. Even if you have experience with carpentry, plumbing, and electrical work, check with your local building inspector to make sure your plan meets code requirements.

This outdoor storage closet has a split personality. The doors closest to the yard (near left) provide access to lawn equipment. The back side holds deck furniture (far left). The closet separates the private sitting area on the deck from the entry area.

OUTDOOR KITCHENS

Everyone knows how much better food tastes when it's cooked and served outdoors. Incorporating an outdoor kitchen in your deck plans requires only a little creativity and perhaps some minor modifications to make the space easy to use, efficient, and pleasurable. You can equip the space with facilities ranging from a plain charcoal grill to a fancy gas range, and complete the kitchen with a sink.

Your deck becomes a favorite dining room if it's conveniently close to the kitchen and offers cooking facilities.

LOCATION, LOCATION...

Because a movable grill—gas or charcoal—will fit just about anywhere, you might think it doesn't make much difference where you put it. But any grill will be most utilized if you plan its location wisely. Find the safest spot. Convenience is important, but safety is more important. Locate a portable grill so flammable surfaces aren't at risk. Construct a built-in grill with fire-prevention methods that conform to your local building codes.

Whether portable or built-in, locate grills out of access routes and views. Take care that they don't pose other safety issues; you don't want anyone to get smoked out. Consider installing a small overhead shelter—with a vent—above the cooking area, or locate the grill under overhanging eaves. This way you can continue grilling if it starts to rain. And if your unit is portable and you don't have room to store it separately, you'll need a waterproof cover when it's not in use.

Your outdoor kitchen should include enough room for preparing and serving food as well as a place for utensils. If you're adding a portable grill to your plans but lack space for full-blown serving areas, you can keep cooking items handy but out of sight by tucking them inside a potting bench or other cabinet or behind a screen. Large potted plants do a good job of hiding a grill, too. Set them on platforms with casters so you can easily roll them out of the way.

BUILT-INS

Permanent fixtures, such as outdoor cooktops, ovens, and refrigerators, offer a host of options that will turn your deck into a summer kitchen. You'll find compact cooktop-only units as well as combination units with a built-in rotisserie, grill, or griddle that fit into a relatively small space.

Look for outdoor-grade equipment that's made to meet building codes and withstand all weather conditions.

Choose from cooktops fueled by wood or charcoal, electricity, or natural gas. Have electrical or gas lines installed before setting up the unit.

Even weather-resistant outdoor appliances need shelter, and waterproof countertops such as those made of marble, metal, or tile will prove to be an investment that gives you plenty of elbow room for preparing meals. Ask your contractor to help you calculate the expense of building the countertop large enough to form a 15- to 18-inch overhang opposite the cooking area—for a bar or buffet. Waterproof cabinets prove useful, too. So will storage made for a kitchen-size garbage can. Close cabinets with screen door hooks or a sliding bolt to keep critters out.

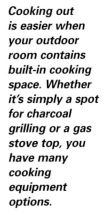

Cooking out is easier when your outdoor room contains built-in cooking space. Whether it's simply a spot for charcoal grilling or a gas stove top, you have many cooking equipment options.

ADDING AN OUTDOOR KITCHEN

When retrofitting a deck for outdoor kitchen space, think small. You may need only a modest extension to the deck surface. Build a grill-size spot from the same materials as your deck. Or add a kitchen patio. Use concrete stepping-stones or precast pavers on a sand base; they seem to complement almost any design scheme.

The best outdoor cooking areas offer plenty of weather-proof storage as well as room to prepare and serve meals. After all, you don't want to tote supplies every time you cook out.

Arranging an outdoor kitchen is a lot like arranging one indoors. But you may need extra countertop room for shared work space if family members enjoy cooking together out-of-doors.

LIGHTING

Low-voltage lights can transform your landscape. They enhance views from within your house and give outdoor spots an after-hours glow.

Lighting extends the use of your deck late into the evening and makes it safer and more secure at night, even when you're not using it.

Adding lights to a deck takes planning and care, but it's not difficult. Choose the lighting system you prefer, review the installation guidelines, and prepare to enjoy your outdoor living space any time of day—and night.

LIGHTING SOURCES

Decorative and concealed light fixtures lend style and atmosphere to outdoor space, as well as bolster home security.

CONCEALED: Concealed light sources focus attention on an object or area. Tucked among plants, in a tree, or at ground level, their strong bulbs typically cast their beams a long distance. Place the fixtures carefully so the bulbs aren't visible from any angle.

DECORATIVE: Decorative fixtures throw a more diffused and weaker light than concealed fixtures; you should be able to look at them without squinting. They come in two forms—either as freestanding units mounted on short pillars, or made-for-mounting units you can attach to posts or walls. Decorative fixtures should fit their setting. For example, small lanterns perched atop chunky pilasters or hanging on a large, empty wall will look out of proportion.

LIGHTING STRATEGIES

Getting the right light in the right places on your deck means combining light from various sources in different strategies.

UPLIGHTING: This technique, in which a concealed fixture casts light up into an object from its base, adds drama to your deck. Use uplighting to draw attention to an area or decorative object. Position the fixture so its

NEW LIGHT FOR AN OLD DECK

When building a new deck, you can lay polyvinyl chloride pipes through the area before installing the paving so you can run wires easily for lighting. But if it's too late for that, you can hide wiring by attaching it to the underside of structures.

You can install perimeter low-voltage lighting at any time. And where the space gets at least six hours of sun, consider installing solar fixtures. They don't require any wires at all.

LIGHTING WITH STYLE

Low-voltage lights are available in styles that range from Victorian Revival to high-tech. Most are designed for in-the-ground installation, but many can be mounted on deck railings, under stairs, or along fences. Halogen bulbs cost more initially but are less expensive to operate.

Lighting steps, stairs, or decking to prevent stumbling requires bright lights wherever there's a change in level.

Concealed fixtures and path lighting (left) combine to illuminate the outdoor room and turn the upper-story deck into a sculptural element.

Conventional path lighting (above left) runs off an electrical system. Solar path lighting (above right) operates on special batteries that store the sun's energy during the day.

beams graze trees or artwork to highlight their shapes. Or aim the light toward a wall or fence silhouetting the shapes of plants, trees, sculptures, or fountains.

Position the fixture in front of the object so the beam shines away from viewing areas. Or use can lights, which are designed to be recessed into the ground and shine upward at an angle while shielding the bulb from view.

DOWNLIGHTING: Downlighting casts a soft, indirect glow on horizontal surfaces such as steps, paths, floors, balconies, and tabletops. Mount the fixtures on tree trunks, branches, or overhead rafters. On arbor rafters, thread wires through the center of hollow columns, or cut a rabbeted groove along the length of a solid post to create a cavity for the wiring.

Keep downlighting fixtures out of sight so that they don't draw attention from the illuminated object. As with other lights,

aim them to illuminate your yard and outdoor rooms, not your neighbor's.

PATH LIGHTING: These short, decorative fixtures cast light downward along a walkway, linking your outdoor room and other parts of your yard, such as the driveway, parking area, or pool. Use a single or matched pair of path lights to illuminate short flights of exterior steps or to mark points of entry.

BEWARE THE GLARE

Artfully placed fixtures cast gentle pools of light that transform your deck into evening-friendly space. Choose lighting that improves the setting and helps guests feel comfortable. Mounting bright spotlights to shine on the deck will provide plenty of light, but that's all. Your guests will feel uncomfortable under the glare.

LINE VOLTAGE OR LOW VOLTAGE?

Lighting systems come in two forms: line voltage, which uses the 120-volt AC power in your house, or low voltage, which uses power reduced by a transformer to 12 volts of direct current. Working with line voltage is easy enough for homeowners with experience doing their own electrical work. But it can be dangerous to use outdoors; you may want to hire professional electricians.

■ Most outdoor line-voltage installations require approval from a building inspector. Low-voltage systems are safer for outdoor use and seldom require inspection unless you add a new 120-volt circuit to feed the low-voltage system.

■ Line voltage is compatible with the wiring you already have, and it's useful for outdoor appliances and power tools, as well as lighting. Low voltage is safe, easy to install, and inexpensive to operate. If you can't decide

which system to use, think about which one matches your needs best.

■ A line-voltage system requires conduit, fittings, junction boxes, receptacles, fixtures, bulbs, wire, and connectors. Your supplier can tell you what other materials, tools, and hardware you'll need. Low-voltage systems are designed for use outdoors and require fewer accessories.

■ Several kinds of fixtures are available for both systems, but low-voltage systems generally offer more options. You can find lights to illuminate deck surfaces, walkways, and stairways. Other lights are made to show off plantings, walls, fountains, and other special features. Fixtures are available in many materials, including molded plastic, hand-finished teak, and cast bronze.

FIRELIGHT

Outdoor fireplaces bring warmth and intimacy to fresh-air rooms. The style of an outdoor fireplace, especially if it's near the house, should match the style of the home. Its design shouldn't look as though you're trying to use up leftover brick.

No artificial light source matches the comforting glow of a controlled fire. Fire brings instant coziness and extends your deck's potential for use.

Firelight is most appealing at night, encouraging after-hours use of your outdoor room. Fires also take the chill out of spring and fall evenings.

Most homeowners don't think about including a fireplace or fire pit when planning their deck. But it's easy enough to do, in either new or existing installations.

and a brick-lined warming oven in the plan, and use your fireplace for cooking and keeping food hot.

Build the outdoor fireplace to suit the way you use your outdoor living area—as a warming place near the pool or the backdrop for an outdoor room. Whether you construct your fireplace of masonry, firebrick, or other material, it should match the style of your home. Choose a rustic look with a wide stone ledge mantel for a log home. Or design a neat

FIREPLACES

An outdoor fireplace makes an excellent addition to an outdoor room. Unlike interior fireplaces, which are built into a wall, most outdoor fireplaces are freestanding, although some are built into walls or hillsides and double as retaining walls. Made of mortared brick or stone, outdoor fireplaces resemble conventional fireplaces. A hearth provides a fireproof safeguard against burning embers that tumble out. Andirons hold logs in place. A fire screen contains sparks that fly from burning logs and exploding embers. A damper controls drafts. If you like, include a rotisserie

FIRES AND CODES

Before building a fireplace or fire pit into your deck plans, check local regulations first.

Many communities have setback and construction requirements as well as seasonal burning rules. Arid, fire-prone areas may restrict outdoor fires altogether.

AN OVERWHELMING ACCENT?

Outdoor fireplaces are imposing features that draw attention year-round. Remember to treat your fireplace as a focal point so its presence doesn't overwhelm your deck. Position it where it won't compete with other accents.

Follow this guideline: Step into your proposed or existing deck space. Glance around. What do you see? An outdoor fireplace and chimney will probably dominate the scene. If that's the case, plan to put other items of interest, such as a sculpture, a fountain, or outstanding specimen plants, where people won't see them within the same initial glance.

Once limited to the Southwest, chimineas are available just about anywhere. These wood-burners cost less than a fireplace and are convenient for open or roofed areas. Use a vent pipe in closed or roofed areas.

A raised pit increases safety. Raised pits contain sparks and prevent guests from accidentally stepping into the fire.

brick structure if your home is more traditional. Cover masonry with a stuccolike finish, if you prefer, but consult a contractor about fire retardation before applying finishes. Cap the chimney as you would a house chimney and screen it to keep out birds and animals. Dress up the mantel with potted greenery, flowers, and natural treasures such as driftwood and attractive stones for summer appeal when the fireplace is not in use.

CHIMINEAS AND FIRE PITS

Chimineas, a portable fire source, resemble potbelly stoves. These kiln-fired ceramic pieces, which originated in Mexico, spread first through the southwestern United States and have become increasingly popular in other regions. A chiminea holds a fire in its rounded base, where there's an opening for feeding logs (and showing flames). It has a chimney tapering upward from the firebox. Usually chimineas sit on a metal stand to prevent overheating the paving or decking.

These decorative fireplaces add comfort with their heat as well as with the sound and scent of burning logs. Chimineas are not designed for cooking. Store them indoors when temperatures fall below freezing. If moisture held by the porous surface of the terra-cotta freezes and expands, the chiminea can crack, flake, or begin deteriorating.

As an alternative, other styles of free-standing gas and wood-burning fire pits have become widely available. Classic, in-ground fire pits open to the sky. Lined with firebricks and surrounded by a wide, fire-resistant coping, such as stone, their open flames resemble campfires. What's more fun than gathering around an inviting fire to toast marshmallows or even cook a meal?

Plan carefully before constructing a fire pit. Because they hold small bonfires, a fire pit requires plenty of floor space on all sides to keep people a safe distance from the flames. Provide seating nearby so you and your guests can gather for conversation in the firelight and warmth.

As with other fireplaces, using fire pits requires common sense. Safety has to be a priority; train everyone in the family so they'll know what to do if a fire grows out of control. Keep an extinguisher handy. Also have a cover for clamping over the pit to smother flames should they grow too large. This also helps contain sparks, which might blow out of the pit after the party is over.

SOFT LIGHT

If fires are not allowed in your community or if your deck space is too small, don't despair. Even the tiniest deck has room for candles, no matter where you live. Their glimmer transforms the plainest spot into a magical world. Lighting groups of candles gives you the satisfaction of settling into your own little retreat. Candlelight sets an intimate mood for dinner under the stars. Candles also complement a low-voltage lighting system and offer just the right touch for nighttime outdoor entertaining.

WATER FEATURES

Natural shapes, materials, and plants make a pond appear comfortable and native to its environment.

Want your deck to really sparkle? Let moving water do the job. Even if you don't need to subdue distracting sounds from beyond your yard, the gentle splashes and trickles will make your deck seem a world apart.

Still water in a shallow reflecting pond, with its glassy surface, acts as a natural mirror and creates a contemplative, calming setting. It's possible to shape an elegant and peaceful reflecting pond with brick, or have a professional pour a concrete base for the pool. Moving water plays with light by catching it, refracting it, and casting it about. Fountainheads spurt water in several basic patterns: glassy mushrooms, multilevel tiers, gurgling bubbles, and simple streams from a spitter. Some fountainheads offer several patterns in one.

INSTALLATION OPTIONS

Putting in a water feature can be as simple as setting up a small pond using a preformed, rigid liner or forming the base of the pond with a flexible liner. Camouflage the liner's edge with landscape timbers or rocks.

All water features must follow one basic guideline: The water should be aerated. Stagnant water breeds mosquitoes, anaerobic (smelly) bacteria, and algae. It also collects silt and debris. Water spilling over the edge of a waterfall or splashing out of a fountain picks up air, which helps it stay fresh.

To keep water moving, install a submersible pump that recirculates the water, sending it to the top of a waterfall, out of a fountainhead, or simply back and forth in the pond. As the name suggests, a submersible pump operates underwater. It must be submerged at all times so it doesn't pump air, which burns out the motor. You must also keep intake filters clean so that debris doesn't clog the pump. Skimming the surface of your pond to remove debris helps prevent clogging, as does setting the pump on a stone or brick on the bottom of the pond.

You can find liners, submersible pumps, and fountainheads readily at home centers, aquatic shops, and nurseries. Ask an employee to help you select the right materials for your water garden and ensure that everything is correctly sized for the volume of water.

MAKING PLANS

When including a water feature in the construction of a deck, plan for the installation of a pair of 2-inch schedule-40 PVC pipes across the deck site. Draw them in your plans so they run like tunnels under the site—from one end of the deck to the other. These pipes—called sleeves—provide a route for electrical wires and smaller pipes

DRAINING THE WATER FEATURE

Drain your pond periodically for cleaning and maintenance, and for winterizing. With a small pond or fountain, simply bail the water by hand. For larger ponds, install a drain valve and drain line that empties into a storm system or natural area; the chore of emptying the pond will be much easier. In areas where ponds can freeze solid, remove the pump and store it temporarily in a bucket of water in a basement or other area where it won't freeze. Once a pump has been used, it's important to keep it wet to prevent the seal from drying out and shrinking.

Straight lines, a raised lip, and an urn-turned-fountain give this water feature a formal air.

ADDING WATER TO AN EXISTING SITE

Retrofitting a deck with a water feature is best done with ground-level decks. To build a pond on an existing deck, you'll need to cut through the decking, excavate beneath the deck, and insert a preformed liner. Make sure the bottom and sides of the liner are fully supported. When installing piping to the pond, pry up sections of dry-set paving on any paths leading to the deck, then replace the paving when you're done.

For mortared pathways, you'll need to cut through the paving to install the sleeves, or hire a contractor to jack and bore under it to install piping. Patch it by laying a band of stone, brick, or other material in the cut (a concrete patch will be obvious). Repeat the banding as a decorative element elsewhere on the deck.

This water feature, with a cantilevered waterfall and raised coping, suggests a natural wetland.

connected to a water source. They also protect wires and pipes from the pressure of any paving, especially if it settles and shifts. If a water line or wire breaks, you can replace it without digging up the deck by snaking the replacement through the sleeve. Any water leaking from a break flows through the conduit and out the ends beyond the site instead of seeping directly into the soil under it. Always run power and water lines through separate sleeves.

WATER FEATURE CONSTRUCTION

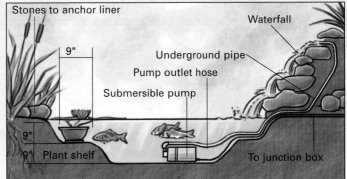

For a natural-looking pond, edge it with materials native to your region. Keep edges irregular to make it look as though the water has cut its own channel through the soil. Set water plants around the edges and stock the pond with fish.

WATER FEATURES
continued

FOUNTAINS

Wall-mounted fountains catch trickling water in prefabricated basins. They work well on upper-story decks because the weight of the structure is borne by a wall, not the floor. And because the wall on which they are mounted shelters these modest-size features, overspray rarely causes a problem.

Wall-mounted fountains require a power source to run the pump that recirculates the water. Have an electrician install an outlet on an exterior wall of your house without disturbing existing flooring.

Running a pump without adequate water will damage the pump. You'll need to regularly replenish the water in a fountain—wall-mounted or freestanding—during hot, dry weather, when evaporation occurs. Simply pour water into the basin of the fountain.

Supply large water features with a source of water that's controlled by a float valve. The float valve automatically monitors water levels so the pool is always full. It turns on the water when levels fall below a preset mark, and shuts it off when the fountain is refilled. Installing a float valve raises the cost

The sound of splashing water soothes and cheers us. Moving water also muffles the noise of an air conditioner, traffic, and other common, annoying sounds.

Pedestal fountains draw attention to their form, not just their sound. Most suit small spaces beautifully.

of the fountain a bit, and a plumber might be required to do the work.

FINE-TUNING

It takes only a moderate volume of moving water to mask unpleasant sounds such as traffic. Even the smallest trickle or drip will buffer noise from the outside world. So if you have to shout to be heard over your waterfall or fountain, too much water is moving through it too quickly. Adjust the flow valve on the pump to reduce the flow and soften the sound.

WATER FEATURE SAFETY

All pumps require electricity—but mixing water and electricity is dangerous. For that reason, you should plug pumps only into waterproof exterior outlets that connect to a power source with a ground fault circuit interrupter (GFCI). The GFCI prevents possible electrocution.

Most building codes classify water features in a special category called "attractive nuisances." That means you'll be held responsible if a child falls into your pool or pond and is injured. Rules regarding attractive nuisances vary locally, so check with the building inspector in your city or county to see how pool depth corresponds to fencing requirements.

STORAGE

Anything you plan to keep on your deck—garbage cans, firewood, furniture covers, pet supplies, garden tools, or barbecue utensils—needs a spot to call home. Finding places to put such items—and keeping the living space from looking like a giant storage box—takes a little creative thinking.

NIFTY STORAGE PLACES

■ When adding a privacy wall, build it with space for firewood.

■ Paint a child's toy box with weatherproof exterior paint and use it as an outdoor coffee table with built-in storage.

■ Keep pet supplies and birdseed in watertight plastic bins, which protect them from weather and pesky critters looking for food.

■ Buy an extra mailbox or decorative bin to provide a dry place for storing small hand tools and garden gloves.

■ Place a baker's rack against a blank wall to store empty flowerpots, harvest baskets, and watering cans.

■ Use everyday yard tools as outdoor art. Mount hooks or handle holders on walls for hanging shovels, rakes, and hoes. The back or side of a garage, where the roof overhangs, provides a protected place. If you have a wall but no eaves, mount a shallow awning overhead to shelter the tools from weather and help prevent rusting.

■ Buy freestanding benches with lids—or build them into the perimeter of your decks.

■ Prefabricated fence sections or lattice panels mounted on posts conceal garbage cans as well as heating and cooling units without obstructing airflow.

■ Mount a trellis to support vines on the side of your home to hide exterior conduit and wires. If a utility meter spoils the look of your outdoor room, build a box around it with a hinged door for the meter reader to open. (Contact your utility company first; some have rules against this.)

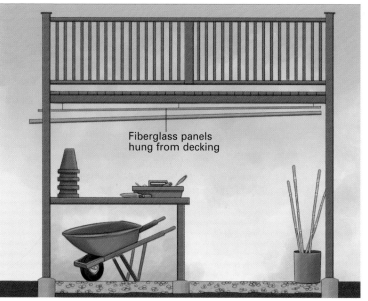

Fiberglass panels hung from decking

Though it won't stay completely dry, the area under your deck can be waterproofed well enough to store many garden tools.

Unused space beneath a built-in bench offers a dry niche for storing firewood conveniently close to a fire pit.

Old shutters create functional as well as stylish screens.

Assessing The Site

Look out at the vast wilderness of your yard. In that space lie both limitations and countless creative possibilities. Before you begin building your deck, you'll want to know exactly what they are.

The features of your landscape can affect both where you put your deck and how you design it. After you've made the basic decisions about style and location, it's time to assess your site to determine what, if any, modifications its characteristics will require.

The terrain of your landscape is perhaps the most important feature. Although no site is perfectly level, a basically flat yard will help keep the job uncomplicated. A slope, especially one that falls off sharply, might call for grading the soil and building a retaining wall to hold back the remaining soil. Or it might mean you should consider moving your proposed deck to another location.

Then there's drainage, existing vegetation, views, and climate. After a rain, for example, do the neighborhood kids come by to marvel at the eroded canyon or to play in the lake that covers your lawn? Are trees making shade or just blocking a view? Or is the view undesirable anyway? How about street noise and privacy?

Many of these features, of course, are beyond your control. Ignoring them can result in an unused and unattractive deck, but if you design your outdoor living space with them in mind, you can minimize their effects. The key is working with nature, not against it.

In some regions, shelter from the sun can become a primary goal of deck design. Assessing the attributes of your site can result in a deck design that overcomes problems caused by climate, as well as the terrain.

A deck can make practical use of terrain that might otherwise prove impractical. Here, the ground-level platforms break the slope into tiers, a solution that minimizes extensive grading.

ON-SITE PHOTOS

Take pictures of your yard when assessing your site. The camera is less forgiving than the eye. It's easy to overlook things you see every day; you'll be surprised how much the photos call attention to details you may have missed. For example, you may discover that the neighbors can see right into your living room window. Or you may not have noticed how unattractive your garbage cans or utility shed is. The deck site shown at the right offers a nice rear view of the woods, but the photo shows how the view to the side yard looks directly onto the neighbors' home. That means that any activity that takes place on the deck is open to the neighbors' view. The deck needs more privacy.

Photos also allow you to bring landscaping problems indoors to your kitchen table, giving you an objective tool to help you plan.

Digital cameras and accompanying computer programs can make your picture planning even more fun. Take several shots end-to-end and let the computer make a panoramic view. With other programs, you can sketch in trees and architectural elements.

CLIMATES AND MICROCLIMATES

Your deck should offer more than privacy, protection, and plenty of seating. It should take advantage of the natural surroundings—cooling breezes, warm sun, shade, subtle garden fragrances. Paying attention to weather patterns and designing your deck for maximum comfort in a variety of conditions can extend its usefulness.

OFF THE AXIS?

Many homes are not situated on a true north-south, east-west axis, and a deck on such a site will get a combination of sun and shade patterns. For example, a deck on the southeast side of a house will get sun much of the day but escape the hot late-afternoon sun.

To get an idea of how your site will be affected, make a rough sketch of your home and experiment with different deck locations, shading in the shadow patterns illustrated on these pages.

SUN AND SHADE

As the sun travels overhead throughout the day and year, it sends down varying amounts of warmth and light. Shadows cast by trees, walls, and rooflines will also shift throughout the day. Place your deck so these natural patterns correspond to the times of the day and the seasons when you'll use the space.

Take an inventory of your shade and sunshine. Watch how the sun moves across your property at various times of the day during warm months. Stakes driven in the yard will help you keep track of moving shade patterns. Make notes about the shade patterns and keep them handy when you begin to draw your plans on paper.

If your proposed site is already shaded during the times you'll use the deck, that makes your decisions about location less complicated But even if you don't have much flexibility in where you put the deck, you can alter the environment.

If you need additional shade, you can make some. Add trees and other plants to shade a site that gets too much afternoon sun. A pergola can filter hot sunlight.

Most north-side locations are in almost constant shade and will probably be cool on all but the hottest days. If you're planning a north-side deck, you may want to build on a detached site, well beyond the shadow line of the house. Or you could extend the surface beyond the shadow line of the house to produce both shady and sunny areas in summer. This site would work well in a year-round hot climate.

Southern sites get sun all day and may need added shade from trees or an overhead structure. Although the south side of the house receives sun most of the day, it does so from different angles, depending on the season. Summer sunlight is high in the sky, but in winter the light comes in at a low angle. A south-facing deck with a lattice-covered pergola would have filtered sun in summer and full sun in winter. Outdoor space on the south side will have the best chance of getting any winter sun in mild-winter climates.

So can a roll-out awning, which can be retracted when it's not needed. Let roses or vines climb up an arbor to create a private shaded spot for outdoor reading—without blocking the breeze. Vines climbing up a lattice wall can cool off a site that gets hot in the late afternoon. Or you could try a compromise— a location that features partial shade and partial sunlight during the hours of greatest deck use.

If you can't find the perfect deck spot that gets both sunlight and shade, create separate areas for each. As shown here, an open table and shaded lounge chair allow you to sit in the sun on cool days and move to a shady spot when it's hot.

For breakfast in the early light or a cool spot for evening meals, an east-facing deck is ideal. The eastern sun warms the cool morning air. But an east-side site will also be shaded sooner than any other location. For example, by 5 p.m., an east-side location will be shaded for several feet, and by 7:30 p.m., even in summer, it will be engulfed in shade. Depending upon your climate, such early shade can be an asset to your deck, or restrict its hours of use.

A west-facing deck will get the hot afternoon sun and, without natural or added shade, may become unbearably hot in the afternoon. The west side starts the day in shade but gets the hot sun from early afternoon until sunset, and deck surfaces will radiate heat long after dusk. To create a deck site that's enjoyable from early afternoon to evening, you may want to consider a wraparound style that takes advantage of both a western and northern exposure.

CLIMATES AND MICROCLIMATES
continued

Trellises invite climbing plants to form screens that provide beauty and privacy without blocking breezes.

TREES, PLANTS, AND MICROCLIMATES

Unless you're building a brand-new house, your choice of deck sites will be affected by what you find on the site: It may be either hilly or flat, sunny or shaded. And although you have very little control over the terrain, you can moderate temperature extremes around your deck by carefully planting trees and shrubs.

Trees can provide shade from sunlight and can break up harsh winds. Deciduous trees—such as oaks, maples, and walnuts—are quite bushy in summer but lose their leaves in winter. The leaves will shade your deck in summer but let sun warm the surface in cooler months. That makes trees a practical investment in moderate climates where the deck is in use most of the year.

No matter where in the country you live, your yard will have prevailing winds, and those winds are likely to come from different directions in summer and winter. Watch to see where the wind comes from, and plant to take advantage of it. In summer you'll want to channel the wind toward the deck; in winter you'll want to block the wind.

As you design your site, keep the variety of trees and bushes to a minimum to unify the design, and don't plant deep-rooted trees or bushes near the house, where they can undermine the foundation.

WIND

The wind will affect your outdoor comfort as much as the sun. A pleasant breeze may bring welcome relief on a hot day, but gusting winds can make it impossible to enjoy the space at all.

Study the wind patterns in your yard and learn to make a distinction between prevailing winds (the general direction of wind currents) and seasonal breezes (those localized to a time of day or season).

If possible, build your deck in a spot that's sheltered from strong prevailing winds. If your site is exposed, a slatted fence or windbreak (trees and hedges) can transform a strong wind into a breeze that flows across your deck, cooling and freshening the air.

RAIN

You can't keep the rain from coming down, but you can build yourself some shelter. A solid roof over a part of your deck can keep you dry outdoors in rainy weather. So can a gazebo or retractable awning.

If you live in an area with harsh winters, construct the roof so it won't be vulnerable to snow buildup or ices dams. And be sure to retract the awning before the first snow. Rain will also affect the relationship of your deck surface to the indoor floor. Build your deck about an inch lower than the floor inside, to keep the rain from seeping in.

SNOW

In snowy climates, you'll want to keep the snow from becoming an uninvited guest in your family room or kitchen. That means that you'll have to build the deck surface 3 to 4 inches below the interior floor. Heavy snowfalls might mean dropping the deck surface to about 8 inches below the inside room, but you can ease this drop with an outdoor landing.

CREATING A MICROCLIMATE

Did you ever notice that the air on a deck feels a bit different from the air a few feet away? That's because the materials that go into a deck and the arrangement of those materials create what's called a microclimate.

Different paving materials, for example, absorb different amounts of heat from the sun each day. They also reflect different amounts of light. A light-colored concrete slab reflects a lot of heat. Although the surface may feel comfortably warm, it may seem harsh and glaring because it also reflects sunlight. By contrast, dark brick won't reflect the harshness of bright sunlight but will absorb a tremendous amount of heat. This can make the deck surface uncomfortable underfoot during the day, but the stored heat radiates during the cool of the evening, prolonging the daytime warmth.

Likewise, a hilltop deck will feel warmer on a calm day than one at the base of a hill because cooler air flows downhill. What's more, if you trap the cold air at the bottom of a hill with retaining walls, fences, or house walls, your deck might be quite cool in the evening.

The construction of a wall or fence can also create a microclimate. Don't expect a solid structure to help reduce winds. Wind-

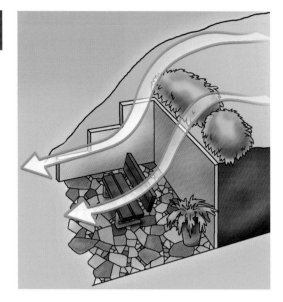

Because cool air is heavier than warm air, it flows downhill, making a deck site at the bottom of a slope cooler than one at the same elevation but on level ground.

control research shows that solid fences create low-pressure pockets that pull the wind down into the very area you want protected. The wind swirls over the top and drops back down at a distance roughly equal to the height of the fence.

This means that if your quiet site is "protected" by a solid 6-foot wall, the force of the wind on your deck about 6 to 12 feet from the wall is about the same as on the other side. Build louvered fences or walls with open areas on top to filter the wind and let it through instead of causing it to vault over the top and come down with a turbulence.

WINDSCREEN/FENCE HEIGHTS

Wind protection drops off at a distance approximately equal to the height of the fence.

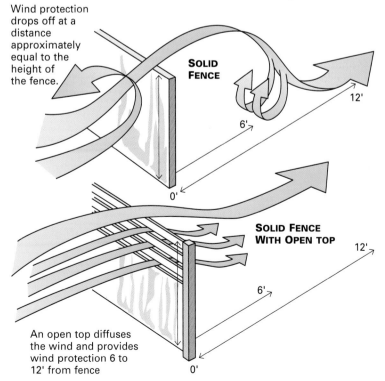

SOLID FENCE

12'

6'

0'

SOLID FENCE WITH OPEN TOP

12'

6'

0'

An open top diffuses the wind and provides wind protection 6 to 12' from fence

FROST AND FOUNDATIONS

In climates that experience frequent freeze-thaw cycles, a mortared deck requires excavation and concrete footings. Without this extra support, the frost will heave and crack the surface.

SLOPES, SOIL, AND DRAINAGE

Raised decks put living space where you want it. This curving bench doubles as a safety rail. Before building a deck around existing trees, check whether the trees are healthy and long-lived species.

Sloping sites, such as hillsides, banks, ravines, and drainage swales, often pose problems, but they can offer you more design opportunities than you might think. If you ignored a slope when you started assessing your site, take a second look.

Land sloping away from a high spot offers a view to the area below. Land that slants uphill generally creates privacy and shelter from harsh winds. A seemingly problematic area might turn out to be the best spot in your yard for a new deck. So even where there's a slope, there's hope—you can usually find a way to grade it level.

LEVELING THE SOIL

To level a slope, either cut into it to remove soil and form a flat area, or fill in a low point, or both.

Both methods will create a level surface suitable for your deck. But untamped fill dirt is not stable and will settle unevenly, causing a ground-level deck to crack. You'll need to tamp and firm the loose surface of a filled area before installing such a design. Use footings, not piers, to support the posts, and dig the holes deep enough so the foundations are in firm, ungraded soil.

If the soil sloughs off when you cut into a slope, you should build a retaining wall to hold it in place. Even if a retaining wall isn't necessary, building one will provide you with a cozy deck nestled into the side of a hill.

TYPES OF SOIL

All soil is not created equal. There are several kinds of soil, and each will have a different effect on your site and how you prepare it.

■ Loose, sandy loam absorbs water and drains well, is good for plantings, and is easy to grade. It erodes easily, however, and does not compact well; you'll need to set posts in concrete.

■ Silted soil is easy to dig and to compact, but posts for overheads and fences will need to be set in concrete.

■ Clay is compact and sheds water so easily that runoff can prove to be a problem. Fix it with grading or with drains that terminate in storm sewers or catch basins.

Each type of soil has a different angle of repose—the steepest angle at which soil on a slope will stay in place and not slough off. In general, soils with a high clay content have a steeper angle of repose and hold together better than loose, sandy soils, which readily give way.

Cutting into a slope created a level area for this snug deck. The brick retaining wall holds back the higher soil and radiates stored heat, which can extend the use of the deck into cooler evening hours.

TIPS FOR RETAINING WALLS

Include weep holes in the design of your retaining walls so groundwater behind the wall can seep through its face. When the water has a place to go, it won't build up pressure behind the wall and crack or topple it.

In general, a wall footing should be twice as wide as the wall is thick, but if your soil is sandy or loose, consult a professional to help you calculate the size of footings.

A trip to your building department can also prove very helpful. The staff can inform you about local codes and tell you which parts of your project require a permit.

SOLUTIONS FOR SLOPES

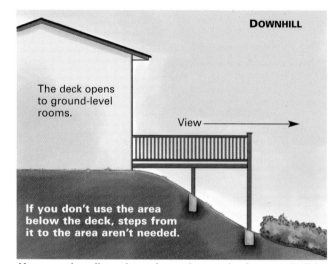

DOWNHILL

The deck opens to ground-level rooms.

View

If you don't use the area below the deck, steps from it to the area aren't needed.

UPHILL

Leave plants undisturbed so slope remains stable.

Privacy

How you handle a slope depends on whether you build the deck above it or below it. Above a slope (above, left), your deck will require additional fill dirt, compacted and held in place with a retaining wall. Below a slope (above right), a deck will often require cutting into the soil and keeping the remaining soil in place with a retaining wall.

WHAT TO DO WITH EXCESS FILL DIRT

Put the soil removed from grading to the best use by leveling other parts of your lawn. This procedure is called cut and fill, and it works best when the grading removes an amount equal to the areas that need additional soil. Cut and fill also eliminates the expense of disposing of excess soil, as well as the cost of purchasing fill dirt.

If cutting into a hillside results in more fill dirt than you need, use the excess topsoil in your landscape—in planting beds, raised or flush with the rest of the lawn. Because you'll probably remove more than just topsoil, not all of the excavated dirt will be suitable for planting beds. Use it instead to construct berms—low mounds of earth in a landscape. Avoid spreading excess soil around trees, even temporarily. Just a few extra inches of dirt over tree roots can suffocate delicate feeder roots and kill the tree.

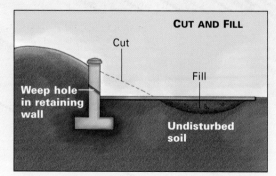

CUT AND FILL

Cut

Fill

Weep hole in retaining wall

Undisturbed soil

SLOPES, SOIL, AND DRAINAGE
continued

RUNOFF AND PLANTS

Runoff from a deck can wreak havoc away from the deck site. Water moving across impermeable surfaces flows quickly. As it gathers speed and runs off the hardscape, it can cut channels through beds, washing away seedlings and topsoil.

Established plants with fibrous roots, such as lawns and ornamental grasses, will probably be able to stand up to this wash of water. But shallow-rooted plants, such as those in recently installed flower beds, will usually wash out of the ground. Runoff flowing into planting areas can also become trapped in puddles, and the overly wet soil drowns plants by suffocating their roots.

You have several options for dealing with excess water:

■ Redirecting the water
■ Planting annuals in raised beds or containers
■ Choosing plants that thrive in wet soil

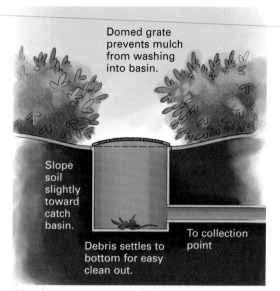

Planting areas surrounded by paving can hold water. Install a catch basin before paving. The basin collects excess water. Underground piping transports the water elsewhere in your yard or into a storm sewer.

GRADING FOR DRAINAGE

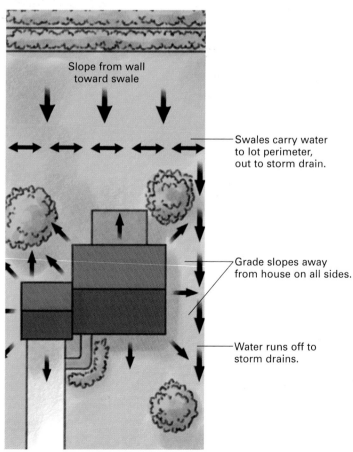

FOUNDATION DRAINAGE

If you have water in your basement, it may be caused by ground sloping toward the foundation. Here's an easy solution:

■ Slope the soil next to the foundation away from the house for a distance of at least 4 feet.
■ Bring in new soil as necessary.
■ Lay landscape fabric over the sloped surface.
■ If you're going to plant the area, cut holes in the landscape fabric for the plants. Spread decorative rock or wood chips to camouflage the fabric.

Build grade-level decks above a gravel bed, using lumber rated for ground contact. Keeping the end grain of wood dry by extending the gravel strip beyond the deck intercepts runoff and looks tidy.

TREES, ROCKS, AND OTHER OBSTACLES

Many existing features of your landscape, such as flower beds, foundation plantings, fences, walls, and walkways, will affect the location of your deck. If you can't part with them, and are certain of your favorite spot, integrate them into your design. The same goes for trees, rocks, and other obstacles. Building trees into your design, however, calls for careful planning.

ENCLOSING A TREE: Decks built around a tree can appear as though nature put them there. Their height and mass will balance the horizontal expanse of your deck surface. But take care to avoid damage to the root system. Your tree can be the life of your deck. Don't let your deck be the death of the tree.

Avoid hemming in trees too tightly with decking. Allow room for trunks to grow, or you'll end up cutting through planks later on to enlarge tree holes.

RETROFITTING FOR DRAINAGE

After heavy rains, water sometimes puddles on decks and other walking surfaces in your landscape. Perpetually damp spots provide ideal conditions for slick moss to grow and for mosquitoes to breed. Even if you've already built your deck or have inherited it as part of the property purchase, it's not too late to remedy these problems.

To stop puddling, divert water away from low areas. During a heavy rain, observe the water's path. Almost anything—debris, excessive mulch, or a poorly placed plant—can block the flow of water and divert it where you don't want it. If the water originates from beyond the surface, change the direction of the flow at its source. For example, relocate downspouts so they don't dump water onto the deck. Or install extensions to the downspouts to carry the water elsewhere.

Use curbing to block the unwelcome flow of water from the lawn or a planting area. Or divert the flow with a swale—a slight depression made to channel water. When installing a curb to redirect storm water, dig a swale along the back side of it. Often, a shallow swale alone keeps water flowing in the right direction. Avoid building a walkway across a swale; it will form a dam and impede drainage.

Removing unused portions of paving is another solution because it reduces the amount of impermeable surface. Removing a section of paving can also pleasantly alter the shape of a patio or path, and create room for low plants within the space. This solution works best if the sections removed aren't in the part of a surface that you use regularly.

TOOLS AND MATERIALS

Building a deck requires a modest collection of tools and a knowledge of lumber, other materials, and fasteners. In this chapter, you'll find all the information you need to get you started, as well as tips that will help you estimate your costs.

Tools fall into three categories—layout, excavation, and carpentry tools. You may already have most of what you need. Some, such as a posthole digger and other excavation tools, you may be able to borrow from friends.

But there are others you'll need to rent (see "Rental Tools, page 75).

The number of retail building supply outlets has mushroomed in the last 10 years to meet the growing do-it-yourself demand. But selecting materials is more than simply a matter of pulling lumber off the rack. The more you know about the wood you'll use—the variety of species, sizes, and finishing techniques— the more rewarding the construction of your deck will be.

ESTIMATING MATERIALS

Use these formulas to estimate the amount of materials you'll need, using the same units— inches or feet—for all measurements.

Rectangular solid

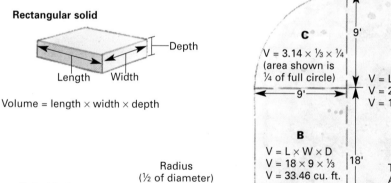

Depth
Length   Width

Volume = length × width × depth

Cylindrical solid

Radius
(½ of diameter)
Depth

Volume = 3.14 × radius² × depth

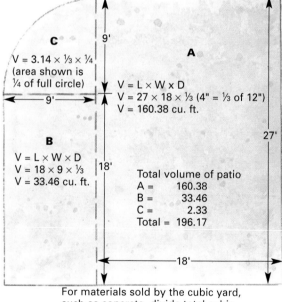

C
$V = 3.14 \times \frac{1}{3} \times \frac{1}{4}$
(area shown is ¼ of full circle)
9'

9'

A
$V = L \times W \times D$
$V = 27 \times 18 \times \frac{1}{3}$ (4" = ⅓ of 12")
$V = 160.38$ cu. ft.

27'

B
$V = L \times W \times D$
$V = 18 \times 9 \times \frac{1}{3}$
$V = 33.46$ cu. ft.
18'

Total volume of patio
A =   160.38
B =   33.46
C =   2.33
Total = 196.17

18'

For materials sold by the cubic yard, such as concrete, divide total cubic feet by 27.

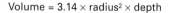

Careful preparation saves time, effort, and money. By having the site ready, and all your tools and materials on hand, you get started right—and you avoid repeat trips to the lumberyard or hardware store.

SHOPPING FOR LUMBER

Because decks are popular projects, you'll find most building supplies readily available and reasonably priced. For the best service, purchase as many items as possible from a single supplier. Get prices from several outlets and ask whether you can get free delivery and quantity discounts. If you prefer the selection or service of one supplier but can get better prices from another, ask the one to match the rival's price. Most suppliers will at least make an effort to be competitive.

MATERIALS CHECKLIST

FOUNDATION:
- ■ Concrete
- ■ Forms
- ■ Sand or gravel
- ■ Precast piers

HARDWARE:
- ■ Post anchors
- ■ Joist hangers
- ■ Angle brackets
- ■ Lag screws
- ■ Carriage and hex-head bolts with nuts and washers
- ■ Decking screws
- ■ Beam saddles
- ■ Galvanized nails
- ■ Stair cleats

DECKING:
- ■ Decking boards

FRAMING:
- ■ Posts
- ■ Ledger
- ■ Beams
- ■ Joists
- ■ Rim joists

FINISH:
- ■ Sealer and stain

STAIRS AND RAILINGS:
- ■ Stair stringers
- ■ Stair treads
- ■ Concrete for stairway landing
- ■ Railing posts
- ■ Railing caps
- ■ Balusters or spindles
- ■ Railings

TOOLS

To build a basic deck, you need basic skills and basic tools. You may already have most of these tools, but you'll probably need to buy or rent a few more as your project proceeds.

Review the list on these pages and look through the instructions for building the kind of deck you have planned. Make a list of the tools you need to buy or rent.

LAYOUT TOOLS

Layout can be the most exacting aspect of deck building, but layout tools need not be expensive. Here's what you'll need.

LINE LEVEL: This small level hooks to mason's line stretched over distances too long to span with a carpenter's level.

MASON'S LINE: The mainstay of layout work. Use nylon; it doesn't stretch.

MEASURING TAPE: This is a do-it-yourselfer's constant companion. A 1-inch blade will extend farther without sagging. Get a 25-footer to be precise and save time.

PLUMB BOB: This makes quick work of marking posthole locations.

EXCAVATION TOOLS

Although there are only a few tools in this category, rent or buy high-quality ones. You don't want any breakdowns.

SHOVELS: Get a round-nosed model for excavating and a square model for removing sod.

GARDEN RAKE: This is for leveling soil and smoothing fill dirt or garden beds.

CLAMSHELL DIGGER: Its hinged shovels will dig clean, straight-sided postholes in almost any soil.

TAMPING BAR: You'll need this to remove rocks that nature put where you want to dig postholes. Tamp the fill with a 2×4.

TOOLS FOR CONCRETE

5-GALLON BUCKET: Use this to measure water for premix and for general hauling of small loads.

WHEELBARROW: It's a must for mixing your own concrete.

SHOVELS: Use the round-nosed model you have for excavating.

HOE: Get a mason's hoe. It has holes that make mixing easier.

CARPENTRY TOOLS

These tools are the backbone of do-it-yourself carpentry. If you're assembling your tool chest for the first time, buy good tools. You'll use them for other projects, many of which won't occur to you until you own the tools.

CARPENTER'S LEVEL: Get a 48-inch model for plumbing and leveling. Shorter versions may give false readings. Buy one with a stiff steel frame.

FRAMING SQUARE: You'll use this for quick, preliminary checks for right angles.

CIRCULAR SAW: These come in different

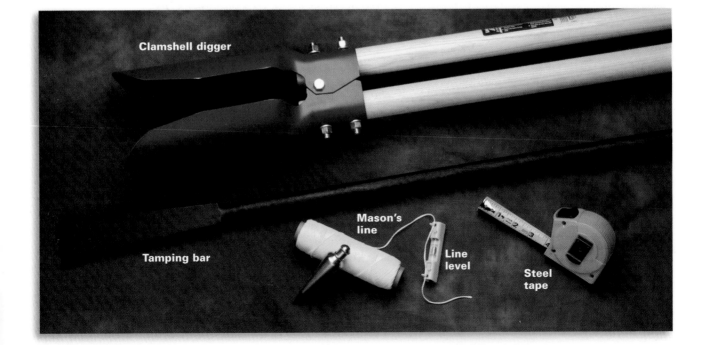

Clamshell digger

Tamping bar

Mason's line

Line level

Steel tape

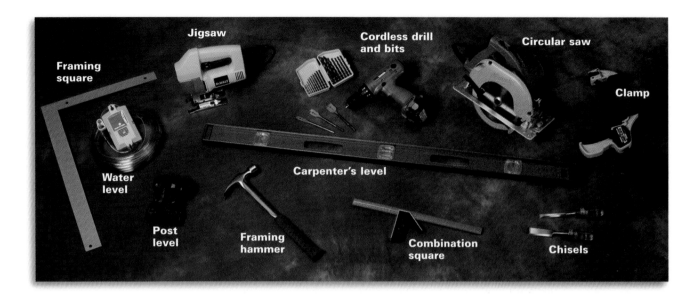

Framing square · Jigsaw · Cordless drill and bits · Circular saw · Clamp · Water level · Carpenter's level · Post level · Framing hammer · Combination square · Chisels

sizes. Get a heavy-duty model with a 7¼-inch carbide-tipped combination blade. The extra power will come in handy on this or any other project that requires you to cut framing members.

JIGSAW: If you're cutting any fancy patterns, you'll need one of these. (Buy a heavy-duty model here too.)

CORDLESS DRILL: This is an essential tool. It drills holes and makes driving screws a snap. Buy a 14.4-volt model and a spare battery. You'll need spade bits of appropriate sizes for larger holes and to start mortises. Twist drills will take care of holes for screws and bolts.

FRAMING HAMMER: Buy a high-quality, 20-ounce hammer. The extra weight may be tiring at first, but you'll be thankful for it after driving a deckful of 10-penny (10d) nails.

POST LEVEL: This is a one-purpose tool, but nothing does it better. Strap it to a post to plumb two sides at once.

WATER LEVEL: This device attaches to the end of your garden hose. Filled with water, it makes long-distance leveling easy.

CHISELS: You'll need chisels to shape mortises and tenons. Buy high-quality chisels and take good care of them. Drive chisels with a mallet, not a metal hammer. Sharp chisels make clean, accurate cuts. Poorly fitting mortises make weak joints.

COMBINATION SQUARE: This is an indispensable tool. It helps you check 90- and 45-degree angles quickly, measure depth from surfaces, and lay out cutting lines.

CHALK LINE: You'll need this to snap lines for cuts.

FLAT PRY BAR: This comes in handy when you need to force a reluctant board in place or to remove mistakes.

NAIL SET: Use this for setting finishing nails in railings or trim.

CHANNEL LOCK PLIERS: This is the universal tool for tightening and loosening fasteners.

SAWHORSES: You'll need these to support lumber when you cut it.

WRENCHES: Buy both sockets and combination wrenches for tightening carriage-bolt nuts and lag screws.

CAULKING GUN: Use this for sealing ledgers and anywhere you need a waterproof joint.

RENTAL TOOLS: YOU'LL NEED THESE—BUT NOT FOREVER

For some homeowners, part of the enjoyment of making home improvements is buying new tools. But there are some tools you won't use after you've built your deck. If you need a tool only once, renting it makes more sense than buying it.

Here are some of the tools you may need to rent for the construction of your deck:
- Excavation equipment to clear the building site
- Hammer drill to install masonry anchors in a brick or stucco wall
- Power auger to dig holes for footings
- Power cement mixer to prepare concrete for footings and piers
- Reciprocating saw to make cuts where a circular saw can't reach
- Hydraulic jacks to hold framing in place during construction
- Framing nailer to make assembly of framing members proceed quickly and with less effort

LUMBER BASICS

Pound for pound, wood is almost as strong as steel. Its warm, natural beauty and remarkable workability make it ideal for decks and other outdoor structures.

The uses of lumber are endless. It can be used to add privacy screens and planters, create ornate railings, build ornamental trellises for climbing plants, or ease the transition between one area of the yard to another with wooden steps.

If you are extending a deck, the lumber you use will probably be similar to the existing structure. But if you're planning to build a shade structure or a deck addition—or to add decorative elements not tied to the deck structure—your lumber choices become more flexible.

Not all woods are alike, of course, so guide your selection by ranking appearance, cost, and durability at the top of your list of lumber-selection "rules." Whatever the scope of your plans, here are some tips to keep in mind when making your selection.

CHOOSING THE RIGHT WOOD

Wood used on exterior surfaces must be rot-resistant; several species are suitable for outdoor use. For example, pine, hemlock, or fir will start to fall apart after a few years if not treated or painted. These woods are fine if a painted surface complements your overall design and if you like how paint looks. But if you want the beauty of the wood grain revealed, you need a naturally resistant species or pressure-treated wood.

TERMITES

Wood has two main enemies—rot and bugs. Rot (even "dry rot") occurs for the most part when wood remains damp for a long time. Termites and other wood-eating insects are often attracted to moist wood. They usually live in the ground and tunnel in through your structure to get food.

Protect against rot and bugs by using pressure-treated lumber or resistant species wherever moisture may be a problem. To protect structural wood from damage, take steps to ensure that it can dry out; sometimes just sweeping away dirt can do the trick. You can also brush the wood with sealer that contains preservative and insecticide.

You can count on the appearance and durability of naturally rot-resistant redwood, cedar, and cypress. These woods are more expensive than others (redwood is the most costly), and their cost (as well as that of any species) increases the farther you live from their natural growth areas.

Redwood

REDWOOD: Beautiful and expensive, redwood is used when cost is not an issue. One of the species used as untreated lumber, redwood has a close grain and is naturally resistant to weathering, warping, cupping, and shrinkage. Its more than 30 grades are based on appearance, strength, and color.

Be careful! Not all redwood is long lasting. The dark heartwood resists rot and insects, but the cream-colored sapwood can be seriously damaged in just a couple of years. Often the two are mixed—in the same board and in the same bin.

"Common" redwood, often sold as "construction common," is partially composed of sapwood. Grades that use the term "heart," such as "B heart" or "construction heart," are heartwood grades with some knots and are as rot-resistant as heartwood grades that are "clear." Common redwood that has been treated is nearly as rot-resistant as pressure-treated lumber.

If you use heartwood, you can let redwood "go gray," meaning that you apply no stain and let it weather to a silvery color. (For staining options and techniques, see page 92.)

CEDAR: Less expensive than redwood, cedar has a lighter color and is generally regarded as less attractive. If you let it "go gray," it will not have

Cedar

the stately sheen of redwood. It works easily, but it's more likely to split than other woods.

Because cedar does not have as many grades as redwood, its quality varies within a grade. Don't rely on grading alone as an indication of quality. Inspect every board for knots and imperfections.

Like redwood, only the darker-colored heartwood of cedar is rot-resistant. Unfortunately, most of the cedar sold today is sapwood, and many homeowners are dismayed to find their cedar decks rotting within a few years. If you use cedar for decking and rails, make sure it can dry out between rainfalls, and give it a thorough coating of sealer-preservative.

CYPRESS: Similar to cedar in several respects, cypress grows in swampy areas of the South, a reason for its natural resistance to rot and decay. Lightweight, strong, and easy to handle, it also weathers to a silvery gray.

EXOTIC WOODS: If you have the budget, any number of exotic woods will add a style to your deck that you cannot match with other means. South American Ipe, for example, wears like iron, is extremely resistant to warping and rot, and requires little maintenance. Some exotic woods are difficult to work, however, so consultation with your wood specialty shop would be wise.

FIR AND PINE: These species are strong, lightweight, widely available, and less expensive than naturally resistant woods. Fir and pine are available in two forms:
■ **Untreated lumber:** Commonly used for

THE NATURE OF LUMBER

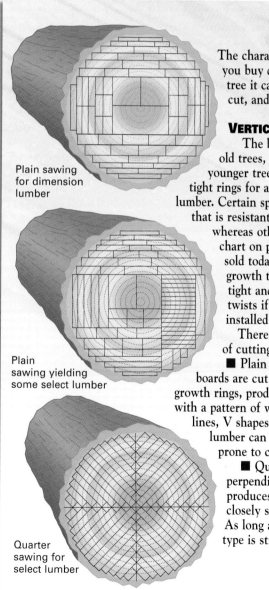

Plain sawing for dimension lumber

Plain sawing yielding some select lumber

Quarter sawing for select lumber

The characteristics of the wood you buy depend on the type of tree it came from, how it was cut, and how it was handled.

VERTICAL AND FLAT GRAIN:
The best lumber comes from old trees, with fewer knots than younger trees, and trees that have tight rings for a close grain in the lumber. Certain species produce wood that is resistant to warping and rot, whereas others do not (see the chart on page 10). Much lumber sold today comes from quick-growth trees, so the grain is not tight and the boards develop twists if not stored and installed carefully.

There are two basic methods of cutting wood:
■ Plain sawing, in which the boards are cut roughly parallel to the growth rings, produces flat-grained wood, with a pattern of widely spaced wavy lines, V shapes, and ovals. This lumber can be strong, but it is prone to cupping and warping.
■ Quarter sawing—cutting perpendicular to the rings—produces vertical grain in closely spaced parallel lines. As long as it has few knots, this type is stronger and more stable than plain-sawn (flat-grained) lumber, making it more desirable for finish work. But if there is a spike-shaped knot extending across much of the width of a board, the board will be seriously weakened. Quartersawn lumber tends to be expensive because it often comes from old-growth trees, and much of the log becomes sawdust and waste wood.

WOOD MOVEMENT AND MOISTURE:
Wood changes with the climate. Freshly cut wood shrinks until it is dry, and dry lumber expands and contracts with changes in humidity. However, given its longitudinal grain, wood can change significantly in width but hardly at all in length.

Most lumber is air-dried after it is cut. This removes much of the moisture, but leaves enough that wood may shrink, bow, and twist after you buy it. For framing and rough work, air-dried lumber is adequate as long as you stack the wood flat and fasten it in place before it has a chance to move.

Kiln-drying removes more moisture, so the boards are more stable. Dry lumber (S-DRY or MC 15) is less likely to warp, works more easily, holds fasteners more tightly, and finishes better. This is your best choice for trim work on your deck.

LUMBER BASICS
continued

forms, batter boards, and disposable bracing, it will withstand the outdoor elements only if finished. Unsuitable for posts, it can be used for rails and fencing infill if painted.

■ **Pressure-treated lumber:** A less expensive substitute for redwood, cedar, and cypress, wood treated with various chemicals under pressure is extremely rot-resistant.

Both chromated copper arsenate (CCA)—identifiable by its green tinge—and ammoniacal copper arsenate (ACA) have been used widely, but wood treated with these and other arsenic compounds is no longer available for residential use. Ammoniacal copper quaternary (ACQ) is a newer preservative with no hazardous ingredients. Grade stamps on the lumber tell you which chemical has been used.

Grade stamps also tell you how much preservative the lumber holds. Posts and boards (skids, joists, and skirts) that are in contact with the ground should have a retention level of 0.60 or higher. Other components can be built with lumber treated to 0.40. Look for a "Ground Contact" or "LP-22" stamp, or both.

SYNTHETIC DECKING: Made of wood by-products, wood and plastic, or 100 percent plastic, composition materials offer long life and extreme rot and insect resistance. They cost more initially, but require less maintenance over time. Some varieties snap together, making installation easy.

One disadvantage of synthetic material is that it can't be used for structural framing. Another is that it doesn't

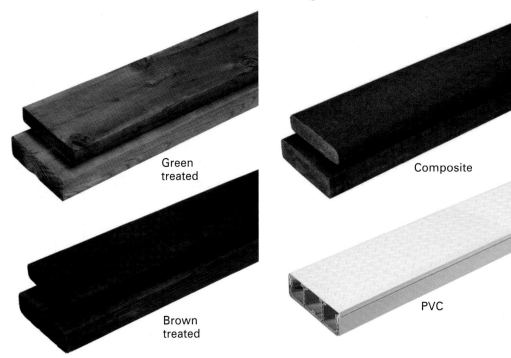

Green treated

Brown treated

Composite

PVC

WORKING WITH PRESSURE-TREATED LUMBER

Pressure treatment is not a substitute for finishing the wood. A couple of weeks after construction, you will need to apply a water-repellent sealer—several coats on surfaces you have cut.

After it dries for two to three months, apply paint or stain. Refinish pressure-treated stock from time to time. An unfinished structure built with treated wood will gradually turn to a pleasant, weathered gray but may not last nearly as long.

Wear gloves when handling treated wood—and a respirator when sawing it. Avoid burning or burying the scrap. Check with your local environmental agency for proper disposal methods.

really look like wood—but it is virtually maintenance-free. Some synthetics weather to a silvery gray color, mimicking cedar.

LUMBER GRADES

Lumber is divided into categories according to its thickness. *Boards* are less than 2 inches thick, and *dimension lumber* is 2 to 4 inches thick. Lumber is graded for its strength and appearance following standards established by independent agencies.

BOARDS: Fir and pine boards are graded in two categories—select and common.
■ **Select:** This is the best—with few or no knots.
   A: contains no knots
   B: has only small blemishes
   C: has some minor defects
   D: has larger blemishes that can be concealed with paint
■ **Common:** Utility grades are ranked from 1 to 5 in descending quality. A middle grade, such as no. 3, is a good choice for many decking projects.

SELECT LUMBER GRADING

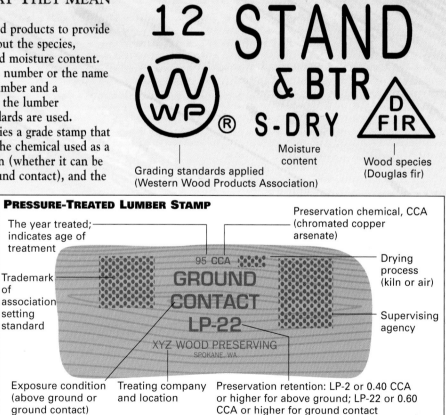

Select lumber is graded according to the prevalence of defects. Grade A is clear and contains no knots. Grades B, C, and D contain an increasing number of knots and blemishes.

GRADE STAMPS: WHAT THEY MEAN

Manufacturers stamp their wood products to provide customers with information about the species, prevalence of defects, grade, and moisture content. A grade stamp may also carry a number or the name of the mill that produced the lumber and a certification symbol that shows the lumber association whose grading standards are used.

   Pressure-treated lumber carries a grade stamp that shows the year it was treated, the chemical used as a preservative, exposure condition (whether it can be used above ground or with ground contact), and the amount of chemical treatment it received. Plywood grade stamps also show whether the wood is suitable for ground contact or only for aboveground use, and whether it can be used as sheathing. The stamp also designates the thickness of the sheet and the distance it can span. If the plywood is made to withstand exposure to the elements, look for a stamp that says "EXTERIOR."

Mill identifier   Grade (Standard)

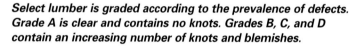

12 STAND
   &BTR
W WP ® S-DRY   D FIR

| | Moisture content | Wood species (Douglas fir) |

Grading standards applied
(Western Wood Products Association)

PRESSURE-TREATED LUMBER STAMP

The year treated; indicates age of treatment

Preservation chemical, CCA (chromated copper arsenate)

Trademark of association setting standard

95 CCA
GROUND
CONTACT
LP-22
XYZ WOOD PRESERVING
SPOKANE, WA

Drying process (kiln or air)

Supervising agency

Exposure condition (above ground or ground contact)

Treating company and location

Preservation retention: LP-2 or 0.40 CCA or higher for above ground; LP-22 or 0.60 CCA or higher for ground contact

LUMBER BASICS

continued

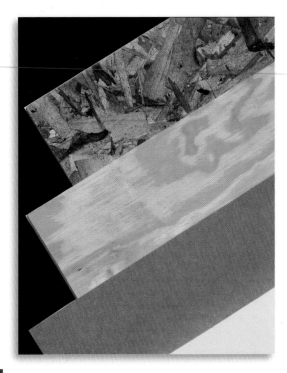

DIMENSION LUMBER: Fir and pine dimension lumber grades are:
- **CONSTRUCTION GRADE:** top of the line
- **STANDARD GRADE:** almost as good but cheaper than construction grade
- **UTILITY GRADE:** low-quality stock, unsuitable for framing

Pressure-treated lumber also comes in a variety of grades, from those treated for ground contact for posts and retaining walls, to lighter treatments for fences or decking boards. Redwood lumber is classified in "garden" or "architectural" grades.

As a rule, buy standard-grade dimension lumber and common-grade no. 3 boards or better if you can afford it. You may choose to save money by buying a cheaper grade and painting it after filling holes and sanding. If you want a rustic look, you may choose a lower grade.

SEASONING

Most wood is either air-dried or kiln-dried before sale. One of three marks tells you its surface moisture content: S-GRN (green lumber), more than 19 percent; S-DRY, up to 19 percent; MC 15, up to 15 percent. For framing and rough work, air-dried lumber is adequate. Dry lumber (S-DRY or MC 15) is less likely to warp, works more easily, holds fasteners more tightly, and finishes better.

PLYWOOD

Manufacturers produce plywood (a sheet material made from thin layers of wood that are glued together for strength) in a variety of sizes, thicknesses, textures, species, and grades. Any plywood used for outdoor construction must be an exterior-grade material—made with glues that will not deteriorate when exposed to moisture—so the veneers stay tightly bonded and the sheets remain flat and strong.

Purchase AA exterior grades (see "Plywood Grades" below) for sheathing that you will stain or paint or that will be visible from both sides. Lesser grades have blemishes that will show through the finish but will work just fine for sheathing covered with another material, such as shingles.

The plywood grade stamp gives you most of the information you need to make purchases. It shows whether the wood is suitable for ground contact or aboveground use, whether it can be used as sheathing, how thick it is, and the distance it can span.

Plywood is stiff and rigid, so it doesn't absorb or filter winds. That's why it should be affixed to a framework that's strong enough to support not only its weight but the lateral forces of wind shear.

PLYWOOD GRADES

Grade	Description
AA	Good on both sides. Highest quality, with no knots, defects, or voids. Readily accepts stains and paint. This is the material to get if both sides of panel fencing are visible.
AB	Good on one side (no knots or holes). The reverse side is smooth but has some defects. It may have patched "football" areas where large knots used to be. There are few voids in the interior. It can be sanded and painted for fences that have both sides visible.
AC	Good on one side. The other side has knots, minor defects, and "footballs." The interior has some small voids. It's suitable for fences that have only one side visible.
BB	Both sides have defects, but most of them can be sanded smooth or patched for painting. Usable for fencing (but not without major effort) where one side is visible, or as sheathing covered by clapboards, shingles, or other material.

DESIGNING WITH WOOD

Although decks share common building materials, differences in color, texture, and harmony make a design distinctive. Color can link the deck with your home and help set the mood. Earth tones generally appear warm and complement traditional settings. Blues, grays, or blacks appear cool and enhance contemporary designs.

Texture also affects the appearance of a deck. Both decking patterns and baluster styles establish a visual texture that can make your design a harmonious addition to your landscape. The photos on this page provide a few examples of how various elements can contribute to the overall effect of your design.

Transform obstacles such as trees into dramatic accents. Here, the enclosed tree trunk adds a visual accent to the horizontal surface of the deck. The lightly stained decking ties the structure to the color of the house, and the angles and narrow boards add variety to the dimensions of the lapped siding. Potted plants add a dash of color to this harmonious design.

Textures abound in this design, from the concrete rounds set in river rock to the vertical lattice planters and the interplay of light from the overhead rafters.

Notice how the painted, slightly formal balusters tie the overall style of this deck to the architecture of the house. The diagonal decking enhances the formal appearance, as do the matched pairs of flower pots.

LOOKS AREN'T EVERYTHING

Solid wood products, such as redwood, cedar, and pressure-treated lumber, have been the choice of deck experts for many years. But that is changing. The chart below lists several things you should consider when choosing materials and ranks them on a scale of 1 (least) to 5 (most).

Type	Cost	Maintenance	Durability	Skill Level Required
Redwood	5	1	5	4
Cedar	4	1	4	4
Pressure-treated pine	2	4	3	4
Composite wood	3	1	5	4

SELECTING LUMBER SIZES

To build a deck that is visually appealing and structurally sound, you need lumber in sizes that fit the scale, strength, and span requirement of your design.

DECKING

Compared to the work of framing your deck, installing decking boards will seem easy. But don't take this part of the project for granted. The surface must endure more weather and wear than any other part of the deck, and it will be the first thing anyone notices about your work. Choose materials and sizes that complement your design.

SIZES: The most common sizes of decking are 2×6 and ⁵⁄₄×6. Because 2×6 lumber is sold for many other purposes, it is usually easier to find and less expensive than ⁵⁄₄×6 lumber. But ⁵⁄₄×6 decking often comes with rounded edges and may be cut from a better grade of wood.

The other important difference between the two sizes is that 2×6 boards are stronger than ⁵⁄₄×6 boards, so you can place joists

farther apart. On a large deck, where you want to maintain a clean appearance with simple lines, 2×6 may be a better choice.

LENGTHS: If possible, buy decking in lengths that will cover the entire deck. If your design requires longer boards than you can

find, scatter the joints randomly on the deck, making sure each joint is centered by a joist.

SPANS: The size of decking you choose also depends on the span between the joists of your deck. Most decking stock is strong enough to span joists set on 16-inch centers. Longer spans require stronger decking. (See the span table, opposite.)

EXPANSION: All wood expands and contracts when it's exposed to the elements, and larger boards tend to expand and contract by greater amounts. Over time, this means that wider decking is more likely to splinter, warp, or expose nails that have pushed out. Pressure-treated lumber, however, will shrink over time, so butt successive boards edge-to-edge when you fasten them.

SPAN TABLES

The tables on the next three pages show specifications for various lumber species and sizes. They offer alternatives that will allow you to tailor the construction of your deck to the size you need. If the tables and data make your eyes glaze, don't worry. A reliable lumber dealer and the local building department will keep you on track.

To use the tables, grab your deck sketch, a calculator, and a sharp pencil. When you actually begin building your deck, you'll work from the bottom up; when you're calculating spans, you'll compute from the top down, starting with the decking.

CALCULATING SPANS

There are four basic parts of a deck structure for which you need to determine the size: decking, joist, beams, and posts. Let's assume you're building a 10×18-foot deck and you're using western pine. Your plans call for a structure 8 feet high, with 1×6 decking laid flat.

USING THE TABLE: Find the species (western pine) and its size (1×6) in the table at right, and note the maximum span appropriate to it (12 inches). This means you'll have to space your joists every 12 inches under the deck. If you want to space them closer, that's OK, but you can't go more

---

LUMBER: WHAT SIZE IS IT REALLY?

After wood is cut, drying, planing, and smoothing reduce its thickness and width. The dimensions used to describe the size of the lumber you will need—2×4, 2×6, and so forth—are its nominal dimensions: the size to which the stock was originally cut. That differs considerably from actual size. The actual size of a 2×4, for example, measures 1½ inches by 3½ inches.

Nominal Size	Actual Size	Nominal Size	Actual Size
⁵⁄₄×6	1¼×5½	4×4	3½×3½
2×4	1½×3½	4×6	3½×5½
2×6	1½×5½	4×8	3½×7¼
2×8	1½×7¼	4×10	3½×9¼
2×10	1½×9¼	4×12	3½×11¼
2×12	1½×11¼	6×6	5½×5½

Reductions in size from nominal to actual dimensions are about the same from one kind of wood to another, although pressure-treated boards may vary slightly from untreated boards. If size is particularly significant to your design, measure the actual dimensions. For example, if you want fencing infill of spaced, rough-sawn, 1¥6s, you'll need to know the actual dimensions of the lumber to compute how many boards and spaces will fit between the posts.

BASIC DECK COMPONENTS

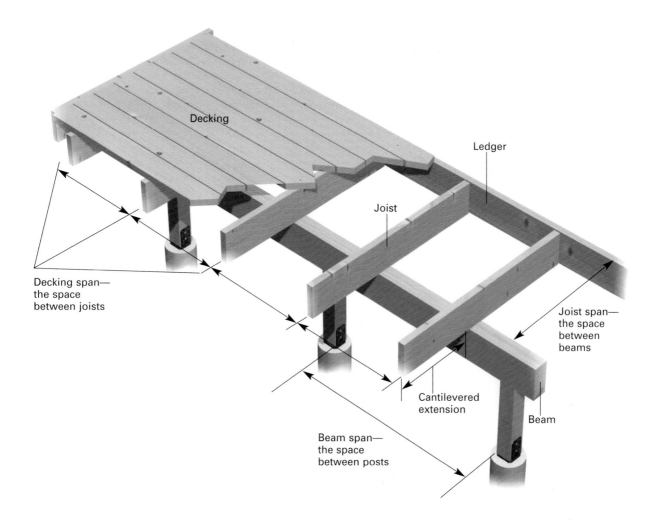

Decking

Ledger

Joist

Decking span—
the space
between joists

Joist span—
the space
between
beams

Cantilevered
extension

Beam

Beam span—
the space
between posts

RECOMMENDED MAXIMUM SPANS FOR SPACED DECKING BOARDS [1]

Species Group	Maximum Allowable Span [2] (inches)					
	Laid flat				Laid on edge	
	1×6	2×3	2×4	2×6	2×3	2×4
Douglas fir, larch, and southern pine	24	28	32	48	84	96
Hem fir and Douglas fir south	16	24	28	42	72	84
Western pines and cedars, redwood, and spruces	16	24	24	36	60	72

[1] These spans are based on the assumption that more than one floorboard carries normal loads. If concentrated loads are a rule, spans should be reduced accordingly.

[2] Based on construction grade or better (Select Structural, Appearance, no. 1 or no. 2).

SELECTING LUMBER SIZES
continued

than 12 inches. If some peculiarity of your design won't allow 12-inch spacing, you'll have to increase the thickness of your decking. For example, increasing the decking to 2×6s will let you set the joists at 32 inches.

DETERMINE JOIST SPANS: Using the same procedures, compute the maximum joist spans. Taking western pine again and using 2×10s for joists, find the appropriate specifications in the "Joist Spans" table, below. Running the numbers again shows you that your 2×10 western pine joists spaced 16 inches (or less) on center will span beams that are set 13 feet apart—more than enough for your 10-foot deck.

If your previous computations had resulted in a joist spacing of 32 inches, you could span only an 8½-foot space between the beams. In this instance, you could still use the lumber of your choice, but you would need a third beam.

CALCULATE POST SPACING: Now you need to figure out how far your beams can span—that is, how far apart you should place the posts. In general, you want your beams to be large enough to keep the number of posts to a minimum, but not so large that they are out of proportion with the rest of the design.

Let's say you like the looks of 6-foot post spacing. Look down the 10-foot column (that's how far your beams are spaced from your previous computations) in the "Beam Spans" table, opposite, until you find the 6-foot spacing for western pine. The table indicates that you'll need a 4×10 beam for

posts spaced every 6 feet. If you change your mind and want posts spaced every 8 feet, you'll have to use a 4×12 beam. The trick is to balance beam size with the number of posts. Too many posts results in undue complexity, difficulty, and expense. Too few posts results in a risk of instability.

COMPUTE POST SIZE: Multiply the spacing between beams (10 feet, in our example) by the spacing between posts (6 feet in our example) to compute the load area in square feet (60 square feet in our example). find this number in the "Sizing Posts" table, opposite, and follow the column down to "Western pine."

The table shows that 4×4 western pine posts will support the deck in our example up to a height of 10 feet, more than enough for a plan that calls for a height of 8 feet.

REMEMBER THE RAILING

You'll perform the most complicated computations when you figure out the sizes of various structural members. Choosing railing stock is less frustrating and pretty much follows standard sizes.

Use 2× stock for rails and 2×2s for balusters, unless your design calls for special stock. Whenever possible, purchase rail and cap pieces long enough to avoid splicing.

JOIST SPANS (BEAM SPACING)[1]

Species Group	Joist Size (inches)	Joist Spacing		
		16"	24"	32"
1 Douglas fir, larch, and southern pine	2×6	9'11"	7'11"	6'2"
	2×8	12'	10'6"	8'1"
	2×10	15'3"	13'4"	10'4"
2 Hem fir and Douglas fir south	2×6	8'7"	7'0"	5'8"
	2×8	11'4"	9'3"	7'6"
	2×10	14'6"	11'10"	9'6"
3 Western pines and cedars, redwood, and spruces	2×6	7'9"	6'2"	5'0"
	2×8	10'2"	8'1"	6'8"
	2×10	13'0"	10'4"	8'6"

[1] *Joists are on edge. Spans are center-to-center distances between beams or supports. Spans are based on 40 psf deck live load plus 10 psf dead load. Grade is no. 2 or better; no. 2 medium-grain southern pine.*

BEAM SPANS (POST SPACING)[1]

Species Group	Beam Size (inches)	Beam Spacing[2] (feet) (joist span)								
		4	5	6	7	8	9	10	11	12
1 Douglas fir, larch, and southern pine	4×6	Up to 6' →								
	3×8	Up to 8' →		Up to 7'	Up to 6' →					
	4×8	Up to 10'	Up to 9'	Up to 8'	Up to 7' →		Up to 6' →			
	3×10	Up to 11'	Up to 10'	Up to 9'	Up to 8' →		Up to 7' →		Up to 6' →	
	4×10	Up to 12'	Up to 11'	Up to 10'	Up to 9' →		Up to 8' →		Up to 7' →	
	3×12			Up to 12'	Up to 11'	Up to 10'	Up to 9' →		Up to 8' →	
	4×12			Up to 12' →		Up to 11'	Up to 10' →		Up to 9' →	
	6×10					Up to 12'	Up to 11'	Up to 10'		
2 Hem fir and Douglas fir south	4×6	Up to 6' →								
	3×8	Up to 7' →		Up to 6' →						
	4×8	Up to 9'	Up to 8'	Up to 7' →		Up to 6'				
	3×10	Up to 10'	Up to 9'	Up to 8'	Up to 7' →		Up to 6' →			
	4×10	Up to 11'	Up to 10'	Up to 9'	Up to 8' →		Up to 7' →		Up to 6'	
	3×12	Up to 12'	Up to 11'	Up to 10'	Up to 9'	Up to 8' →		Up to 7' →		
	4×12			Up to 12'	Up to 11'	Up to 10'	Up to 9' →		Up to 8' →	
	6×10					Up to 12'	Up to 11'	Up to 10'	Up to 9' →	
3 Western pines and cedars, redwood, and spruces	4×6	Up to 6'								
	3×8	Up to 7'	Up to 6'							
	4×8	Up to 8'	Up to 7'	Up to 6' →						
	3×10	Up to 9'	Up to 8'	Up to 7'	Up to 6' →					
	4×10	Up to 10'	Up to 9'	Up to 8' →		Up to 7' →		Up to 6' →		
	3×12	Up to 11'	Up to 10'	Up to 9'	Up to 8'	Up to 7' →			Up to 6' →	
	4×12	Up to 12'	Up to 11'	Up to 10'	Up to 9' →		Up to 8' →		Up to 7' →	
	6×10			Up to 12'	Up to 11'	Up to 10'	Up to 9' →		Up to 8' →	

[1] *Beams are on edge. Spans are center-to-center distances between posts or supports. (Based on 40 psf deck live load plus 10 psf dead load. Grade is no. 2 or better; no. 2, medium-grain southern pine.)*

[2] *Example: If the beams are 9'8" apart and the species is Group 2, use the 10' column; 3×10 up to 6' spans, 4×10 up to 7', etc.*

SIZING POSTS[1] (WOOD BEAM SUPPORTS)

Species Group	Post Size (inches)	Load Area[2] : beam spacing x post spacing (square feet)									
		36	48	60	72	84	96	108	120	132	144
1 Douglas fir, larch, and southern pine	4×4	Up to 12' high →			Up to 10' high			Up to 8' high			
	4×6					Up to 12' →				Up to 10'	
	6×6									Up to 12'	
2 Hem fir and Douglas fir south	4×4	Up to 12'		Up to 10' →		Up to 8' →					
	4×6				Up to 12'			Up to 10' →			
	6×6							Up to 12' →			
3 Western pines and cedars, redwood, and spruces	4×4	Up to 12'		Up to 10' →	Up to 8' →	Up to 6' →					
	4×6				Up to 12' →		Up to 10' →	Up to 8' →			
	6×6						Up to 12' →				

[1] *Based on 40 psf deck live load plus 10 psf dead load. Grade is standard and better for 4×4 posts and no. 1 and better for larger sizes.*

[2] *Example: If the beam supports are spaced 8'6" on center and the posts are 11'6", then the load area is 98. Use next larger area, 108.*

BUYING LUMBER

No lumber is perfect, so to get the materials that are right for your deck, take an exploratory trip through your lumberyard. Look at the different species and examine their color and grain patterns. Assess quality differences among the grades.

Compare pressure-treated with untreated products. If you don't have a good idea of what you'd like to use, take your scaled plans with you and ask a salesperson to give you recommendations and an idea of costs. Then take a second look.

Keep in mind that stains and sealers will make the finished wood look darker. There's no general guideline that can help you estimate the exact effect of finishes. Each product "takes" differently on each species. To get a rough idea of how your deck will look when finished, look for samples displayed with the finishing products. The samples will represent the approximate outcome of the finish on your wood.

ASSESSING DEFECTS

Go through the lumber racks, pick up each board, and check for defects. Sight down the length of boards on both the flat side and the edge. Are they crooked? Warped? Or square and flat? Check for knots. Are they small and tight? Or loose and large? Look for checks and splits. If the wood hasn't been kiln-dried, you can expect more checks and splits to develop as the lumber seasons.

Take time to inspect every board before you buy it, and be careful how many imperfections you accept. Flaws in decking boards or the stock you'll use for railings will detract from the appearance of the deck and may cause premature wear. Some defects in framing lumber won't affect the strength of the structure. Others can be structurally dangerous and may be hidden once you install them.

Some defects—such as knots, shakes, checks, or splits—are natural (that doesn't make an abundance of them acceptable,

however). Others, such as torn grain or warping, are the result of milling errors or poor drying conditions.

ESTIMATING

If you're planning a simple project, the best way to estimate your lumber needs is to use your dimension plan and count all the pieces of each size. That way you can give your supplier a list of the exact number of 2×4s, 2×6s, and so forth.

Keep your costs down by keeping the waste to a minimum. Most lumber comes in even lengths, so if you need a 3-foot and a 6½-foot 2×10, you'll need to order a 10-foot board from which to cut them.

ORDERING

Ordering lumber requires attention to detail. You'll need a list of each size stock, the species, what kind of footings (if any) you'll be pouring, and how you will finish the structure. You may be able to negotiate a better price for materials if you place the full order with one supplier.

When you've sorted everything out and have a good idea of what material you need, shop around to compare both material costs and service. You can quickly get an idea of

Before choosing lumber, decide which defects will not harm your project and which are unacceptable. Sight along a board to spot twists, bows, and crowns. Many carpenters set joists crown edge up for a structural advantage.

costs by visiting your lumberyard and asking the salesperson to give you the materials cost for a basic deck of your size. Ask for estimates from several suppliers.

You might find that a higher-grade stock costs less at one yard than lower-grade materials at another. If you can't get the material to the site yourself, factor in delivery costs before ordering.

STORING LUMBER

When your materials arrive, protect them from direct sunlight and moisture. If the lumber has not been kiln-dried, let it dry for several weeks. Stack the boards so that they are flat and evenly weighted, inserting spacers (called "stickers") between them. Store them under a cover or in the shade. Kiln-dried lumber should be dry enough to use right away, but it, too, needs to be protected from direct sunlight before you begin construction.

WASTE NOT, WANT NOT

This is an adage that does not apply to construction work. You'll waste a certain amount—it's unavoidable. Order 5 percent more than your materials list calls for.

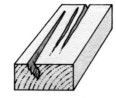

Checks: Splits that run perpendicular to the grain are called checks. They are a cosmetic—not a structural—flaw.

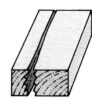

Shakes: Splits following the grain will probably grow larger. Avoid using boards with splits that extend halfway or more.

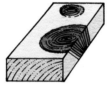

Knots: Use these rules when using boards with knots for joists and rafters. Apply the rules to both sides of the board. 1. Tight knots are OK in the top third of the board. 2. Missing knots are OK in the middle third. 3. No knots larger than an inch in the bottom third. Loose knots will probably fall out in time.

Wane: Boards with a wane can still be very strong but may not provide enough nailing surface for sheathing joints.

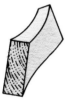

Twist: If you use a twisted board, one or more corners will stick out. Eliminate minor twists by installing blocking and strategic fastening.

Crown: The high part in the middle of a board . Orient all the crowns the same way on a wall frame. On joists or rafters, put the crown up. Avoid badly crowned lumber or cut it in to shorter lengths.

Bow: Bowed lumber is usually not a problem unless the bow is very pronounced. Straighten bowed studs or joists with blocking.

Cup: Cupped wood is strong but unsightly. If the cup is severe, the board may crack when you fasten it.

FASTENERS

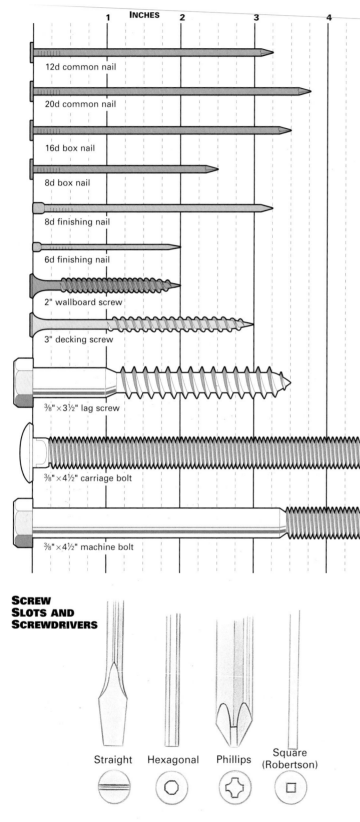

INCHES 1 2 3 4

12d common nail

20d common nail

16d box nail

8d box nail

8d finishing nail

6d finishing nail

2" wallboard screw

3" decking screw

3/8" × 3½" lag screw

3/8" × 4½" carriage bolt

3/8" × 4½" machine bolt

SCREW SLOTS AND SCREWDRIVERS

Straight Hexagonal Phillips Square (Robertson)

Avoid scrimping on the quality and quantity of fasteners in your project. After all, it's the fasteners that hold all your hard work together. Framing fasteners come in a variety of forms—nails, screws, lag screws, bolts, and metal framing connectors. You may need one or more masonry fasteners, too, if you build your deck on a slab or otherwise attach it to a concrete surface.

NAILS

Nails hold things together by the friction they generate against wood fibers. The size of a nail is determined by its length expressed as pennyweight, abbreviated as d (which stands for denarius, an ancient coin; it referred to the cost of 100 nails of a given size).

■ **COMMON NAILS,** used for general construction, have large heads and thick shanks. They hold well but are hard to drive and may split the wood.

■ **BOX NAILS,** thinner than their common cousins, reduce splitting in stock that measures ¾-inch or thinner.

■ **RINGSHANK AND SPIRAL-SHANKED NAILS** grip the wood fibers better than common or box nails and don't easily work their way out. They are very difficult to remove.

■ **FINISHING NAILS** have slender shanks and small, barrel-shaped heads that can be countersunk. Use them for trim work and wherever you don't want the heads to show.

■ **CASING NAILS** are heftier versions of finishing nails with more holding power.

■ **BRADS** are miniature finishing nails used for attaching thin, fragile pieces.

■ **DUPLEX NAILS** come in handy as

NAILS OR SCREWS?

For most projects, nails will prove the least expensive fastener. Screws cost more, but they create a stronger joint, and ultimately that can mean a longer-lasting structure. And even though driving an individual screw may take slightly longer than pounding nails, screws can save you time in the long run. An air or power nailer makes nailing go extremely fast and can be well worth the cost of the rental fee. You may want to practice on scrap before engaging this tool in construction. (See page 75.)

PREDRILLING FASTENERS

Once a board is split by a nail or screw, not only is the board unsightly, the fastener has lost almost all its holding power. Small splits will almost certainly grow in time. Save time and disappointment by drilling pilot holes wherever there is a possibility of splitting—especially close to the end of a board.

Drill a pilot hole using a drill bit slightly smaller than the nail. Test by drilling a hole and driving the nail. It should be snug enough so it takes some hammering to drive it in.

Try this trick for attaching softwood trim: Insert the finishing nail in the chuck of your drill. Drive the nail with the drill until it contacts the framing. Finish driving the nail with a hammer.

Use the chart below for predrilling pilot holes for screws. Drill through the top piece and into the bottom piece to a depth equal to the screw length. Clamp or hold the parts together as you drive in the screw.

Screw Diameter	Pilot hole Diameter
4	$1/16$"
6	$3/32$"
8	$7/64$"
10	$1/8$"
12	$9/64$"
14	$5/32$"

temporary fasteners. They have a double head, which makes them easy to pull out when you strip away framing braces, for example.

The metal used to fabricate a nail makes a difference. Some nails rust readily; others won't ever rust.
■ **GALVANIZED NAILS** are the most common type. Hot-dipped galvanized (HDG) nails are more reliable than electrogalvanized (EG). They resist rust, but no galvanized nail can guarantee rust-free performance. The coating often flakes off.
■ **ALUMINUM NAILS** won't rust, although they aren't quite as strong as HDG nails and can be very difficult to drive (they bend), especially in hard woods.
■ **STAINLESS STEEL NAILS** won't rust, but they are very expensive, and not all suppliers stock them. They're a good choice and worth their expense for projects built near salt water.

SCREWS

Screws hold better than nails, they don't pop out of the wood, and they are easier to remove. They also come in a bewildering array of styles. What you're looking for are decking screws—generally in $2\frac{1}{2}$- to $3\frac{1}{2}$-inch lengths. Decking screws are coated for resistance to the elements and are sharp, tapered, and self-sinking. With a cordless drill, you can drive them about as fast as nails.

Regardless of what size you use, predrill them (see chart above) when driving them within 2 inches of the end of a board. Predrilling keeps the wood from splitting.

Be sure to match your screwdriver bit to the type of screw head (or vice versa). Straight-slot screws are available only as round-head wood screws, and you won't use them in your outdoor structure. The same holds true for hex-head screws. Decking screws generally are machined with a phillips or square head or a combination head.

Many types of combination heads will not hold a phillips tip securely against the torque of a cordless drill, especially when fastening 2× framing. If you're stripping your combination-head screws when you go to sink them, switch to a square tip.

HEAVY FASTENERS

Nails and screws are the mainstay fasteners, but bigger connections call for heavy-duty hardware:

BOLTS: Bolts, nuts, and washers provide a solid connection with excellent load-bearing strength. They hold parts together by compressing their surfaces, and their size is designated by their shank diameter (under the head) and their length. Use only those with a hot-dipped galvanized finish, and predrill them with a drill bit of the same diameter.
■ **MACHINE BOLTS** have a hex or square head.
■ **CARRIAGE BOLTS** have a rounded head for a decorative or finished appearance.

WHAT SIZE FASTENER?

The longer and thicker a nail, the better it holds. However, if a nail is too thick for the stock, it will split the wood and have almost no holding power at all.

Although it might seem that building a deck calls for a wide selection of fasteners, those listed below will get you through most projects.
■ Common, spiral, or ringshank nails (10d or 16d) for framing—in 2× or thicker stock
■ Box or ringshank nails (8d or 10d) in 1× or thinner stock
■ Finish nails (8d or 10d) for trim
■ Decking screws (#10, in appropriate lengths)

FASTENERS
continued

Tighten machine screws with two wrenches (putting washers under the head and nut). Carriage bolts have a square shank under the head that pulls into the wood and keeps the bolt from turning. Tighten both fasteners until they are just snug and make the slightest indentation in the surface of the wood.

LAG SCREWS: A lag screw is a bolt in a screw's clothing. Its large size will attach heavy framing members and hardware. Lag screws have a hexhead (square heads are available but uncommon). Tighten them with a wrench.

MASONRY FASTENERS: Masonry fasteners are similar to nails or screws. Some are made of hardened steel; others rely on expansion and friction to grip the masonry. Refer to the illustrations on this page for installation methods.

MASONRY ANCHORS

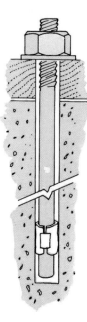

Anchor bolts expand against the concrete when the bolt is tightened. Drill a hole of the same diameter and at least ½" longer than the bolt. Blow the dust from the hole and drive the bolt in with the nut turned just to the top of the threads. Make sure the bolt doesn't turn when tightening.

GET A GRIP

Whether you assemble your deck with nails or screws, make sure that two-thirds of the fastener shank is in the lower (usually the thicker) member of the joint. Where possible, and to get the best holding power, drive the fasteners at an angle, toward or away from each other.

FRAMING CONNECTORS: Framing connectors are designed for a number of special purposes. Those available from your distributor may not look exactly like the styles illustrated here, but their general shape should be the same.

Most manufacturers supply nails (usually blunted to reduce splitting) for framing connectors, but you can use common nails of the closest size, cinching the nail if it's longer than the framing.

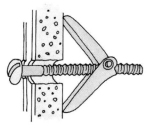

Hollow wall anchors can be used to fasten lumber between the recesses of concrete block. Drill a hole of the same diameter, insert the anchor, and tighten the screw to draw the flanges against the rear of the recess. Remove the screw, insert it through the material to be fastened, and retighten the screw in the anchor.

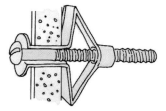

Toggle bolts have wings that expand against the rear of a concrete surface and can also be used to fasten material to concrete block. Drill a hole of the same diameter; insert the wings through the material to be fastened and into the block. Tighten the bolt to draw the wings snug.

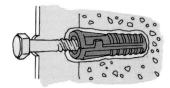

Expansion shields are made of soft metal or plastic whose sides expand as a screw or lag screw is tightened.

Drill a hole of the same diameter and length, set the shield in the hole, and tighten the screw.

FRAMING CONNECTORS

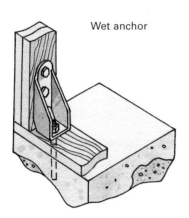

Wet anchor

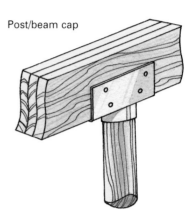

Heavy column base

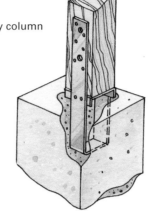

Post/beam cap

WET ANCHORS are a form of post connector inserted into a concrete foundation, slab, or post footing while the concrete is still wet.

HEAVY COLUMN BASES are also a form of post anchor inserted into wet concrete.

POST/BEAM CAPS tie a beam to a post of equal size.

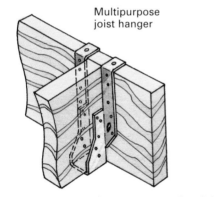

Multipurpose joist hanger

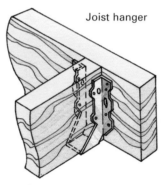

Joist hanger

Angle bracket

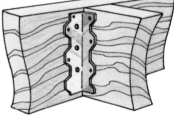

JOIST HANGERS butt joists to beams or headers. Single and double sizes are available.

ANGLE BRACKETS strengthen perpendicular joints—at rim joists and stair stringers, for example.

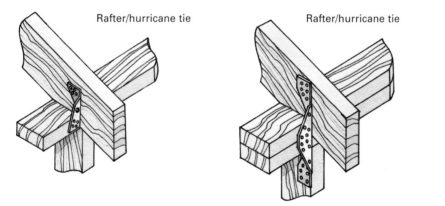

Rafter/hurricane tie   Rafter/hurricane tie   Rafter/hurricane tie

RAFTER/HURRICANE TIES connect rafters to top plates.

FINISHING

WOOD FINISHES

Whitewash

Natural

Wood preservative

Clear stain

Tinted stains

Paints

If it weren't for the weather, you wouldn't have to worry much about the durability of your deck. But wind, rain, snow, ice, and sun exact a heavy toll on wood. The right finish can help protect your deck and enhance its look.

There are many ways you can finish your deck, depending on the type of lumber, your preference of color, and the deck's environment. Here are some guidelines you can use in selecting a finish and applying it.

CHOOSING THE FINISH

Ask yourself how you want your deck to look. Do you want to paint it, stain it, or let it weather? With a clear finish, redwood and cedar show off their natural color. They also look good when left to weather. On the one hand, some designs seem made for paint. Others, especially those in woodland settings, might look better weathered. What about your design?

■ First consider the style of the deck and its setting, including colors on your home.

■ Then turn your attention to what color, tone, and surface sheen (flat or glossy) complements the overall landscape design theme.

■ Finally, research the durability and ease of application of various products.

If you mix finishes, make sure they're compatible. Your supplier will be able to help you choose the right combination.

SEALERS: Sealers, also called water repellents, seal wood against water penetration. You have two basic options—clear or pigmented sealer. Both protect the

---

THE WEATHERED LOOK

If you want your deck to have a gray, weathered look, the easiest "finish" is to do nothing. Just let the wood weather naturally. This process works best with all-heartwood grades of a durable species, such as cedar, cypress, or redwood.

The final color and length of the aging process varies with the species and its exposure, but generally cedar and cypress weather to a light, silver gray; redwood turns dark gray; and pressure-treated lumber turns a soft gray, while retaining a hint of its original green or tan coloring.

wood but don't change its appearance appreciably.

A wide range of additives increases the effectiveness of sealers.

■ Fungicides and insect repellents ward off mildew, insects, and fungi.

■ Ultraviolet blockers diminish the effect of the sun's rays and help maintain the natural color of the wood.

All-purpose sealers usually contain water repellents, preservative, and ultraviolet blockers.

A clear sealer has the least effect on the wood's natural color. It may slow the graying of wood but won't stop it. Pigmented sealers provide the same protection but change the color of the wood slightly. You can apply sealers over or under stains and under primer and paint for extra protection.

STAINS: Stains change the look of a surface, but most are not designed to protect the wood. Stains are somewhat less expensive than paints, and application goes faster than painting because stains don't require an undercoat. They go on easily over rough or smooth surfaces.

Stains fall into two general categories based on the concentration of pigment:

■ **SEMITRANSPARENT STAINS** allow the wood grain to show, but they wear away more quickly. They are particularly suitable for highlighting the beauty of wood grain.

■ **HEAVY-BODIED** stains contain more pigment and tend to obscure the grain more.

No matter what their pigment level, stains don't offer much variation in sheen. They tend to retain the wood's low-luster, natural look.

Both kinds of stain come as oil-based or water-based products. In general, oil-based stains are more durable than their water-based counterparts. But new chemical techniques are producing water-based products that rival oil-based stains. Ask your retailer for recommendations. On redwood and red cedar, however, apply oil-based stains.

Even if you've decided on a heavy-bodied stain for the frame of your deck, consider a semitransparent product for the decking. The inevitable wear won't be as noticeable on a light color, and the slight difference in tone can often produce a pleasing contrast with the rest of the deck. Periodic restaining will give you a more even color.

In any case, make sure you apply a nonchalking stain or sealer-stain to eliminate the possibility of tracking a powdery film into the house.

Stain can add a colorful character to your deck design. Stains are easy to apply and dramatic in effect.

SAFETY GEAR

Wear rubber gloves and safety glasses or goggles when you work with any finish. Carefully follow all safety instructions for products that include solvents or other volatile organic compounds (VOCs). To avoid excessive waste and spatter, treat smaller pieces by dipping them in a container of the sealer or preservative.

PAINTS: Painting a deck creates an elegant, refined look. Unlike stain, its opaque film can mask some of the defects in the wood, making it an ideal finish for lower grades of lumber.

Paint offers an unlimited choice of colors and looks the same on all species. Paint takes more time to apply, however, is more expensive, and is harder to maintain than other finishes. All of this inconvenience is balanced by the fact that it offers the most complete protection. But once you have painted a deck, you can't change your mind and apply any other finish.

If you're painting, apply primer first. Painted finishes tend to last longer and look better on smooth surfaces than on rough ones. And, of course, they can be recoated.

Here again, you have choices:

■ **EXTERIOR ALKYDS** (oil-based products) are costly, require solvents for cleanup, and dry slowly.

FINISHING
continued

Paint can change the character as well as the color of a deck. Keep in mind that paint will show wear patterns earlier than other finishes and requires more frequent care.

SAMPLE A SECTION

Before applying any finish, test the final color by applying a small sample in an out-of-the-way spot on your deck. Let the finish dry to make sure it produces the color you want. In general, paints dry darker than when wet. Stains dry lighter.

■ **WATER-BASED LATEX** paints don't cost as much as alkyds, clean up easily with water, and dry quickly.

Both kinds come in a range of sheens: gloss, semigloss, flat, or matte.

Oil-based primers provide better protection on raw wood than water-based primers. You can add stain blockers to stop bleed-through from redwood and cedar. A good-quality acrylic-latex top coat applied over an alkyd primer is probably the most durable and protective finish.

When painting the decking itself, choose a product specified for outdoor decks or porches so it will withstand heavy wear. Like painted porches and steps, a painted deck surface can be slippery when wet. As an extra safety precaution, especially around doorways and stairs, you can mix a handful or so of clean sand (play sand for sandboxes) with the paint used for the final coat.

FINISHES AND PRESSURE TREATMENTS

Most pressure-treated wood is kiln-dried before preservative is applied. This means that a great many boards are still soaked when they get to the lumberyard—and when you bring them home. Wet wood won't take a finish and will cause it to blister and peel. Some boards may be dry to the touch but still contain enough moist chemicals to resist finishing. You can build your deck with freshly treated lumber, but you'll have to let it dry—sometimes several weeks—before applying a finish. Try the "bead" test (see "The Bead Test," opposite).

BLEACHING TREATMENTS

These treatments change the appearance of wood by lightening its natural tones.

Bleaching treatments offer an intermediate solution to the problem of toning down the jarring look of a brand-new deck. They soften the raw-wood look and help the varying shades of natural wood to blend in. You get the effect of two seasons of natural weathering in one application because, like the sun, the treatments strip color from the wood fibers. These treatments don't protect the wood, and some products are harmful to plants and grasses.

Sealers stop the bleach from working. So if you plan to bleach the wood, don't seal it first. Wait two months after applying the bleach to seal the wood.

APPLYING FINISHES

It's best to apply finishes to the wood before assembling the deck. That way you're assured of preserving all of the surfaces. It's also easier to apply finish when the deck is in pieces, as you won't have to crawl underneath the deck, for instance, to finish the bottom of the decking. For most do-it-yourself decks, this step will prove impractical, especially if you're curring materials as you assemble the deck. But at a minimum, coat at least the exposed end grains that will be hidden in joints. It's th end grain that tends to wick up water and rot first, so give these board-ends a good soaking. Some deck builders prefer to dip end grain in a shallow pan of preservative rather than to apply the preservative with an applicator.

Whether the components are assembled or unassembled, however, it's important that the wood is dry. Pressure-treated wood might require several weeks before the moist preservative cures out of the wood. Even with naturally resistant species, it's wise to wait a week or so before applying the finish.

If you're applying a sealer, use a good-quality roller that has a 1-inch nap. That way you'll get good coverage and better penetration than with other applicators. You can recoat most clear sealers while they are still wet.

Roller

For all other finishes, you can use a brush, pad, roller, or sprayer. Larger projects will go more quickly with a sprayer. Rent an airless model—they produce less overspray—but practice on scrap wood first.

If you're recoating an existing surface, give it a good cleaning. Scrub it with a moderately stiff brush and a solution of 1 cup household chlorine bleach and 1 gallon water, then rinse it well. If the deck has weathered naturally for some time and you would like to restore the original wood color, use a bleaching agent, and be sure to protect any nearby plantings.

As an alternative, you can use a pressure washer to remove surface dirt and restore the wood's natural color prior to restaining or resealing.

Brush

Pad

THE BEAD TEST

To see whether your deck is ready for a finish, sprinkle water on the wood. If the water soaks into the surface, the wood is dry enough to take a finish. If the water beads up in droplets, put the finish away, wait a few weeks, and test it again.

Rollers spread a lot of finish over a large area, but they won't get in tight spots and don't apply oil-based paints well. Brushes will put finish anywhere, but not as quickly. Brushing also ensures a solid adhesion of paint to the surface. Pads are good for tight spots and for trimming edges. Sprayers put finish on quickly but be sure to mask off surfaces you don't want sprayed.

Preservative sprayer

FOUNDATIONS

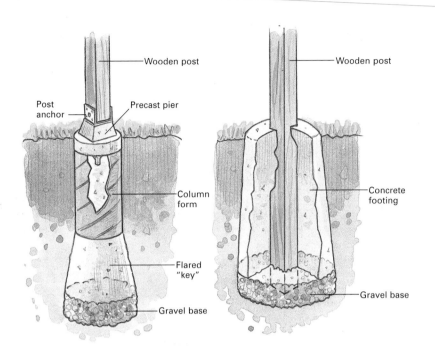

Decks and overheads require a foundation for each load-bearing post. The type and dimensions of the foundation you'll need depends on the height of the structure, the types of materials you plan to use, how deep the ground freezes, and the load-bearing capacity of the soil.

Because they support wood posts or beams, which deteriorate with ground contact, post supports typically extend above grade. They are usually cylinders or blocks, at least 8 inches across, with straight or beveled sides.

Footings are typically 18 inches square and at least 6 inches thick. You should dig the holes for them to a depth prescribed by local building codes—anywhere from 1 to 6 feet or more, depending on the local depth of the frost and the stability of the soils in your area.

FOOTINGS AND PIERS

When it comes to supporting the posts for your deck or overhead, you have several options.

PRECAST PIERS: A precast pier generally looks like a pyramid with its top cut off. You can purchase precast piers at your local materials supplier in sizes that are appropriate to your installation. The better piers have post anchors already embedded and are ready-made for setting in a poured footing while the concrete is still wet.

POURED-IN-PLACE PIERS: These are piers that you make yourself, molded in a form and poured at the same time you pour the footings.

You can buy prefabricated forms (usually they are large cylinders that you place in the footing hole) or make your own configurations with wooden forms. Poured-in-place piers offer decorative options that precast varieties do not.

POST ANCHORS: Some post anchors are designed to be set in the footings or piers while the concrete is still wet; others can be added later by drilling through the concrete, but these tend to be less stable.

PRE-MIX FOR FOOTINGS

Mixing concrete for postholes is usually easier with premixed bags; you just add water and provide the muscle power to mix it. Using premix is slightly more costly than mixing your own concrete from dry materials, but the expense is more than offset by the convenience.

Holes for 4×4 posts (3 feet deep) require only a little more than 2 cubic feet each—two 60-pound sacks per posthole. You can fill about three postholes with four 90-pound sacks of premix. Make sure to buy extra. Concrete isn't expensive, and you won't want to come up short in the middle of pouring.

FENCING MATERIALS

Wood is not the only material you can use for fencing, of course. Other materials may make a better fit with your landscape design and your budget.

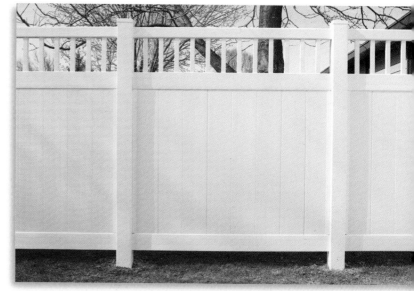

■ Vinyl fencing, made of the same PVC as siding and plumbing pipe, comes in a variety of styles that resemble wood and metal. You can get vinyl pickets, lattice, boards—even vinyl basket weave. It comes in prefabricated panels (some require assembly). A few styles are designed to follow the contour of a slope, and you can modify end posts to install stepped styles.

Although its lateral and load-bearing strength is not as great as wood or metal, PVC is otherwise virtually indestructible. Vinyl fencing comes in colors (typically whites and browns), doesn't need painting, and won't peel, rust, or decay.

Most styles come as kits with posts, rails, and infill cut to the right lengths. Panels are usually 72 to 96 inches long.

■ Prefabricated wood-fence panels are made for fence builders in a hurry. They are usually available in 6- and 8-foot lengths. All you have to do is install posts, nail on the bays, and apply the finish. You may even find that it is less expensive to buy prefabricated bays than to build your own.

Before you decide to use prefabricated bays, examine them carefully. They are available in a wide variety of styles, prices, grades—and quality. Lower cost may mean that shortcuts have been taken in quality of materials, construction, or both.

Buy panels made with pressure-treated lumber and 2×4 rails. They should be assembled with galvanized nails or screws, not staples. Make sure the product is a worthwhile investment that will give you years of service and not require excessive maintenance.

■ Tubular aluminum and steel fences are manufactured in many sizes, designs, and colors. Kits usually come complete with posts, rails, prefabricated panels (in 72- to 96-inch lengths and various heights), and the hardware needed to fasten the parts together.

If you're fencing a moderate slope, use a style with a frame you can rack to match the angle of the ground. Steep slopes require angled panels. Stepped fencing must be custom-made. You'll find prepainted metal fencing in black, white, or brown (make sure the finish is a poly-powder coating). If you buy unpainted fencing, apply a rust-resistant paint before putting up the fence.

Most tubular fences attach to metal posts that are set in concrete. Some prefab panels, however, attach to wooden posts or masonry columns with special brackets. What is consistent among all tubular fencing is the necessity to install it one panel (and one post) at a time.

These fences require careful planning, but assembly is easy. Most suppliers will build the fence for an additional fee.

COMPARING MATERIALS

Choosing materials is a balancing act. Listed below are some of the factors to consider. They are ranked on a scale of 1 (least) to 5 (most). The rankings are generalized because local costs may vary, and climate may affect the life of the material and the maintenance required.

Material	Cost	Maintenance	Life Expectancy
Wrought iron	5	4	5
Steel, aluminum	3–4	2	4–5
Chain link	3	1	4
Wire mesh	2–3	3–4	3
Vinyl	2–3	1	5

FINALIZING COSTS

Getting help with your project will save you time and money. It's best, however, to find friends who have some deck-building or carpentry experience, and to assign those with less experience to tasks requiring less skill. Your work will proceed more smoothly and will be safer for all.

Once your design has been approved by everyone who needs to review it, you're ready to start gathering bids. Get bids from at least two or three major suppliers, and ask friends and relatives for recommendations.

You can divide your costs into several parts. Here are a few suggestions:

■ **YOUR TIME:** How much do you want to do yourself, and can you afford that much time? Of course, you can put a value on your time, based on what you earn, but you won't simply be "spending" your time. You will get some exercise, learn new skills, stay in control of the project, and benefit from the results of your work and the sense of accomplishment.

■ **CONTRACTOR COSTS:** You can get a rough estimate of contractor costs without seeking bids. Double your material costs for any section of the project (or the whole thing). The result will be in the ballpark.

■ **SITE PREP:** Include building permits, excavation, drainage, and landscaping. Site preparation costs may not apply to your project, but if your lot needs considerable grading, that expense should be included as part of the cost of your deck.

■ **MATERIAL:** Concrete, lumber, hardware, equipment rentals, other building supplies—

it all adds up at computer speed. Fortunately, material costs are the easiest to compare. You can create a materials list, then give copies to several suppliers, asking for item prices and a package price.

WHAT'S YOUR TIME WORTH?

The time you spend building a deck probably isn't time taken from your job. It's weekends, evenings, or vacation days that you could be spending with your family or friends. How do you put a value on that?

The best approach to this question is to focus on satisfaction and not dollars. Set aside briefly the prospect of saving money by doing the work yourself. Save that as a tie-breaker. Here's the real issue: If you want to give yourself a challenge, enjoy working with your hands, or just want to call your deck your own in every way possible, the time you spend on it won't be lost. Instead, it will be an investment in personal accomplishment and pride of ownership. The only question remaining about your time is whether you have enough.

SITE PREPARATION

You may not have thought much about preparing the site, but that little pond that forms in your yard after a rain can be real trouble if it's located right where you plan to put a deck post. You may have to grade your site to improve drainage.

If grading is necessary, get estimates from landscape contractors. Their equipment can make short work of jobs that would wear you out. Also, their speed means you can schedule site preparation to take place just before you start building.

SAVE YOURSELF A TRIP

When you get bids for materials, ask each lumberyard or building supply center about its return policy. Look for a business that will exchange defective goods and accept returns. Then buy more of each bulk item— such as fasteners and decking boards—than your plan requires. It's easier to return the extras after the project is finished than to make a separate trip each time you run short of materials.

SHOULD YOU HIRE A CONTRACTOR?

The explosive growth of the do-it-yourself industry shows that many homeowners can handle all but the most extensive landscape projects. When you're deciding whether to do the work yourself or hire it out, consider these points:

■ **DON'T KID YOURSELF ABOUT SKILLS:** Weigh your skill level and experience against the scope of the project. You can do minor excavating with a posthole digger or shovel. Slabs require heavy equipment. If your carpentry skills are weak, buy precut kits for fences and overheads.

■ **WILL FRIENDS HELP?** Many construction projects require at least two pairs of hands—lifting framing lumber into position on an overhead or pouring and leveling concrete slabs, for example

■ **POWER TOOLS:** Power tools save time. So does proper planning. Buy a power drill/driver if you don't have one. It will be a valuable addition to your tool kit. Rent a reciprocating saw for cutting posts or timbers.

■ **LOGICAL ORDER:** Don't build fences until the major projects are completed, and have materials dropped next to the project. Anything you can do to reduce your labor will make the job more enjoyable.

■ **ADD IT UP:** What will your total cost be? Make sure your materials list is complete and get prices for everything. Add subcontractor bids for any work you will definitely contract, such as excavation or electrical wiring. Include the cost of tools you'll have to buy or rent, as well as waste removal, permits, and inspections. Add these costs together and compare them with a general contractor's bid.

Are the savings large enough to warrant taking the project on? Even if the savings are small, remember that doing it yourself can be an enjoyable and rewarding experience.

CONTRACTOR CONSIDERATIONS

If you've decided to contract all or some of the job, how do you find a contractor? Friends and neighbors are good for references. So are local garden shops. But don't work with any contractor whose references you have not checked.

You may also need to enlist the services of landscape professionals such as:

Landscape architects: They completely design and plan your landscape, producing detailed drawings, plans, and written work descriptions. They will also supervise the construction.

Landscape designers: They will assist you with the design of your project and will provide drawings for your deck's general look. These drawings do not include construction details.

Landscape contractors: These builders have particular expertise in landscape construction. Some firms describe themselves as "Designers and Builders" and have professional architects, designers, and builders on staff.

The best way to find a reputable design professional is through the satisfied references of friends and family. Ask at work or parties: Anyone who has a new landscape will be happy to talk about it and the professionals who made it happen.

■ **NARROWING THE FIELD:** Once you've selected your prospective contractors, ask each one for job references; then check them. Visit job sites and inspect the quality of work.

Get several bids, and be wary of any that are significantly higher or lower than average. The bids of reputable contractors bidding for the same work with the same materials should be close.

■ **CONTRACTS:** Get everything in writing— everything. Read the contract carefully, and insert any information that you feel is needed. If you have any uncertainty, have a lawyer review the documents before you sign. The contract should specify the following:
• The work to be done.
• Materials to be used.
• A start date and a completion schedule.
• Procedures for making changes.
• Stipulations that the contractor will obtain building permits and lien waivers.
• Methods for resolving disputes.

■ **OTHER DOCUMENTS:** Often required by local laws, your contractor should provide evidence of the following:
• Licensing: showing government standards to do the work have been met.
• Bonding: evidence that if the contractor fails to perform the work, a bonding company will pay another contractor to finish the job.
• Insurance: liability for nonworkers and compensation for workers injured on the job.

■ **FINAL PAYMENT:** Before you make final payment, obtain signed lien waivers from the contractor for every subcontractor and supplier. You'll avoid liability in case the contractor fails to pay them.

When the job is completed, inspect it carefully. If anything looks questionable, make a note of it. Ask the contractor to do a walk-through with you so you can point out problems; then both of you can see firsthand what needs to be corrected. The contractor should either correct any defects or explain why they really aren't problems.

Many cities provide recourse for resolution of future problems—usually within a year. Check with your local building department. If problems arise, appeal first to the contractors involved; then allow a reasonable time for repairs. If the problem is still not resolved, appeal to the professional associations to which the contractor belongs or consult a lawyer.

PUTTING YOUR PLANS
ON PAPER

You've pondered your deck's function and style, and you've chosen the materials you'll use to build it. Before you bring out the shovels and levels, however, it's important to refine your plan, to clarify and map out precisely where all the final elements will go.

This is the time for you to put your plans on paper. Taking a little time now to set down all the details will save you lots of time in the long run—to say nothing of money and frustration. Plans will also help keep you on schedule throughout the construction process—and they will increase your satisfaction with your finished deck. Drawing a deck plan before you begin building saves you from having to make hurried decisions in the field. It allows you to experiment with the location of the deck, its contours, and the pattern of its materials. Paper plans can also give you a bird's-eye view of the landscape, helping you discover design ideas you might not otherwise have seen.

On the following pages, you'll find tips and illustrations that demonstrate how the pros go about developing a complete landscape plan. If your project is small, you may not need to invest time in such elaborate plans. But large or small, your deck will profit from including each step of the design process.

CRITICAL MEASUREMENTS

Planning a deck requires more detail than planning other landscaping projects because of the complexity of deck construction. In addition to the base map and other plans illustrated on the following pages, you'll need construction drawings, such as framing plans and elevations, to keep you or your contractor on target.

When measuring, focus on one feature at a time. Some dimensions are more critical than others. For example, if you plan to enclose an existing tree, the deck must be correctly sized to fit properly. Measure the edge of the deck starting from the tree.

Other dimensions are less critical. Label these measurements with a plus or minus sign. For example, the length of the deck from the tree to the house is better measured exactly when you install the framing. Placing the symbol in front of this measurement indicates that the deck must reach from the tree to the house, but the exact length is subject to on-site adjustment.

DECK FRAMING PLAN

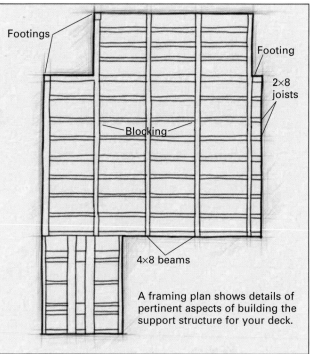

Footings

Footing

2×8 joists

Blocking

4×8 beams

A framing plan shows details of pertinent aspects of building the support structure for your deck.

ELEVATION

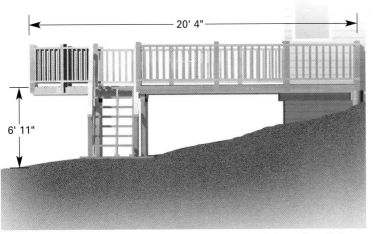

An elevation shows the deck from one side—and the other, if they are different. Show how far above the ground the deck will be built, and indicate any grading or other ground-level changes.

CONSTRUCTION DETAILS

FOOTINGS

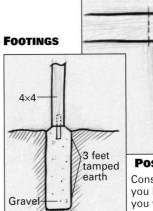

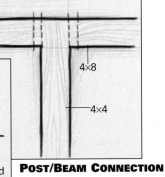

POST/BEAM CONNECTION

Construction details help you keep track of methods you will use when building your deck.

KEEP YOUR CONNECTIONS

While you are planning the location and placement of your deck, check the outside of your house to make sure you won't lose access to important connections, such as a hose spigot or line to a furnace. If you can't move a connection, remember to create an access panel in the deck that will allow you to reach it when necessary.

DRAFTING TOOLBOX

Here's what you'll need to get your paper plans on their way:
- An engineer's scale
- A roll or sheets of tracing paper
- 2 circle templates ranging from ¼" to 3½" in diameter
- Thick and thin black felt-tipped pens
- Rulers (6" and 12")
- Pencils with erasers
- Drafting or masking tape (drafting tape comes off surfaces more easily and doesn't leave marks)
- T square
- Pencil sharpener

MAKING A BASE MAP

As with any decisionmaking process, you'll simplify the task (and reduce your confusion) by taking the planning process one step at a time. The first step is to draw a base map of your property.

FIRST: SKETCH

Begin by walking around the outside of your house with a clipboard and a 100-foot steel measuring tape. You'll be measuring and sketching in the outlines of structures and plantings and other major details. Later you will transfer these sketches more exactly to a graph-paper map. Even though you're familiar with your own house and lot, avoid taking anything for granted.

BOUNDARIES: Start with the exact location of your property lines (look for metal markers, or use a metal detector to find them). Sketch in the outline of your yard and house, noting its distance from the property lines. Take accurate measurements from all property lines. Measure and record the dimensions of each wall of your house and the size of other structures, such as detached garages or sheds. Your sketch should include the distances structures are from one another.

LOOK AT SMALLER ELEMENTS: Include the little things on your sketch. They will matter when you build your deck. Here's a sample list of items to watch for:
■ Location of doors and windows, including width, height, distance from the ground, and what rooms they lead from
■ Extension of roof eaves beyond the exterior walls of the house
■ Location of downspouts and direction of runoff
■ Where existing trees, shrubs, and gardens are planted
■ Location of outdoor walls, fences, steps, walks, and driveways

NEXT: DETAILED MAP

Once your sketch is complete, take it back indoors and transfer it to graph paper (24×36 inches is a good size, with a scale of ¼ inch=1 foot). Include all the elements on your sketch, and note all the dimensions you've recorded.

Be sure to include the location of windows, doors, hose bibs, and electrical outlets. Use dotted lines for any buried cable.

This is the time for precision. If you're in doubt about any measurement, go back outside and measure again. This small step can save you hours of actual construction time. When you're done, you'll have an accurate map of your property drawn to scale.

BASE-MAP SHORTCUTS

You may be able to shorten the base-map process by using existing maps of your property. Start with the existing legal maps and descriptions of your house and lot. These documents—called deed maps, house plans, plat plans, or contour plans—are typically available from your title company, bank, mortgage lender, city hall, or county recorder's office. You may even have a copy filed in your records along with the other papers you received when you bought the house. Plot maps do not, however, show every measurement. You'll still have to measure the dimensions of your house and the elements listed on page 103.

Another, though more costly, option is to commission a survey of your property (a necessity if your plan includes extensive grading), but expect to pay several hundred dollars.

HIGH-TECH HELP

Computerized landscape-design programs take the pencil (and eraser) out of planning. They're easy to use and flexible, and can speed your progress from base plan to final design. One of a computer's more appealing features is deletion—an electronic eraser that allows you to change your design without redrawing it.

The features are slick: Programs calculate dimensions of each of your proposed structures and areas of use. Most programs have a number of symbols for trees and shrubs, as well as elements such as furniture, pools, and decks. Some will even create side elevations and three-dimensional views of your plan. Other programs prepare materials lists and cost estimates.

Check your home improvement center, too. Many offer computer design services. If you're not familiar with computers, you can take your rough drawings (including dimensions), and the store's staff will computerize your project and produce a materials list and cost estimates. Ask for extra copies; your local building department will need them when you apply for permits.

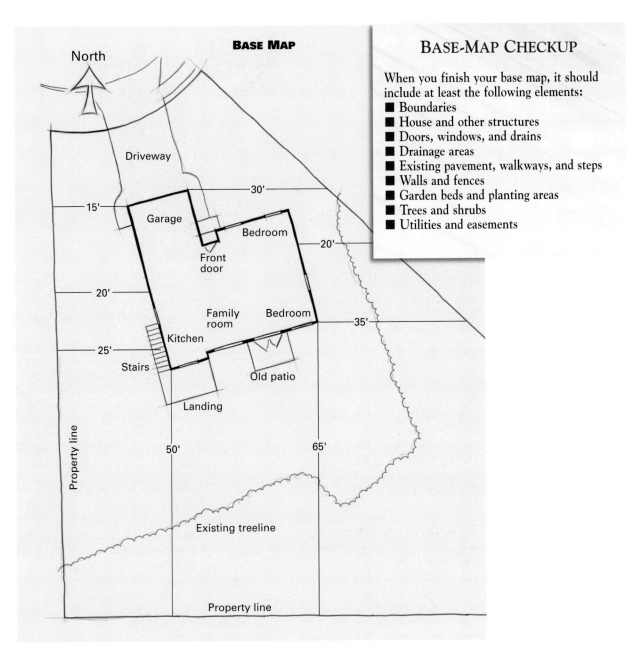

BASE MAP

North

Driveway

Garage

Front door

Bedroom

30'

15'

20'

20'

Family room

Bedroom

Kitchen

35'

25'

Stairs

Old patio

Landing

Property line

50'

65'

Existing treeline

Property line

BASE-MAP CHECKUP

When you finish your base map, it should include at least the following elements:
- Boundaries
- House and other structures
- Doors, windows, and drains
- Drainage areas
- Existing pavement, walkways, and steps
- Walls and fences
- Garden beds and planting areas
- Trees and shrubs
- Utilities and easements

WHEN IT'S TIME FOR A CHANGE

Did you inherit a dysfunctional patio or deck when you bought your house? Perhaps you built one years ago when your family's needs were different. When it's time for a change, here are some ideas for retrofitting a worn-out or out-of-date design.

■ Is your deck larger than you need? Consider dividing it into smaller spaces with raised planters. Or cut through the decking and plant trees.

■ Do you entertain on a regular basis, but your deck is too small to hold all your guests? Convert a flower bed near the deck to lawn where you can easily set up tents or party tables. Build a second deck and link the old and new spaces with a boardwalk or path so guests can move between the areas to socialize. Enlarge the space by installing a brick patio at the foot of a deck.

■ Make the deck seem larger by removing hedges, fencing, or other obstructions whose primary purpose is decorative. That will open up the view and make the space seem larger. Be careful not to take out plantings or structures that were put there to increase privacy.

■ Improve the view: Bring compost bins, garbage cans, yard tools, and heating and cooling equipment into a single service area rather than leaving them scattered throughout the yard. Then hide them all behind an attractive screen.

ANALYZE YOUR SITE

A base map gives you a picture of the outline of your property and its contents—just as they are. A site analysis takes that picture one step further.

A site analysis enables you to view the components of your yard as though you were in a helicopter. It will help you evaluate the relationships between landscape elements and record what you consider to be assets (things that work well with your lifestyle) and liabilities (the things that don't).

CONSIDERATIONS

Take your sketch (not the base map) out in your yard and step back so you can evaluate its assets and liabilities (use the checklist, opposite, for tips on what to look for). Ask yourself the following questions:

■ What works well?
■ What do I want to change?
■ Is the route to the deck site pleasant?
■ Is the site easily accessible, or will I have to take a circuitous route to reach it?
■ Is the best part of the yard visible from the seating on the proposed deck space?
■ Is this site private enough to feel comfortable when I relax?

Go through the checklist item by item and make judgments about how each of these features of your yard will either enhance or detract from your comfort and convenience.

Make notes about your evaluation on your landscape sketch and include the following concerns:

■ How does the distance from your proposed deck to streets, alleys, and sidewalks affect your need for quiet and privacy?
■ Will streetlights and light from the neighbors encroach upon your use of the deck in the evening?
■ What views do you want to keep?
■ What views do you want to block?
■ Are there sources of noise nearby—day and night?
■ Are there drainage problems you need to correct?
■ Do neighbors' trees or bushes overhang or shade your yard?

Take your sketch and notes back inside, trace your base map on a piece of tracing paper, and transfer your notes to it. When you're done, it should look something like the site analysis shown at left.

SITE ANALYSIS

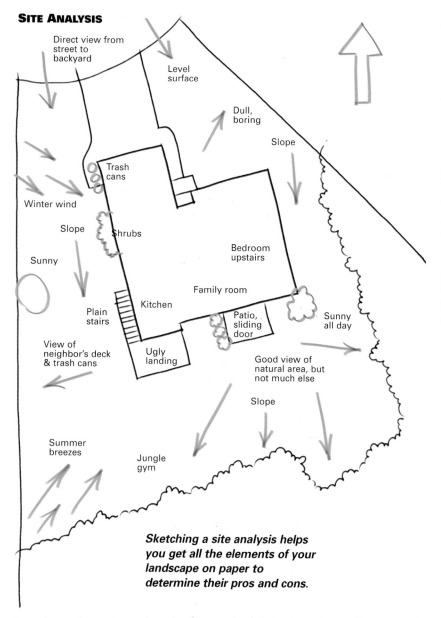

Direct view from street to backyard

Level surface

Dull, boring

Slope

Trash cans

Winter wind

Slope

Shrubs

Sunny

Plain stairs

Kitchen

Bedroom upstairs

Family room

Patio, sliding door

Sunny all day

View of neighbor's deck & trash cans

Ugly landing

Good view of natural area, but not much else

Slope

Summer breezes

Jungle gym

Sketching a site analysis helps you get all the elements of your landscape on paper to determine their pros and cons.

Notes for Site Analysis
✓ Too much sun on patio space
✓ Don't block view to woods
✓ Yard slopes steeply at rear
✓ Deck will shade patio
✓ Neighbor has too much view of patio (screen view)
✓ Improve visual access
✓ Good view from kitchen window

LOOK FOR UTILITY LINES

No matter where you build, consider utilities carefully. Verify with the local utilities where their gas, water, sewer, electrical, or communication lines are located. Make sure construction won't cut into them or that you won't cover them with paving.

Even if safety isn't an issue, your deck should not prevent future access. Rights of access by utility companies are called easements, and easements apply even if you don't receive the service of a particular utility. For example, even if you use a satellite dish for television, you need to find out whether the cable company uses underground lines. Note all easements on your base map or site analysis.

CHECKLIST FOR SITE ANALYSIS

Effective deck planning means more than simply drawing plans and erecting a wood structure. A good plan should take into account the details of the total environment. When you are sketching your plans, it's easy to overlook details that you'll later find important. Here's a checklist for the elements to include while you're sketching your deck site. Use the list as a guide. Many items may not apply, and you will add other items specific to your needs.

STRUCTURES
- Dimensions of house, garage, and any other permanent buildings
- Roof overhangs
- Walls, fences, and trellises
- Columns
- Built-in furnishings and appliances (benches, tables, grills, counters)

PAVED SURFACES
- Existing and proposed deck pavings
- Driveways
- Walkways and paths
- Steps
- Edging

AMENITIES (DECORATIVE AND FUNCTIONAL)
- Freestanding furniture and grills
- Lighting
- Play areas
- Poolside areas
- Birdhouses
- Wind chimes
- Sculpture and decorative elements

ACCESS
- Foot traffic patterns
- Doors and windows

DRAINAGE
- Spouts
- Gutters
- Current runoff areas and patterns

SLOPES OR STEEP GRADES
- Dips in ground
- Slope direction
- Steep grades that may need retaining walls
- Stairs and steps

PLACEMENT OF UTILITIES
- Electrical supply lines, overhead or underground
- Telephone lines, overhead or underground
- Television cable
- Natural gas supply lines
- Water supply pipes
- Wastewater pipes
- Hose bibs
- Sewage pipes and catch basins
- Septic tanks
- Utility easements (access for utilities)

PRIVACY AND VIEW
- Open and closed areas within your property
- Views to preserve
- Views to block
- Privacy walls, fences, plants

PLANTS (EXISTING AND PROPOSED)
- Trees
- Shrubs and bushes
- Ground cover
- Ground-level flower beds
- Raised flower beds
- Vegetable or herb gardens
- Edging

WATER AND ROCK
- Erosion
- Natural ponds
- Streams
- Constructed pools and fountains
- Boulders or rock outcroppings

CLIMATE AND MICROCLIMATE
- Prevailing winds
- Precipitation
- Sun and shade
- Heating and cooling

CREATING A BUBBLE PLAN

Your site analysis is a snapshot of the existing landscape with all its attributes and drawbacks. The next step—*bubble diagrams*—will reflect how things could be.

THE DIAGRAM

Making bubble diagrams means using more tracing paper. Lay a fresh sheet over your site analysis and retrace the basic outlines of your property, including the house, fence, property lines, and driveway.

BUBBLE DIAGRAM 1

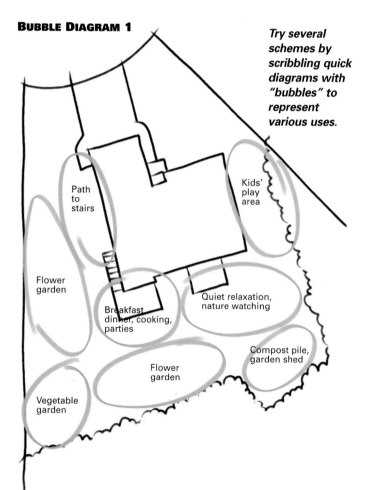

Try several schemes by scribbling quick diagrams with "bubbles" to represent various uses.

Path to stairs

Kids' play area

Flower garden

Breakfast dinner, cooking, parties

Quiet relaxation, nature watching

Compost pile, garden shed

Flower garden

Vegetable garden

BUBBLES FOR AN OLD DECK

Sketching bubble diagrams is equally valuable when reevaluating an existing deck. You might want to change adjacent areas to complement your present space. For example, if you want flowers nearby when you relax or entertain out-of-doors, sketch a flower garden bubble next to the deck. Rough out several schemes before selecting the sketch that illustrates the ideas that work best for your home.

Next make circles, or "bubbles," on the tracing paper to represent various areas in your yard, labeling each bubble with a brief description of that intended use. If you don't like your first design, make another one. Repeat the process with new sheets of tracing paper to rearrange the bubbles. Try different schemes. Draw as many bubble diagrams as it takes to find one that works for you.

You don't have to be an artist to use this technique. It is simply a tool to help you organize your ideas and get you started in the right direction.

BRAINSTORM WITH BUBBLES

Using bubble diagrams as a design tool works like brainstorming. Many of your ideas may seem extreme, but in the end you'll find a creative solution that contains practical and affordable elements.

Feel free to move bubbles from place to place. And forget about budget limitations at this stage. Some ideas may require more effort or expense than you want to put into this project. That isn't your concern now; just let the ideas flow.

By allowing yourself to dream at this point, you might find other ways to achieve your goals. Perhaps you can't tear down an old deck and rebuild it in a new location, even if the new site is *the* ideal spot. But you might be able to put in an inexpensive sitting area.

Here's another possibility: An existing deck might be open to the lawn, but you want a more intimate space. Use bubble diagrams to find a way to separate the deck from the activities on the lawn and to open views. Perhaps you could leave the lawn and the deck where they are and draw a bubble to represent a privacy planting between the two. Or you could move the deck bubble to another part of the diagram, or move the lawn to a different spot. Or how about adding a fence and planting along the outer edge of the lawn to give the entire yard more privacy?

REALITY CHECK

As you sketch bubble diagrams, watch for one that stands out as the most appealing and appropriate to your needs. Take time to study this "final" diagram thoroughly. Apply the realities of your site to it by comparing the bubble diagrams. Look at your site analysis and transfer the notes on it to your bubble diagram. Compare the proposed use of each bubble to the physical description of its location. Are they compatible?

BUBBLE DIAGRAM 2

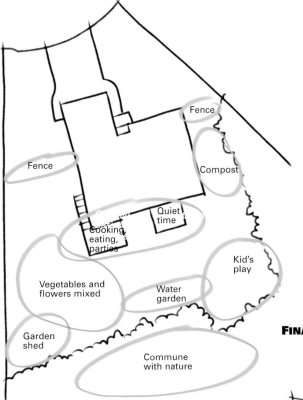

was a good start, but the site analysis reveals that it's back to the drawing board. Thinking about the trees, however, could lead you to consider using foliage to screen the parking lot or building a plant-covered arbor over the parking area.

Notice the changes from Diagram 1 to the plan at left. The areas for cooking, dining, and quiet relaxation are left pretty much unchanged—accessible to compatible indoor rooms. But the children's playground is now moved to the corner of the yard, allowing easy supervision from the house and relaxation area. Other areas have been rearranged for both functional and aesthetic reasons. Even this diagram may not be the final plan. Note the differences between it and the final diagram, below.

FINAL BUBBLE DIAGRAM

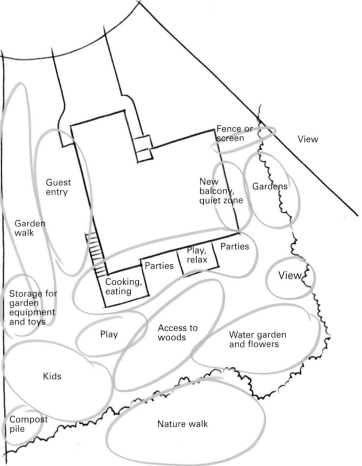

Comparing reality with desire is a critical step in design decisionmaking. It helps you make sure that the planned use for the space is compatible with the site's characteristics.

For example, you may have selected the ideal spot for a new deck. You like the connection between indoors and out, the view from the area, and the size of the space. However, your site analysis reveals that this location slopes steeply, and building a deck there will prove expensive.

If you had failed to analyze the site and started the project without considering its limitations, you could have incurred excessive construction expenses. At the same time, if you abandon this scheme for a flatter but otherwise less desirable area, you might not use your new deck as much as you expect. Looking at site conditions before deciding on a final plan allows you to find a solution that works with existing assets and liabilities.

Evaluate your entire scheme, bubble by bubble, considering the assets and limitations of each part of the site. Rearranging the bubbles may inspire a new strategy. For example, you might want to move a parking area because the cars ruin the view. When you combine the notes from the site analysis with the bubble diagram, however, you realize that you'll have to cut down several lovely, mature trees. In this case, the bubble diagram

Sketch as many bubble diagrams as you want before selecting the one that combines the best ideas for an attractive and practical landscape that works with your home.

MAKING A MASTER PLAN

Now that you're sure where everything in your new landscape will be, it's time to get a little more specific.

THE DESIGN CONCEPT

A design concept includes every decision you've made about your landscape—for example, where you intend to add shade, wind protection, privacy, or overhead shelter. In one way it is the final bubble diagram—with instructions—and these instructions will be the key to drawing your master plan.

Note the differences between a concept diagram and a bubble plan. The design concept tells you specifically what you need to build or add to accomplish the goals you've set out in earlier plans. To make a design concept, trace your house and property on a fresh sheet of paper and write descriptions of plantings and construction.

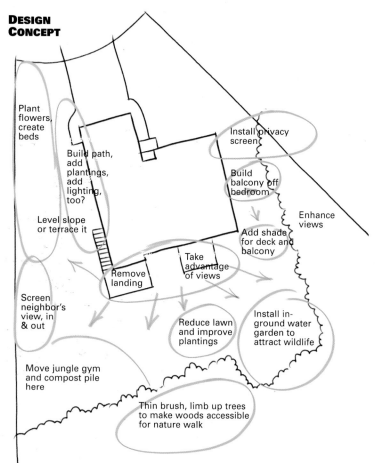

DESIGN CONCEPT

Plant flowers, create beds

Build path, add plantings, add lighting, too?

Level slope or terrace it

Screen neighbor's view, in & out

Move jungle gym and compost pile here

Install privacy screen

Build balcony off bedroom

Enhance views

Add shade for deck and balcony

Remove landing

Take advantage of views

Reduce lawn and improve plantings

Install in-ground water garden to attract wildlife

Thin brush, limb up trees to make woods accessible for nature walk

Combining the ideas of your favorite bubble plan with the realities in your site analysis will yield a design concept—a diagram of your landscape showing what you plan to build, plant, or add to your site.

THE MASTER PLAN

Lay a piece of tracing paper over your base map and trace the outlines of your house and other existing features. Now make rough drawings of the new structures you will build, using your bubble diagrams to help you decide where everything will go.

STRUCTURES FIRST: Start with the structural elements—the parking areas, landings, and pathways. Designers call this *hardscape*. Play with different shapes and lines, but keep the basic configurations to scale.

There's still time to explore some ideas freely. If a square-cornered deck doesn't look just right—or if it won't quite fit the space—round the corners. If a straight walk to your goldfish pond is too direct or needs to follow the contours of the land, bend it. This is still a time for experimentation; things are easy to change on paper.

PLANTS AND TREES: Once you draw in the hardscape, add lawn and planting areas with their bed lines. Because they are used as separations, bed lines shape two adjacent spaces at one time. You can make them formal and geometric or curve them with a flowing informality.

Next sketch circles to represent any trees you plan to plant, referring to your design concept to remind you of any view you want to frame or areas that need privacy or shade.

Finally, put labels on your renderings and include the rooms of your home. Make one last check of the relationship each area has with the interior of your home. You may have forgotten that you had planned to remove a tree to open up a view or add high shrubbery to make an interior room more private.

A WALK-THROUGH

Now take your plan outside and walk it through your property. Make sure you haven't forgotten anything.
■ Are all the access routes workable?
■ Have you accounted for screening?
■ Do the axis lines call attention to the desired focal points?
■ Can you move a structure within your plan to a spot where you won't have to excavate—without botching the rest of your design?

Even if you intend to build your landscape in stages over a period of years, the master plan will keep your design unified, both now and in the future.

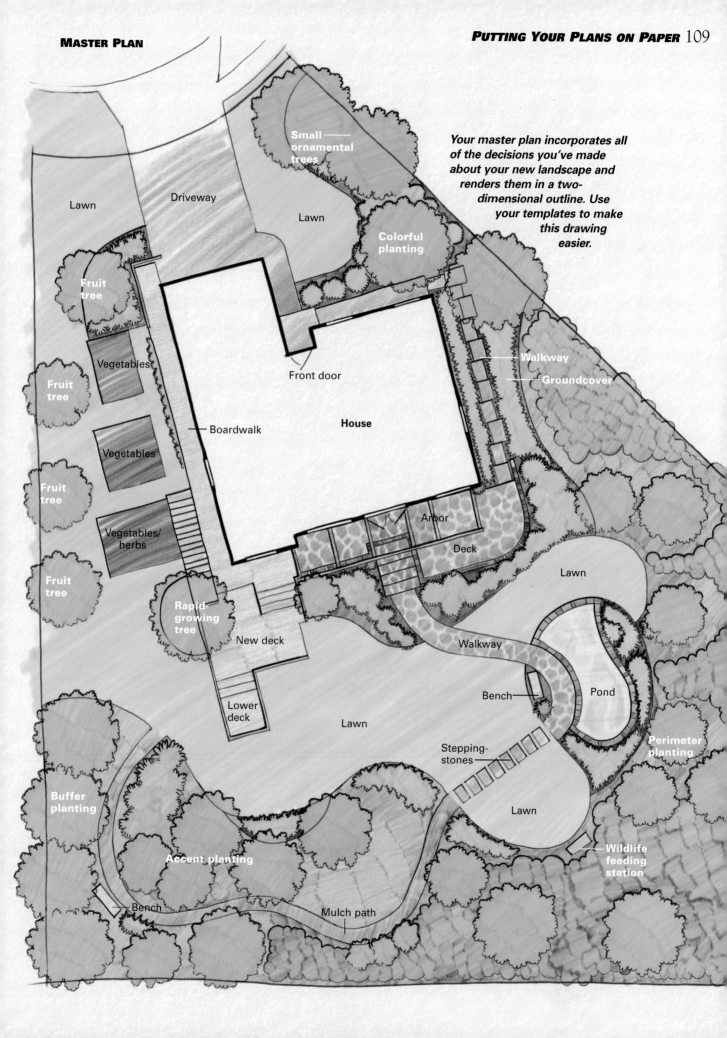

Small ornamental trees

Lawn

Driveway

Lawn

Colorful planting

Your master plan incorporates all of the decisions you've made about your new landscape and renders them in a two-dimensional outline. Use your templates to make this drawing easier.

Fruit tree

Fruit tree

Vegetables

Fruit tree

Vegetables

Walkway

Groundcover

Front door

Boardwalk

House

Vegetables/herbs

Arbor

Deck

Rapid-growing tree

New deck

Lawn

Walkway

Bench

Pond

Lower deck

Lawn

Perimeter planting

Stepping-stones

Buffer planting

Lawn

Accent planting

Wildlife feeding station

Bench

Mulch path

SAFETY FIRST

Building a deck can be great fun. Make the experience an enjoyable one by keeping safety a top priority. If you're not sure how to handle certain tasks or tools, get advice from someone who knows. If you need to rent tools, ask the rental center staff for complete instructions or a demonstration. Remember that your most valuable tool is common sense.

Avoid accidents by following standard safety precautions:

■ Wear safety glasses when hammering, sawing, or doing any other task that might send something into your eyes.

■ Always keep your eyes on your work—especially when using any power tool.

■ Wear hard-soled work boots. Those with steel toes are safest.

■ Wear a dust mask when sawing or doing anything that raises dust.

■ Wear knee pads when kneeling.

■ Avoid loose-fitting clothes that could trip you or get caught in machinery.

■ Avoid leaving tools on top of a stepladder. You'll regret it when you move the ladder.

■ Know your limitations. Take regular breaks, even if you don't feel tired.

A well-planned deck is constructed in orderly steps. Here, the site has been laid out and squared, postholes have been dug, footings have been poured, and framing for all sections has been completed. Decking for each section will be laid next, followed by railings, balusters, and steps.

CONSTRUCTION BASICS

You've decided on your deck design. You've selected the materials. You have all the permits and plans in hand. You know what you need to do, and why. If your site is graded for drainage, your supplies have been delivered, and you have your brother-in-law lined up to help, it's time to build.

Construction is different from planning in several key ways: Mistakes are more expensive, can be dangerous, and take longer to correct. So work carefully, at an easy, steady pace, and use help from others whenever you can. The extra time you spend will pay off in reduced frustration and well-built results.

This chapter describes principles and techniques that apply to any deck project. Instructions, though, do not account for every building site, all materials, or varied skill levels. Get more details or experienced help before taking on a task you don't understand.

WATCH WHERE YOU'RE GOING

By now you should have a complete list, or construction schedule, that organizes the tasks to be accomplished. If you haven't made one, do it now. Make sure your list includes every step of the project, from applying for your building permit to sending invitations to your first deck party. Then review the list to see how much time each step will take, and add cost estimates and dates. Here's a sample list:

- Order materials
- Grade building site for drainage
- Prepare outside of house
- Set up materials at work site
- Attach ledger board
- Set up batter boards
- Locate and pour footings and piers

- Set anchors and posts
- Install beams and joists
- Attach decking boards
- Install railings and balusters
- Build stairs
- Build additions such as benches
- Finish deck surface

Be sure to complete each task before starting the next one. Put everything away when you stop work each day. Even if your neighborhood is secure and the weather won't harm materials left out overnight, keep the site orderly so you can start work right away instead of hunting for materials buried under yesterday's scrap heap.

ANATOMY OF A DECK

The first step in building a deck is to familiarize yourself with some terms. So here's a quick deck-builder's dictionary:

BEAMS OR GIRDERS: Hefty framing members attached horizontally to the posts to support the deck structure.

DECKING BOARDS: Attached to the joists to form the floor of the deck.

JOISTS: Horizontal framing members that sit atop the beam or girder and support the decking boards. Joists can be either 16 or 24 inches *on center* (the distance between the centers of adjacent, parallel framing members in a series).

LATTICE: A gridwork of plastic or wood slats that conceals base framing and keeps out windblown debris while permitting free airflow for ventilation.

LEDGER: A horizontal support attached to the house to hold up one side of the deck.

PIERS: Masonry columns that support the posts and the structure above. They protect the posts from water and insect damage at ground level. On sites subject to frost heaves, concrete is poured in a hole dug to frost depth. Consult your building department for frost depth in your area. Precast concrete piers may be set on shallower bases, or footings, where frost heaves are not a factor.

POSTS: Timbers set on end (vertically) to support the structure above.

RAILINGS: The horizontal timbers that extend from one deck post to another to form a safety barrier at the perimeter of the deck. The term often refers to the entire rail structure, including posts, top rails, and balusters/spindles. The balusters, the smallest vertical components, are positioned to fill the space between the top and bottom rails and between rail posts. Minimum baluster spacing for child safety is 4 inches.

RAILS: Components that provide a safety barrier at the edge of the steps. Rails should be built so the handrail can be completely gripped by the person's hand, and should be securely attached so they are strong enough to support a falling person's weight.

RISERS: Boards that enclose the vertical spaces between stairway treads. Risers are often omitted on deck and other exterior steps.

SKIRT BOARDS: Finished lumber that covers and finishes the exposed face of rough perimeter joists.

STRINGERS: The long wood components that support the weight of the step load and to which the treads are attached.

TREADS: The horizontal stepping surfaces of a stairway.

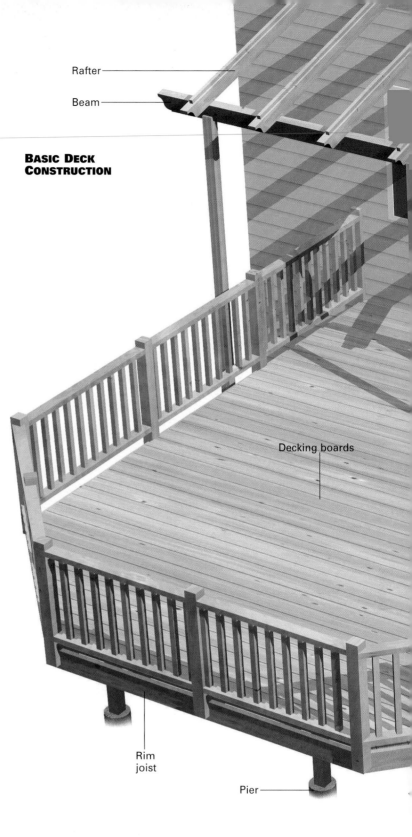

Rafter

Beam

BASIC DECK CONSTRUCTION

Decking boards

Rim joist

Pier

Overhead ledger

SKILL CHECK

If your deck will include outdoor lighting, a pool, or a hot tub, you need to be familiar with plumbing and electrical work. These advanced projects require a greater knowledge of structural support, so take them on only if you have confidence and experience. Be honest with yourself in this assessment. Remember, electrical and plumbing installations need to meet building code requirements and will be inspected very closely.

If you have concerns about your skills, strength, or how much time a task will take, talk to a contractor before you start. Expect to pay for any consultation time. The contractor can check your construction schedule to see whether it makes sense, and give you information on the costs of hiring out certain parts of the job. Some contractors will work with clients who want to do some of the labor themselves. Good advice from a professional can save you a great deal of time, money, and frustration.

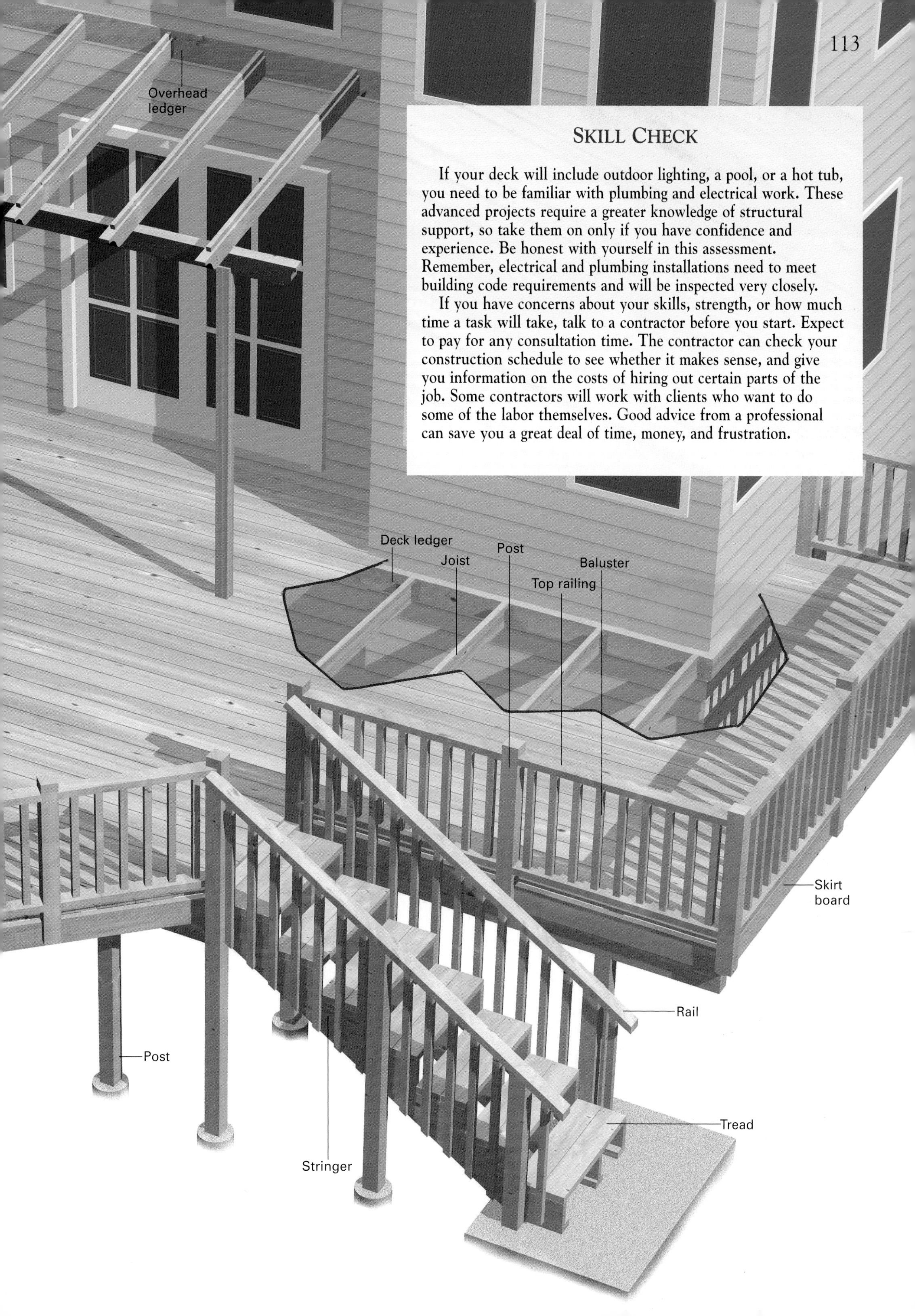

Deck ledger

Joist

Post

Baluster

Top railing

Skirt board

Rail

Post

Tread

Stringer

GRADING AND DRAINAGE

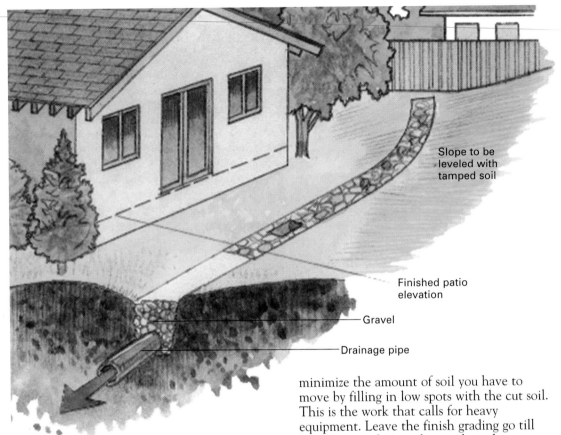

If your yard has only a minor slope that will interfere with the location of your structure, constructing a swale may be a sufficient remedy. Large-scale drainage problems, however, may require a full-fledged drainage plan such as the one shown here—and probably the help of a landscape professional. Arrows on the plan show the direction of water flow.

Slope to be leveled with tamped soil

Finished patio elevation

Gravel

Drainage pipe

No matter what size or style deck you're building, the first step is to prepare the site. The amount of site preparation will vary from landscape to landscape and from deck to deck, but it generally includes removal of debris, trees, weeds, and structures.

GRADING

Making changes to the grade is often the first—and sometimes the only—step in preparing the site for a landscape project. If your deck site abuts a slope, you'll have to remove some—or all—of the slope to make the site level. Even a perfectly flat site can often benefit from the addition of contours to the land.

Begin all the rough grading before laying out the site, and minimize the amount of soil you have to move by filling in low spots with the cut soil. This is the work that calls for heavy equipment. Leave the finish grading go till last. You can do it with a garden rake.

Lay conduit sleeves that lie outside the site after the rough grading is done and continue their run in the site itself after you've excavated it.

You can often make minor changes by eyeballing the grade, but for greater precision, stake out the site to mark changes in the grade, making sure the slope you leave runs downhill slightly— ¼ inch per linear foot.

SITE SAFETY

Site preparation can leave an area temporarily hazardous. Take the following precautions:
■ **PROTECT YOUR TREES:** Use flagging tape to mark trees you want to keep. Siltation fences keep displaced soil from covering root zones.
■ **LIMIT ACCESS:** Designate and mark heavy equipment access points. Barricade driveways against heavy equipment, which can crack the concrete.
■ **KEEP IT SAFE:** Barricade holes (even shallow excavations), and make sure tools are removed at the end of each workday.

CALL IN THE PROS

Although you can do finish grading and many small excavations yourself, rough grading and major excavation call for earth-moving equipment.

Even if you can do the work by hand, it may be more efficient to spend $500 to have it done all at once than to spend four weekends at hard labor. You'll free your time to work on things you can easily do yourself.

Costs include an hourly equipment fee plus an operator expense—another reason for scheduling grading and excavation for the same time.

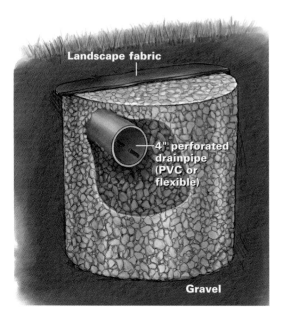

Landscape fabric

4" perforated drainpipe (PVC or flexible)

Gravel

DRY WELL

A dry well is a large, gravel-filled hole located at a spot lower than the deck (but above the water table) and removed from the deck site. A dry well collects water and lets it slowly disperse into the surrounding soil. It must be connected to the site by drainpipe sloped 1 inch every 4 feet. Dig a hole 3 feet deep and 2 to 4 feet wide. Fill it with coarse gravel, and cover the gravel with landscape fabric, then topsoil and sod. Landscape fabric keeps soil from washing into the gravel.

WEED CONTROL

For ground-level or low-lying decks, you will have to install weed control. Otherwise you will have vegetation crashing your parties. Prepare the site as described below, either immediately before or after setting posts—certainly before building the frame. The same goes for decks whose sides will be enclosed—with latticework, for example.

When you remove the sod, take it up in rolls and use it elsewhere in your landscape. Store it out of the sun and keep it moist if you're not ready to use it right away.

Once the sod is up, lay down landscape fabric, which blocks sunlight but allows water to flow through. Cover the fabric with loose gravel.

CROSS SECTION OF A FRENCH DRAIN

Landscape fabric (lay across pipe) 4" perforated pipe (PVC or flexible) Washed gravel (coarse aggregate)

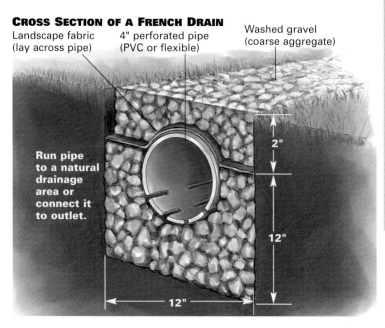

Run pipe to a natural drainage area or connect it to outlet.

2"

12"

12"

DRAINAGE TRENCH

A typical drainage trench is 12 inches wide and as deep as needed to maintain a slope of ⅛ inch per foot. Fill half of the trench with gravel, install perforated drainpipe (holes down), and add more gravel. Cover the gravel with landscape fabric, soil, and sod.

CATCH BASIN

A catch basin is an open surface drain with a receptacle that holds water and disperses it through piping when it reaches a certain level. Install a catch basin to collect water from terrain that is too low to drain elsewhere. Concrete catch basins are sold ready to install. The drainpipe can empty into a distant dry well or—if local codes allow—into the storm sewer system.

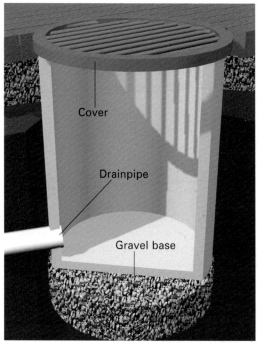

Cover

Drainpipe

Gravel base

INSTALLING THE LEDGER

ATTACHING A LEDGER TO SIDING

Deck layout begins with a ledger or an existing rim joist. A ledger bears the weight of a deck and carries it to the house foundation. This firm bond, supporting one side of the deck, reduces the number of posts that would be required if the deck were free-standing.

In addition to support, the ledger provides the starting point from which the deck will be built. So it must be level and positioned precisely. The ledger should be cut from the same dimension lumber as the joists. Cut its length 3 inches shorter than the width of the deck to allow space for the end joists.

Keep in mind that a poorly attached ledger would be a serious safety hazard, especially on an elevated deck. So study the attachment methods carefully:

■ If you have siding, cut it as shown at right. This will provide access to attach the ledger directly to the framing of the house.

■ If you have a masonry wall (opposite), attach the ledger flush with the surface. Lag screws must go all the way through the sheathing into the band joist, which sits on top of the foundation around the perimeter of the house.

Mark for ledger.

You can tack a 2×4 here as a guide to increase the accuracy of your cut.

1 *To remove siding, hold the ledger level on the siding and mark its outline. Check it with a carpenter's level. Set the blade on a circular saw to cut through the depth of the siding but not through the sheathing. Make the ledger cutout 3 inches longer than the ledger board so the end joists will fit against the ends of the ledger.*

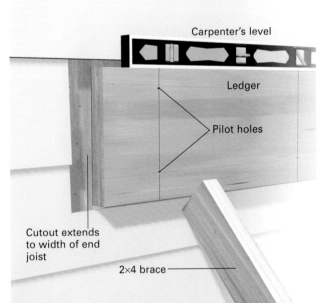

Carpenter's level

Ledger

Pilot holes

Cutout extends to width of end joist

2×4 brace

2 *Pry the cutout away and center the ledger in the recess. Then tack it in place with duplex nails. Drill ¼-inch pilot holes in the ledger. In highly grained woods, offset the holes to avoid splitting the ledger.*

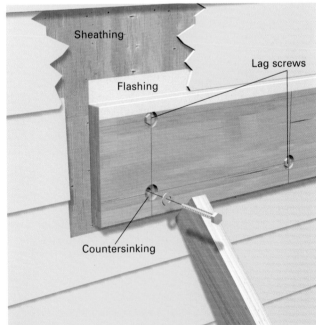

Sheathing

Lag screws

Flashing

Countersinking

3 *Countersink the ledger pilot holes by ½ inch with a 1-inch spade bit. Slide metal flashing under the siding at the top of the opening and lift the ledger into position. Attach the ledger to the house with ½×5-inch lag screws and washers. Seal the screw heads with siliconized caulk.*

ATTACHING A LEDGER TO BRICK

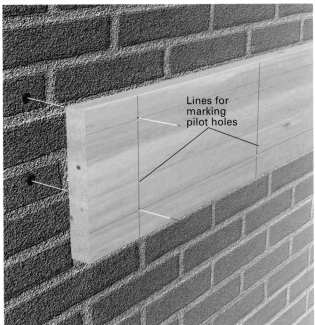

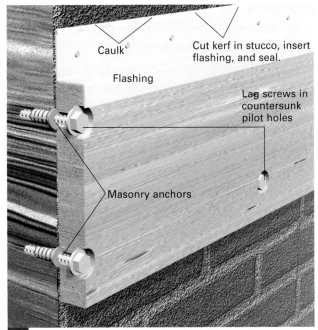

1 *Brace the ledger in place (leveling it) and drill pilot holes for the lag screws. Stop drilling when the bit strikes masonry. Mark the pilot hole locations with a hammer and cold chisel. Remove the ledger and drill ⅝-inch holes in the brick 3 to 3½ inches deep. Use a masonry bit. Insert masonry anchors in the holes and fasten the ledger with ⅜×5-inch lag screws.*

2 *To protect a ledger against moisture damage on a masonry house, you must keep water out from between the ledger and the side of the house. Use spacers to allow water to pass behind the ledger, and attach metal flashing to the wall with masonry nails. Seal the nailheads and the top of the flashing with siliconized caulk.*

POSITIONING THE LEDGER

Place the ledger so the deck surface will be set below the door at the height your plans indicate). Typically this means 1 inch to keep rain out, 3 inches to keep snow at bay. Be sure to allow for the thickness of the decking when setting the ledger.

KEEP IT DRY: Rainwater that collects between the ledger and house will eventually rot the siding and the ledger. Use flashing or spacers to keep the joint dry.

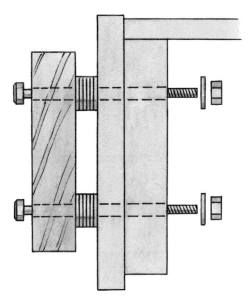

As an alternative to flashing, attach the ledger to siding, using spacers to promote air circulation.

LAYING OUT THE SITE

Whether you start the layout of your deck with a ledger or are expanding an old deck from an existing framing member, the next step is laying out the site for footings and post locations.

Here's how to get things right.

THE STAKE-OUT

Drive temporary stakes at the corners of your layout. If you're building a cantilevered deck where the joist will extend beyond the

MAKING BATTER BOARDS

Batter boards are a homemade tool that will help you make both the layout and excavation of the site more precise.

To make a set of batter boards (you'll need two for each corner, except where the deck abuts the house directly), cut scrap 2×4 lumber to 2-foot lengths, and point the ends so you can drive them into the ground.

Fasten a 15- to 18-inch crosspiece to the legs a couple of inches below the tops. The crosspiece will let you move the mason's line so you can position it where you need it.

beams, allow for the extension when you place the stakes.

SET BATTER BOARDS

Drive batter boards in the ground about 2 feet beyond the temporary stakes. Stretch mason's lines from the ledger (or a framing member, if you're expanding a deck) to the batter boards in all directions. Then tie a line between the other set of batter boards, across what will be the front edge of the deck. This line will be parallel to the ledger and will help you mark the footing locations. Don't worry if your angles aren't right on the money yet. That comes after you have all the lines tied.

Then square the corners with a 3-4-5 triangle as discussed on the opposite page. Keep the lines level with a line level as you square them.

MARK THE POST LOCATIONS

When the mason's lines are square and level, you are ready to transfer the footing locations to the ground.

Depending on how you've drawn your plans, the intersection of the mason's lines represents one of two points—either the corner of your posts or their centers. It doesn't

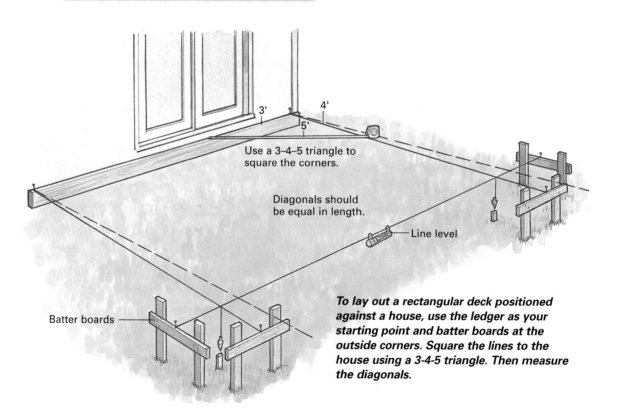

Use a 3–4–5 triangle to square the corners.

Diagonals should be equal in length.

Line level

Batter boards

To lay out a rectangular deck positioned against a house, use the ledger as your starting point and batter boards at the outside corners. Square the lines to the house using a 3-4-5 triangle. Then measure the diagonals.

matter which, but you need to refer to your plan to make sure.

Drop a plumb bob at the intersection of the lines and mark the spot with a small stake. If this point represents the center of the posts, that's where you'll start digging footing holes. If the point is at the post corners, measure in from that joint by half the diagonal width of the post and remark that point. Mark the location of each footing this way.

MARKING THE GROUND

If your project calls for an excavation for a section of patio, for example, use the same methods described above to lay it out. After you have marked your corner locations with stakes, tie a taut line at ground level between the corners, and paint the line with spray paint. This provides a straight line on the ground for excavation.

SQUARE? IT'S AS SIMPLE AS 3-4-5

To ensure that your layout is straight and square, align the mason's lines so that they are square on all four sides. Even if your deck is not square, you'll want a square reference to set posts, beams, and joists. You can do this easily by calculating a right triangle.

■ **DO THE MATH:** The method is simple: When a right triangle measures 3 feet on one side and 4 feet on the other side, the long, diagonal side will be exactly 5 feet. Use this knowledge to check the position of your mason's lines to be sure they are square.

This step is critical. Every part of your deck will depend on it being square and accurately measured.

■ **MEASURING:** Measure and mark a point 3 feet from the intersection on one of the lines. Then measure and mark a point 4 feet out along the other. Finally, measure the distance between the two points you have marked. It should be 5 feet.

It is? Congratulations. If it isn't, shift the strings along your batter boards until all corners pass this test.

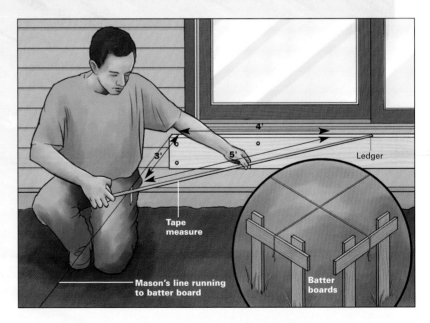

Long spans can be difficult to measure by yourself, so recruit someone to help you hold the tape.

FOOTINGS AND PIERS

Clamshell digger

A clamshell digger can be awkward to use at first, but it digs postholes accurately. Postholes may seem deeper than they really are when your arms get tired, so check with a measuring tape before you declare a hole finished.

INSPECTION

Many towns' building codes require that footing holes be inspected before you fill them. Schedule an inspection, and don't mix any concrete until the holes are approved.

When all the footing locations have been marked, remove the mason's lines and dig the footing holes with a posthole digger or power auger.

The building codes in your area may have a lot to say about the kind of footings you need and how deep they should be. In some localities, posts set in concrete or tamped earth and gravel may be OK. Other municipalities require above-grade posts to be set on piers and footings. In this case, footings must reach below the frost line to prevent them from heaving when the ground freezes. (See page 96.)

To prevent moisture damage to the posts, set your finished footings and piers slightly above grade. If you plan to set post anchors directly in wet concrete without piers, use tube forms. If you plan to pour the footings first and add piers later, make sure your footings are high enough so the piers will keep the posts above ground level.

DIGGING THE HOLES

With a clamshell digger or an auger, dig the footing holes to the size required by local codes and your design. (See page 148 for typical footing dimensions.)

Pour 4 inches of loose gravel in the hole to help water drain away from the footings. If you are using prefab forms, attach them to a 2×4 frame as illustrated on the opposite page, so they are set at the correct level—the bottom of the form should be approximately 8 inches above the bottom of the hole.

If you're installing posts below grade, put them in and brace them, as shown on page 122, before pouring the concrete or tamping in earth and gravel.

POURING FOOTINGS

No matter what kind of concrete you use— premix bags or mix you own—it's best to mix it in batches one hole at a time, unless you have a crew of helpers.

Shovel the mixed concrete carefully into the footing hole, pushing the mixture down with a scrap 2×2 to force out any air bubbles. Once the hole is filled, smooth the concrete with a trowel and, if you haven't used tube

CONCRETE MIXES

You can buy concrete in premixed bags (just add water) or purchase and mix the dry ingredients from scratch. Here's what you should consider:

QUALITY: If you mix dry ingredients from scratch—in the correct proportions— the quality will equal that of premix.
CONVENIENCE: Premix is much more convenient. No mixing is required— except for water, of course.
COST: Premix costs more than mixing from scratch, but the extra cost buys you convenience and time.

GET READY

Have your hardware and piers handy before you mix and pour the concrete. You will be setting them in wet concrete. This is no time to run to the building supply store.

Precast pier

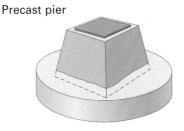

To improve the bond between a precast pier and its footing, soak the pier for a few hours before placing it in the wet footing.

MIXING YOUR OWN CONCRETE

Here's the recipe to use if you're mixing your own concrete from scratch: 1 part portland cement, 1 part sand, and 1½ parts gravel. Use a wheelbarrow, a mortar box, or a power mixer.

Measure shovelfuls of sand and cement first and mix them thoroughly, then add the gravel and mix again. Hollow out the center of the mix and add a little water. Pull the dry ingredients into the center a little at a time, adding just enough water so the mix is stiff.

After you dig the footing holes, suspend tube forms with 2×4s.

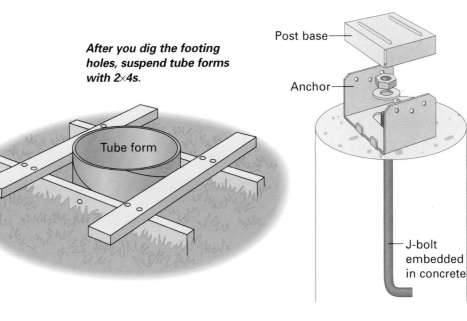

Tube form

Post base

Anchor

J-bolt embedded in concrete

Use a post anchor to attach a deck post to a concrete footing. Adjustable anchors let you shift the position of the post slightly. Make sure all the post anchors face the correct direction as you place them.

forms, slope its surface to let water drain away. Install the post anchor or J bolt. Once the footings and piers or anchors are in place, the concrete needs three days to a week to cure.

SETTING CORNER POSTS

Treat the bottom of each post with a protective sealer at least one day before you set the posts in the anchors. This guards the posts against rot, infestation, and moisture damage. Pour the sealer in a shallow pan and soak each post for a few minutes before setting it up to dry.

Set the corner posts first. That way you will have a benchmark from which to level all the posts with the ledger.

SOFTEN UP HARD SOIL

Wet soil is easier to dig than dry soil. If you run into hard, dense soil, pour a bucket of water into the hole. Water makes the soil softer, which lets the blades of a manual digger or a power auger cut through more quickly. Lifting the wet soil will be more difficult, but still easier than trying to cut through the hard earth. Let water drain out of the hole before pouring concrete.

FOOTINGS AND PIERS
continued

1 **Set the post in the anchor and hold it in place with one or two nails or screws. Stake two braces in the ground and tack the other ends to the post.**

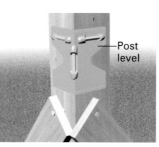
Post level

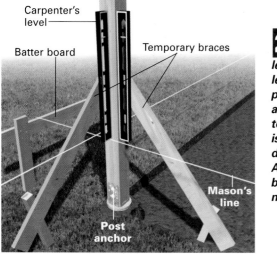
Carpenter's level
Batter board
Temporary braces
Mason's line
Post anchor

2 **Using a carpenter's level or post level, check the post on two adjacent sides to make sure it is plumb in all directions. Adjust the braces as needed.**

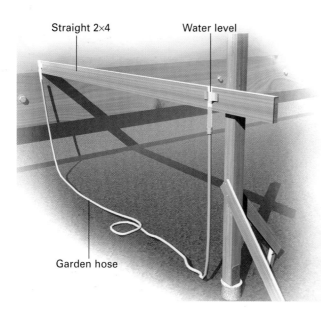
Straight 2×4
Water level
Garden hose

3 **For any deck larger than 10×12 feet, checking for level between the ledger and a corner post can be a difficult job. One person can hardly hold both ends of the level, read it, and adjust it all at once. An inexpensive water level makes this task easy. For smaller decks, use mason's line and a line level, or a straight board and a carpenter's level.**

■ Place a corner post in an anchor; hold it temporarily with decking screws.
■ Brace the post with scrap 1×4 lumber angled to ground stakes, as shown at left.
■ Check the post on two adjacent sides for plumb with a post level or a carpenter's level.
■ Adjust the bracing as needed until the post stands plumb.

If you plan to cut the post in place, fasten its base securely with lag screws. If you are going to remove posts for cutting, don't fasten them securely. In either case, leave the braces in place as you continue.

■ Using a water level, a line level on a taut mason's line, or a 48-inch carpenter's level placed on a long, straight 2×4, mark the post level with the top edges of the ledger.

If your posts will extend above the deck, use this line as a reference when you install the beams and joists. If the posts won't extend above the deck, mark them as follows:

■ Measure down from the line by the depth of the joists and mark this point.
■ Use a combination square to make a line and to transfer the line to all four faces of the post. This is where you will cut.
■ Mark an × on one side of a line to indicate the waste portion.
■ Set and mark the remaining corner posts in the same way.
■ Cut the corner posts as illustrated.

LEVEL THE REST

Once you have the corner posts plumb, marked, and cut, install the remaining posts and use the following method to mark them:
■ Stretch a chalk line between the tops of the corner posts and snap it on the uncut posts. This puts your cutting line level on all posts.
■ Cut the post using the technique shown on the facing page.

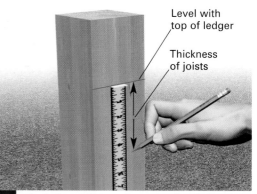
Level with top of ledger
Thickness of joists

4 **Mark the point on the post that is level with the top edge of the ledger. Measure down by the thickness of the joists, and mark the post.**

MEASURE TWICE, CUT ONCE

Use this old carpenter's adage when preparing to cut posts. If your deck design includes any unusual features—cantilevers, extended posts, special hardware, or beams longer than the ledger—keep them in mind as you measure the posts for cutting. These features can affect post length. To avoid time-consuming mistakes, remember:

■ You can cut a post shorter, never longer.

■ The mark on the post that is level with the top edge of the ledger is where the decking boards will be fastened to the joists. Your cutting line represents the top of the cut posts, on which beams and joists will rest.

Combination square

5 *Transfer the cut mark to all four sides of the post using a combination square. Check the post height against the ledger for level one more time before cutting.*

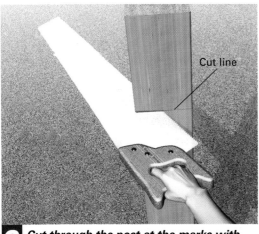

Cut line

6 *Cut through the post at the marks with a handsaw, reciprocating saw, or circular saw. Check the opposite side often as you cut to make sure the blade doesn't wander.*

Nails used for first setting

Lag screw used for final installation

7 *After marking and cutting the posts, and while the braces are still attached, fasten the post to the anchor with the hardware recommended by the manufacturer. In the absence of specific directions, ask your hardware retailer for information.*

CUTTING TIPS

You can cut the posts in place or take them down to cut them. Each method has advantages and drawbacks.

■ Cutting posts in place is difficult because you are sawing at an awkward angle. You risk making cuts that aren't straight, but you avoid taking the posts down and resetting them.

■ Cutting posts on the ground—on sawhorses— will likely give you a cleaner cut because your position is more balanced. But you'll have to rebrace and replumb posts when you put them back up.

Either way, there are common difficulties:

■ Using a circular saw is difficult because 4×4s are too wide to cut in a single pass.

■ Treated lumber gums up saw blades.

Whatever method, consider these tools:

CIRCULAR SAWS usually make the fastest and cleanest cuts but can be awkward to use sideways. Make two passes.

RECIPROCATING SAWS are easier to handle if both hands are free to hold on, but their blades can wander. These aggressive, hardworking saws are anything but subtle.

HANDSAWS take longer, but they're simple and safe. Use a sharp crosscut saw with teeth no smaller than 8 points. Some come with large teeth to cut through large framing.

INSTALLING BEAMS AND JOISTS

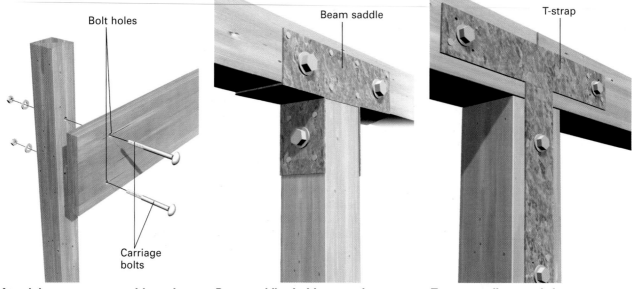

Bolt holes

Carriage bolts

Beam saddle

T-strap

Attach beams to posts with carriage bolts or countersunk lag screws. Seal with siliconized caulk. Use this design when posts extend above the deck surface.

Beam saddles hold post-to-beam joints stable in two directions. They can be fastened to tall posts before the beams are lifted into place.

T-straps, splices, and cleats are required when the ends of two beams meet on top of a post. Make sure any end-to-end joists are centered on a post.

SEEING DOUBLE

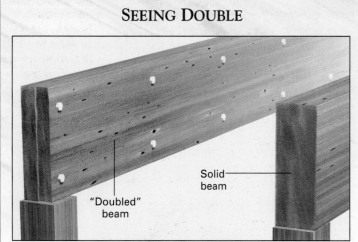

Solid beam

"Doubled" beam

Larger beams, such as 4×12s, can be hard to find. They also are expensive. Make your own from doubled 2× stock fastened side by side. Install ½-inch plywood spacers every 2 to 3 feet to strengthen the beam and to make it the same size as the post that will support it. Fasten the beam from both sides with 3-inch galvanized lag screws.

CROWNING

Beams (or any lumber for that matter) might display a slight crown (the high point of a curvature). Install crowned lumber crownside up. The weight of the deck will force the board straight.

Once the ledger and posts are in place, install the beam(s) that support(s) the joists and decking. Beams run parallel to the ledger and fasten to the posts. The number of beams increases as the span away from the house increases.

MOUNTING

Mount the beams on the sides of the posts or on top, using the method that best suits the specific requirements of your design and construction details. Study the illustrations above to see how these framing members can be held together. Make certain that any joints fall directly over the center of a post so they get adequate support.

FASTENERS

In general, hex-head or carriage bolts provide more strength to structural joints than lag screws. However, if you can't get wrenches on one or both sides of the joint because a joist or bracket is in the way, use lag screws. Bolts give you the chance to tighten joints that loosen.

INSTALLING RIM JOISTS

Rim joists are the outer joists of the deck frame and typically define its edges. They include end joists and headers. End joists are attached to the ends of the ledger. A header ties the ends of the joists together.

Use angle brackets to attach end joists to the ledger and the header to the end joists.

Brace each end joist against the ledger and the beam or corner post. Level it and fasten it with an angle bracket. Fasten the end joists to the beam or corner post with lag screws or bolts. Brace the header against the end joists, and nail it.

INSTALLING INNER JOISTS

Inner joists bear the weight of the decking and everything that goes on it.

MEASURE AND MARK: Measure from the outside edge of the end joist and on the ledger, then mark the location of the center of the first joist hanger (use the spacing you derived from your span calculations—usually 16 inches). Then mark the center points for the remaining joists at the same interval.

Using a combination square, mark the ledger for the edges of the joist hangers.

TEST ALIGNMENT: Place a scrap piece in a joist hanger, and line up the top edge flush with the ledger. Remove the scrap and nail one side of the hanger in place. Fit the scrap in the hanger again to make sure it has not spread, and nail the other side.

Measure and mark the joist locations on the beam or header joist. Insert each inner joist in its hanger, and nail the hangers to the joists.

LAPPING JOINTS: If your deck design requires joists longer than standard lengths, lap or splice two joists over a beam. To lap them, allow each joist to extend 8 to 12 inches beyond the beam, nail them together from both sides, and anchor them with seismic ties. If you lap the joists, be sure you shift the markings on the header before installing the hangers.

To splice joists, butt the ends on the center of an interior beam. Nail cleats of the same stock to both sides of the butt joint.

Fasten the end joists to the ledger with angle brackets inside the corners, and toenail the joints from outside. Fasten joist hangers to the ledger before installing the inner joists.

DECK FRAMING

Ledger

Joist hanger

Joist

Angle bracket

Joist hanger

Ledger

End joist

Inner joist

Chalk line to mark joist ends for cutting

Beam/post anchor

Beam

Post anchor

Attach beams to posts with beam/post hangers or seismic ties. After marking the joist ends, cut them and attach the header joist.

INSTALLING BEAMS AND JOISTS
continued

DECKING PATTERNS

In the simplest and most straightforward decking pattern, the boards are laid perpendicular to the joists, but there are many ways to vary this layout.

Some variations won't require you to alter the subframing. Others will. Most diagonal patterns, for example, won't require framing modifications, but alternating diagonal modules will.

The key to making decking patterns safe is to recognize that offset patterns mean that decking boards have to span a longer distance than perpendicular decking. This may require closer joist spacing or stronger decking. If you want to change the direction of the pattern within the surface of the deck, or if you wish to lay out an elaborate design, you will have to plan the direction of the joists accordingly.

When planning unusual decking patterns, remember to design structural framing members carefully. The cut ends of each board must always be centered on a joist.

For simple patterns, such as perpendiculars and diagonals, install the joists and scatter the butted ends of decking randomly across the surface.

For more complex styles, such as basket weaves and herringbones, support each modular decking unit with framing. Typically, this means installing blocking at regular intervals, with joists often doubled to receive the edge of the decking pattern.

BLOCKING AND BRIDGING

To stabilize joists more than 8 feet long, install blocking or bridges.

To block joists, nail pieces of the joist stock between them.

For bridging, cut the ends of 1× or 2×4 sections at an angle to fit diagonally between the joists.

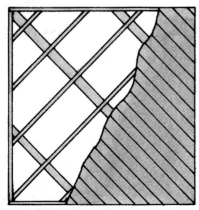

Diagonal decking installed across diagonal framing

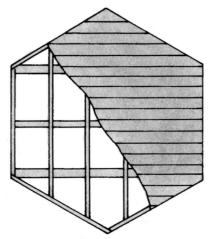

Freestanding hexagonal deck

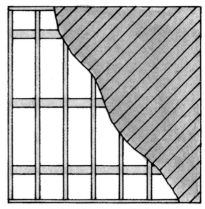

Diagonal decking installed across normal framing

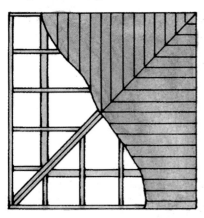

Bidirectional with mitered joints

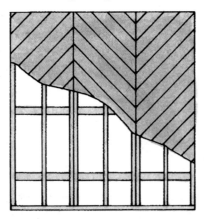

Herringbone on normal framing

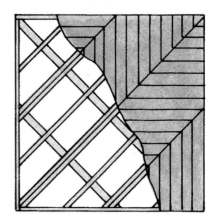

Herringbone on diagonal framing

BUILDING A CANTILEVERED DECK

Not all decks have their edges neatly corresponding to the edges of the posts and beams. Cantilevered decks have joists that extend past their beams. The header joist, parallel to the ledger and tying together the ends of the extended joists, is not supported directly by the beams or posts.

ADVANTAGES: This design is often very attractive and can make it possible for you to build a larger deck than you could with a corner-post design.

For example, cantilevering can extend a deck over a slope that is too steep or rocky to allow footings and posts at the corners. Such an extension creates space that otherwise might not be usable.

Cantilevering creates a floating effect on a deck of any size. With footings inside the perimeter of the deck, the structure appears to hang in space.

PRIME RULE: Local codes govern the length of the overhang, but in general no more than a third of the deck's total area should extend beyond the outer beam. The distance from the ledger to the beam should be at least twice the distance of the overhang.

The beam that supports a cantilevered deck can be a single board, a pair of boards mounted on either side of the posts, or a laminated beam of two or three boards fastened together. Such laminated beams can likewise rest in post caps or flank the posts.

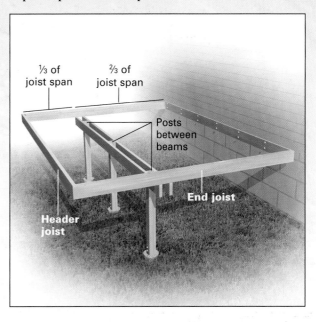

BRACING

Decks more than 5 feet tall or those in regions with loose soil, earthquakes, or periodic high winds may need permanent bracing, and the time to do it is now—after you've tied the posts and beams together. Even if your deck is not subject to such forces, bracing can make it more stable. Most bracing is diagonal, providing increased stiffness at joints. Review the illustrations and install bracing that meets local codes and conditions.

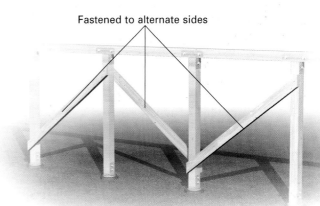

To add stability without adding too much lumber, brace posts in a diagonal pattern as shown. Use 2×6s for braces more than 8 feet long.

Tall posts need the strongest bracing possible to provide stability. X-bracing creates extra support in two directions. For even greater strength, nail or screw spacer blocks between the braces.

Y-bracing is easy to add even after the rest of the deck is finished. This design works best with beams mounted directly on top of posts, but it also can be used with posts sandwiched between beams.

INSTALLING DECKING

Width of decking board, plus gap

As you approach the ledger or header, check the remaining distance to make sure the last board will fit. Remember to include the gaps in your measurements. Adjust the gaps between the last few decking boards so everything fits. If the differences are too great to correct with small adjustments, rip the last board to fit.

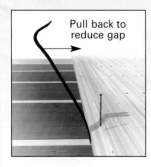

Pull back to increase gap

Pull back to reduce gap

FIXING BOW AND WARP

If some decking boards have slight bows (and they will), you can correct them during installation.

Fasten the bowed board at each end, then insert a flat pry bar along the bow.

For an inward bow *(top left)*, fit the pry bar between the last finished board and the bowed one, and pull back until the bowed board is straight. Fasten before you let go.

For an outward bow *(bottom left)*, drive the pry bar into the joist next to the bow, pull back on the bar to straighten the board, and nail or screw it in place.

Because decking provides the surface appearance of your deck, you may want to invest a little more for high quality lumber such as cedar or redwood. Even if you choose to use pressure-treated lumber for your decking, measure and install it with care.

STARTER BOARD

This is the first board laid either at the header joist or along the house. Starting at the header allows you to make minor adjustments to spacing next to the house, where it won't be as noticeable.

In either case, measure and cut the starter board to the exact length of the deck and fasten it in place.

THE REST OF THE DECK

Lay out the remaining decking with ends overhanging the joists; you will cut them off later. Before you start to fasten the decking, arrange it so joints are centered on joists and fall in a random pattern.

Space untreated lumber ⅛ inch apart (an 8d nail makes a handy spacer). Butt treated lumber together; it will shrink the first year.

Fasten each board with nails or decking screws, drilling pilot holes at butt joints (or on all of the ends) to avoid splitting.

As you approach the ledger (or the header, if you started at the house), lay the boards exactly as you will fasten them and make adjustments in the spacing. (You may have to rip the final boards to fit.) Leave ¼-inch space between the last board and the house to allow for expansion.

TRIM THE ENDS: When all the decking is fastened, snap a chalk line from the starter board to the ledger, and trim the ends of the decking with a circular saw. Tack a 1×4 on the decking to keep the saw on the line. Set the saw to the exact depth of the decking to avoid scoring the face of the end joists.

OTHER PATTERNS

The instructions above describe the most common decking pattern. A diagonal pattern requires some exceptions: Joists must typically be spaced 12 inches on center.

To lay your starter board, measure 3 feet from a corner on both the header and end joist. Start at this point and lay decking on either side of the starter board. Cut the boards to fit at the ledger, and trim the excess as above. A herringbone pattern also requires joists on 12-inch centers. Double every other joist so the decking joints meet on them at right angles. Measure from a corner to the first double joist, and mark this distance on the header. Lay the starter board at a 45-degree angle on this mark, and the next board at 90 degrees to the first one.

Chalk line — Cut notches to thickness of post.

If the posts in your deck design extend upward to support a canopy or railing, notch the decking to fit around the posts. Cut into the decking board by the thickness of the post, then chisel out the material between cuts.

FASTENER TIPS

Cordless tools are convenient, but a variable-speed corded drill won't stop you when batteries need charging. It will keep going as long as you do.

You can get a good idea where to drive nails or screws by watching the joist beyond the boards. But to line nails up consistently, lay a carpenter's square against the decking and parallel to the joist.

If the nails you're using tend to split the decking boards, and you can't always drill pilot holes, try blunting the tip of each nail before driving it. This prevents most minor splits.

TRIMMING DECKING BOARDS

JOINTS

Use full-length boards where possible. Make sure joints butt together over the center of the joists, and nail 2×4 cleats to the joists under the decking. Staggering the joints will also increase their strength and greatly improve the appearance of the deck.

To reduce squeaks and fastener pops, use a deck adhesive and spiral or ringshank nails or deck screws—two fasteners for 4-inch stock, and three for 6-inch boards. Drive the fasteners at a slight angle toward each other.

Treated lumber is dense, so it may help to predrill it before putting in fasteners. If any wood is splitting, predrill it.

After you've snapped a chalk line, use a circular saw to trim the edges of the decking. Set the saw to just the thickness of the decking.

STAIR BASICS

A stairway adds visual interest as well as utility. These pages contain instructions for building a standard stairway. On pages 134–135, we show you how to create deeper stairways. Stairways should come to rest on a firm, slightly sloped concrete or masonry surface (or the next level of a multitiered deck).

All steps in a stairway must be the same height and depth or they will feel awkward—and may be dangerous. Getting them consistent will require a bit of calculation; but first, some terminology.

ADDING STAIRS TO AN EXISTING DECK

If you need to add a new stairway to an existing deck that already has a railing, remove the railing to the posts that are on either side of the stairway. Build the stairs first, then attach railings correctly sized for the stairway.

RISE AND RUN

The terms "rise" and "run" describe the physical characteristics of stairs.

■ **RISE** refers to the height from one tread to the next.

■ **RUN** is the horizontal depth of each tread, front to back.

The following terms are used to further designate the dimensions of each step or the total stairway:

■ *Unit rise* or *unit run* designates the dimensions of a single step.

■ *Total rise* or *total run* indicates the entire vertical and horizontal distance traveled by the stairway.

Each step in a standard stairway should typically have a rise of 6 to 8 inches and a run of 10 to 12 inches. There's a formula for the ideal relationship between the rise and run—

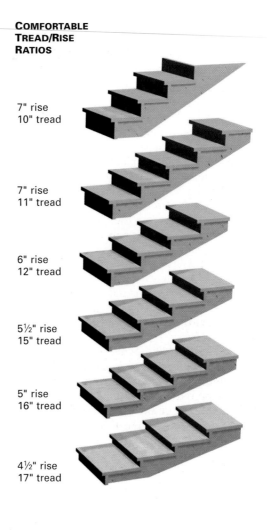

7" rise
10" tread

7" rise
11" tread

6" rise
12" tread

5½" rise
15" tread

5" rise
16" tread

4½" rise
17" tread

If your site is sloped, use straight boards and levels to help measure the rise and run and to locate the end of the stairs and the landing.

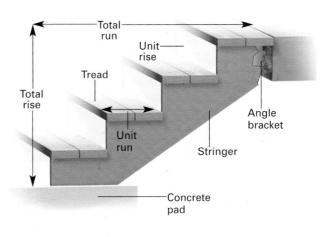

Total run

Unit rise

Tread

Total rise

Unit run

Angle bracket

Stringer

Concrete pad

Carefully plan your stair layout. You may need fewer or more steps than you had anticipated; if so, adjust the dimensions to fit.

twice the rise plus the run should be between 24 and 26 inches. The formula is the same whether you build stairs with standard or more generous dimensions (see page 134).

ESTIMATING RISE AND RUN

Calculating the rise and run requires slightly different techniques, depending on whether the ground below the deck is level or sloped. In any case, your first round of calculations will result in estimates.

LEVEL GRADE: To calculate the rise on a level grade, measure from the deck surface to the ground and subtract 1 inch (the aboveground height of the landing). To calculate the run, measure from the base of the deck out to your proposed landing site.

SLOPED GRADE: If the ground slopes, use a level and straight boards, as illustrated, *opposite*.

Either way, your calculations will proceed as follows. Assume, for this example, that your measurements result in stairs with a 38-inch rise.

■ Divide the total rise by the approximate riser height you want—for example, 7 inches —to give you an idea of how many steps you need—approximately five.

■ Multiply the result by the tread depth you want (in this case, 10 to 12 inches) to estimate the total run—50 to 60 inches.

■ Using the estimated total run, drive temporary stakes in the ground to mark the end of your stairway.

Now it's time to fine-tune the results.

MAKING FINAL ADJUSTMENTS

Adjust the height of the individual risers so they are even. In our example, the calculations resulted in five steps with each step about 7.6, or 7⅝ inches high. Adjust the individual runs (staying within the formula above) so the total run will put the bottom of the stairway where you want it. In our example, the calculations result in a tread that is 8.8 to 10.8 inches (8¾ to 10¼ inches) deep.

BUILDING THE LANDING PAD

To make a concrete landing pad, mark an area 6 inches wider than your steps and 30 inches from front to back.

■ Lay out the area with stakes so the bottom of the stairs is about a foot from the rear of the pad.

■ Excavate it to a depth of 6 to 8 inches, depending on local codes.

SIMPLE STEPS

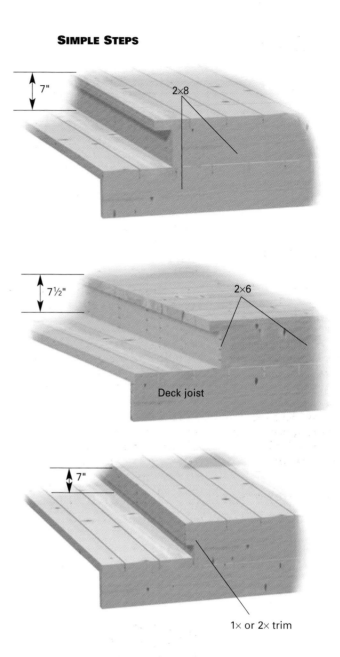

To incorporate steps on tiered decks, calculate the rise and run and build steps to fit the dimensions of your plan. Use the same size stock for the step support as you did in building the deck frame.

HOW WIDE?

Outdoor stairs need to be at least 36 inches wide. But if you entertain large groups, you may want to build them as wide as 5 feet to let two people pass side by side.

STAIR BASICS
continued

■ Line the excavation with 2×6 forms, and tamp in a 3- to 4-inch gravel base.

■ Lay in reinforcing mesh, then pour in 3 inches of concrete, and level it with a straight board.

■ Trowel it smooth and insert J bolts where you will install angle iron to anchor the stair base.

■ Let the concrete cure for at least 48 hours.

You also can set bricks or pavers in sand, or tamp gravel or stone inside timber edgings.

EASY SPEED AND ACCURACY

Stair gauges—small, hexagonal brass blocks with setscrews—can speed up your measuring and marking jobs. Available at building supply stores, they fasten on the sides of a carpenter's square, providing consistent measurements from one step to the next.

LAYING OUT A STRINGER

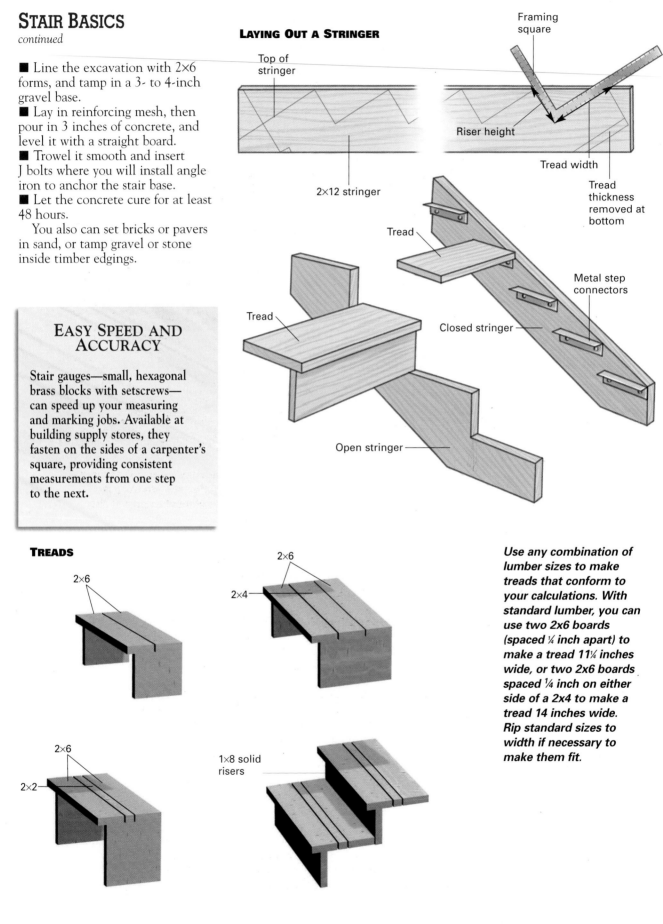

Top of stringer

Framing square

Riser height

Tread width

Tread thickness removed at bottom

2×12 stringer

Tread

Tread

Metal step connectors

Closed stringer

Open stringer

TREADS

2×6

2×6

2×4

2×6

2×2

1×8 solid risers

Use any combination of lumber sizes to make treads that conform to your calculations. With standard lumber, you can use two 2x6 boards (spaced ¼ inch apart) to make a tread 11¼ inches wide, or two 2x6 boards spaced ¼ inch on either side of a 2x4 to make a tread 14 inches wide. Rip standard sizes to width if necessary to make them fit.

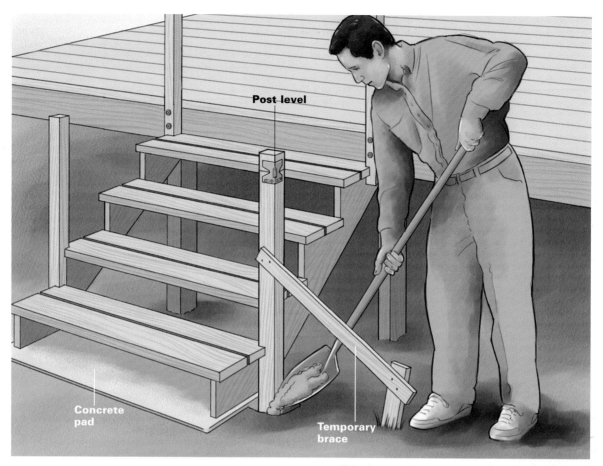

Post level

Concrete
pad

Temporary
brace

Dig the postholes before you set the stringers,
but install the posts after the stairway is
framed, leaving enough post to trim to the
correct height.

CONSTRUCT THE STAIRS

The hefty beams that support your steps are
called stringers. You'll need a 2×12 stringer
on each end and, for stairs wider than
36 inches, a third in the middle. Purchase
straight, clear 2×12s.

Stringers are either closed or open.
■ Closed stringer are easier to make; you
don't have to notch them for the treads.
■ Open stringers will need notches cut for
the treads.

MAKE THE STRINGERS: Mark the unit
rise and run with tape on a framing square.
With the 2×12 crown side up, draw light
pencil lines. Start at the top, where the
stringer will attach to the deck, and work
downward. Mark the bottom step 1½ inches
shorter than the others to allow for the
thickness of the tread.
■ To make a notched stringer (with treads
resting on the top of cut-out notches), cut on
your marks with a circular saw, stopping just
short of the corners. Finish the cuts with a
handsaw. Apply sealer to newly cut surfaces.
■ To make a closed stringer, cut only the top

and bottom of the stringer. Attach stair cleats
at the lines with 1¼-inch decking screws
driven through pilot holes.

ASSEMBLE THE STAIRS: Tack the
stringers to the deck, then mark the ground
for post holes at the second or third step.
Take the stringers down and dig holes at least
3 feet deep, or to the level specified by local
codes. Attach the stringers to the deck joist
or the framing you've added to provide firm
support. Use joist hangers to attach the
stringers to the header, and angle iron to
anchor the stringers to the concrete pad.
Square the stringers, plumb and attach the
posts, then cut and attach the treads
(notched, if necessary).

On closed stringers, attach the treads
with 1¼-inch decking screws.

On open stringers, screw the treads down
on top of the cutouts. Attach riser backings,
or leave the space behind the treads open.

Then fill the holes with concrete.

BUILDING DEEP STAIRS

Standard 3-foot-wide stairs with treads 11 inches deep are fine for taking out the garbage or other normal traffic. But if you want a pleasant place to sit and enjoy the view or if you want a more gracious access to the yard, consider more spacious steps.

These deep-tread stairways all have rise-to-run ratios that follow the "rule of 24-26." Twice the rise plus the run equals 24 to 26 inches.

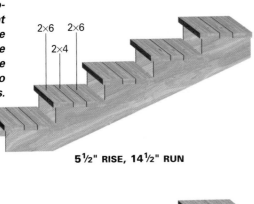

2×6 2×6
2×4

5¹⁄₂" RISE, 14¹⁄₂" RUN

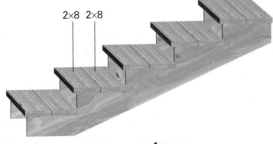

2×8 2×8

5" RISE, 14¹⁄₂" RUN

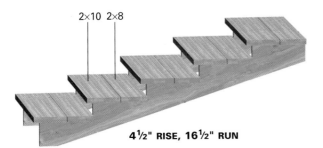

2×10 2×8

4¹⁄₂" RISE, 16¹⁄₂" RUN

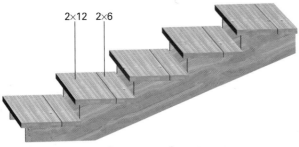

2×12 2×6

4¹⁄₂" RISE, 16³⁄₄" RUN

CALCULATING FOR COMFORT

As stair treads become deeper, the rise should become shorter; otherwise, climbing them will be uncomfortable. Although the dimensions of most stairs—even those with larger treads—should comply with the 24-26 rise-to-run ratio when possible, some situations may not fit the "rule." These deeper steps can still be comfortable to use.

LONG STEPS

To construct these stairs, use the same techniques as you would for a "formula" stairway, but adjust the placement of the lower end of the stairway to fit your site—even if such adjustment puts the stair dimensions slightly outside the 24-26 ratio. Construction is similar, but the stringers will be longer and may need a support post on each side at the middle of the run.

FIGURING RISE AND RUN: First decide where you want the steps to end in the yard; then decide on a rise-run ratio. For instance, if you want to descend to a point that is 32 inches below the deck (total rise) and 70 inches away from the deck (total run), you could have five steps with a rise of 6¹⁄₂ inches (5×6¹⁄₂=32) and a run of 14 inches (5×14=70). Of course, moving the landing pad a few inches in or out will simplify the calculations without affecting ease of use.

SUPPORTING THE STRINGERS: Use a framing square to mark 2×12s as you would for standard stringers, and cut them with a circular saw and a saber saw or handsaw.

Stringers for deep stairs have a large "foot," so make sure the landing pad is wide enough to support all of it. The longer and more horizontal the stringer, the weaker it will be. As a general rule, if a stringer will not have support for more than 7 feet, it needs a third stringer in the middle—perhaps with a separate footing and post (in addition to the railing post near the bottom of the stairs).

TREAD COMBINATIONS: To get the width of tread you want, use any combination of boards that works. For instance, a 2×12 (11¹⁄₄ inches wide) plus a 2×6 (5¹⁄₂ inches wide) with a ¹⁄₈-inch gap between them form a 16⁷⁄₈-inch-wide tread.

GENTLE LANDINGS

For a more gradual descent, build several landings—either in succession or separated by a short flight of steps. Landings extending more than 2 feet are no longer bound by the "rule of 24-26." Just be sure that all steps from one level to another—stairs or landings—are the same height, no more than 7½ inches.

In most cases, you will frame these landings separately—as you would a deck surface—but without an underlying beam. When calculating heights, remember to include the thickness of the decking.

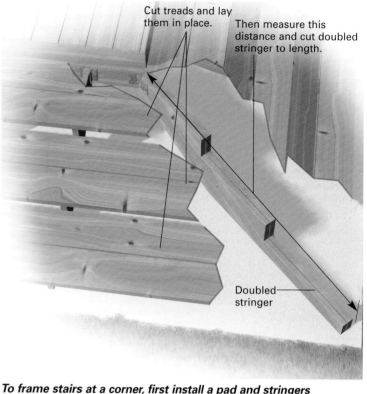

Cut treads and lay them in place.

Then measure this distance and cut doubled stringer to length.

Doubled stringer

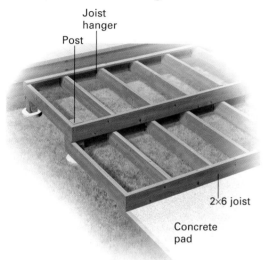

Joist hanger

Post

2×6 joist

Concrete pad

Frame descending landings as you would a deck surface, with joists, joist hangers, and posts with footings.

To frame stairs at a corner, first install a pad and stringers at the ends of each descent. Install a doubled stringer (two stringers nailed together, side by side) at an angle at the corner. It will be longer than the other stringers. Here's how to measure its length: First cut, miter, and temporarily set the treads in place, meeting in a miter joint at the corner. Remove the treads from one side and measure the length that will support the bottom tread at the corner. Mark the stringers (the runs equal to the length of the miter), nail them together, then attach them to the deck frame.

HANDRAILS FOR SAFETY

A 2×6 or 2×8 is not comfortable to use as a stairway cap rail. Attached handrails are safer; you can buy ready-made materials or make your own.

To make your own, use the same stock as the rest of the railing. Rip a 2×3 from a 2×4 and round off the edges with a sander or a router with a roundover bit. Attach a 2×4 so it spans the inside edge of the stair rail posts a couple of inches below the rail cap. Cut 2×3 supports to hold the handrail, 2 inches out from the rail. That way, you'll have plenty of room to grab. Carefully drill pilot holes in the rail and the supports and attach them to the 2×4 with 3½-inch screws every 3 feet.

If you're buying your rail ready-made, purchase standard brass handrail hardware and rounded rail stock. The rail stock is usually available only in pine or oak. Apply at least two coats of sealer to the wood (it's not designed for outdoor use) and secure the rail hardware to the post with extra-long screws.

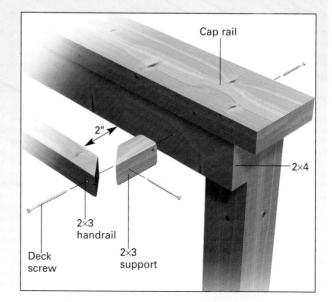

Cap rail

2"

2×4

2×3 handrail

Deck screw

2×3 support

BUILDING RAILINGS

If you plan to extend the posts above the surface of the deck (right), fasten the end and header joists to the posts, and add fascia boards for a finished appearance. Lattice panels (below) make inexpensive and attractive infill for railings.

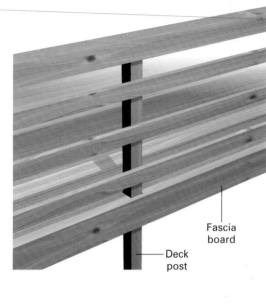

Fascia board

Deck post

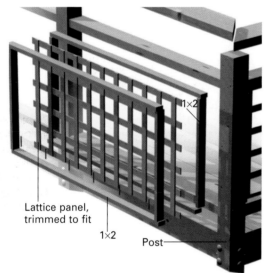

1×2

Lattice panel, trimmed to fit

1×2

Post

In addition to providing safety, railings are an important design element of your deck. They help convert the flat surface to a three-dimensional enclosure. For most railings, install the posts first, then the rails, then the balusters, and finally any decorative trim. The balusters illustrated on these pages are cut from 2×2s, but you can use other styles as well—spindled, turned, and even 2× stock set edge out.

ESSENTIALS

Most building codes require railings on decks built 18 inches or more above the ground—in some areas even less than that.

Typical codes also set a minimum height for railings, usually 36 or 42 inches. Your local codes also specify the distance between posts, the openings under the railings, and baluster spacing (usually no less than 4 inches and no more than 6 inches).

MATERIALS: Use the same wood on the railings as you used for the decking. If you have splurged on the decking, maintain that quality in the railings. Using different materials can often destroy the continuity of your design.

EASY DOES IT: You can build railings between the posts using one of three methods.
■ Use the same posts that support the deck (extended above the decking).
■ Add posts to create the proper spacing between supports—typically 4 to 6 feet.
■ Empty posts using a combination of the two methods above.

DECORATIVE POSTS

Finish the posts by making a decorative detail. You'll want to do this work before you put the posts in. Here are several ideas for creating your own styles:
■ With a router or table saw, make band cuts near the top of each post. Chamfer the top of the post at an angle that corresponds to your overall design, and make sure not to make the point dangerously sharp.
■ Turn the top of each post into a decorative finial using your lathe or shaper.
■ Bevel the bottom of each post with a table saw. You'll be surprised at how much interest this simple detail will add to your deck design.

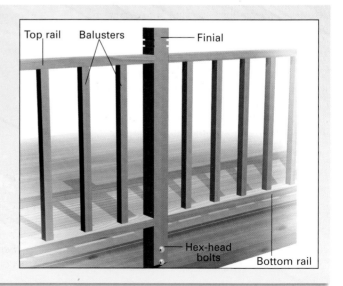

Top rail   Balusters   Finial

Hex-head bolts

Bottom rail

In a popular railing installation, and one of the easiest to build, posts are attached to the header and end joists. This system allows you to add the railings after installing the framing and decking. Because you'll be working along the outside edges of the deck, you'll have easy access to each post.

INSTALLING POSTS

If the posts don't already extend above the deck, add new posts beginning at the house and corners. Attach 4×4 railing posts to the facing at least every 6 feet. Install posts at your stair location, too, cutting their tops to match the stair angle.

Installation is the same no matter where you locate the posts. Here's what you do:

■ Mark each post location. Then cut the posts to length and predrill them for ⅜ hex-head bolts (offset and countersink the holes) or carriage bolts. If you can't get a bolt in, use lag screws. Then make any decorative cuts.

■ Set each post plumb at its location, and run the drill bit through the holes to mark the joist. Drill ⅜-inch holes through the joist (pilot holes for lag screws), and fasten the post in place with ⅜×7-inch fasteners.

■ When the corner posts are in place, divide the space between them equally and at a spacing that conforms to local codes. Snap a chalk line between the bottom of the corner posts so their outside faces will lie in the same plane. Then mark, cut, and install the remaining posts using the fasteners for which you predrilled the holes.

Use the same marking methods for top-mounted posts set in anchors on the decking.

INSTALLING RAILINGS

To set the railings, first mark the rail locations on the posts, then cut the rail stock so it will fit snugly.

■ Attach the bottom rail first, about 3 inches above the decking.

■ Fasten the top rail from the underside or sides to hide the screw holes—flush with the top of the posts.

■ Hold side-mounted rails in position and cut the joints so they are centered on a post.

Predrill the rails and drive two 3-inch galvanized decking screws just through the other side. Place the rail at the mark and press the screw tip into the post, then drive one screw at one end and one at the other. Finish by driving all screws home.

Alternatively you can attach the railings with rail hangers, or toenail them, using blocks underneath for increased support.

The simplest method of installing posts is to attach them to the faces of end and header joists. Drill and countersink pilot holes in the posts, then fasten the posts to the joists with lag screws, hex-head bolts, or carriage bolts.

Bolt holes

Carriage bolts

Overlap cut at a 45° angle

If you must splice the rails, cut the ends at a 45-degree angle and join the boards in the middle of a post.

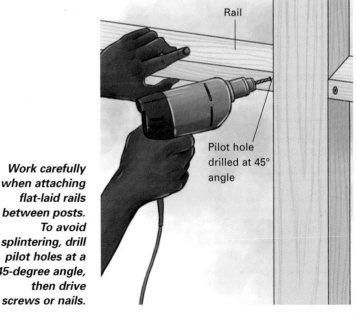

Rail

Work carefully when attaching flat-laid rails between posts. To avoid splintering, drill pilot holes at a 45-degree angle, then drive screws or nails.

Pilot hole drilled at 45° angle

BUILDING RAILINGS
continued

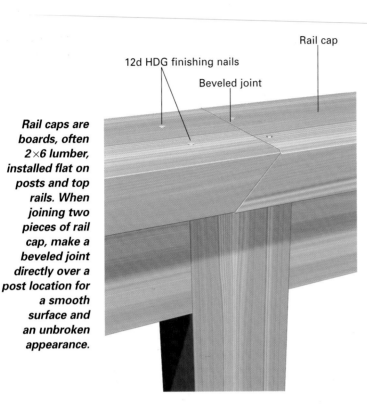

12d HDG finishing nails

Beveled joint

Rail cap

Rail caps are boards, often 2×6 lumber, installed flat on posts and top rails. When joining two pieces of rail cap, make a beveled joint directly over a post location for a smooth surface and an unbroken appearance.

SPACING BALUSTERS

In most areas, building codes require that balusters be spaced less than 4 inches apart. Codes also specify the spacing between the deck surface and the bottom rail.

Some railing designs, including those that use screening material or latticework between the posts, have openings small enough to meet most building codes. Others, including many popular designs, should be approved before you start building.

SAVING TIME

Here are a few ways to reduce the amount of time and effort you spend on installing railings:
■ To make the railing parts consistent, cut all the pieces of each kind at the same time, using a 10-inch power miter saw with a stop installed at the length of your finished pieces.
■ Work off site on a flat surface—or on your deck if there is room. Cut a plywood scrap and use it as a spacer to set the balusters at a consistent distance apart.
■ Instead of toenailing the balusters to the bottom rail, fasten them from underneath with decking screws. This is almost impossible to do once the bottom rail is in place, but it's easy if you assemble the entire railing section before you install it.

INSTALLING THE CAP

A rail cap protects the cut ends of the posts from the weather and adds an important decorative element to your deck design.

Use a straight 2×6 or 2×8 that is low in moisture content and free of large knots. Buy the longest boards you can find, and center any joints over posts. Bevel the joints and seal the cut ends to reduce moisture damage. The rail caps should be wider than the combined width of a post and rail.
■ Position each piece so it overhangs the post and the top rail, and mark it for cutting.
■ Attach it with 12d finishing nails or screws driven into the posts—and into the top rail if it is flush with the top of the post—driving a fastener every 8 inches.
■ Countersink the screws heads or use a nail set to drive the finishing nails below the surface.
■ Fill the holes with putty and sand them smooth.

Outside corners are best mitered to keep them from separating, warping, or splitting over time. To make the 45-degree cuts, use a power miter box or work carefully with a circular saw. Even if you consider your saw accurate, practice on scrap first to get the correct angle. Attach the pieces by drilling pilot holes and driving screws. If you have a biscuit joiner, use it to make a tight joint, as shown, *below*.

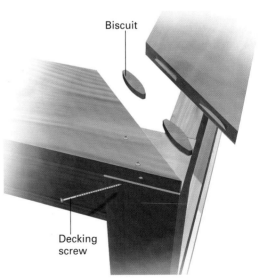

Biscuit

Decking screw

The mitered outside corner of a rail cap is often a trouble spot; it can come apart after a few years. Use a biscuit joiner to strengthen the joint. Drill a pilot hole and drive a screw to hold the pieces together.

INSTALLING THE BALUSTERS

Purchase ready-cut balusters or make your own from 2×2s. You may want to angle-cut one or both ends on the outside faces. Determine where you will drive the fasteners. Set a group of balusters side by side. Use a framing square to mark fastener positions, and drill pilot holes.

Construct a jig to help maintain consistent spacing between the balusters.

■ Attach the balusters with 2½-inch fasteners, bottom first, flush with the bottom of the lower rail.

■ Install the first baluster plumb, then align the next few.

■ Check every five or six balusters to see that they are still plumb, and reposition an errant baluster, if necessary.

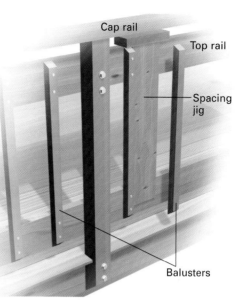

Cap rail

Top rail

Spacing jig

Balusters

A simple spacing jig keeps balusters evenly spaced. Place each baluster tightly against the jig, then fasten the baluster to the rails with nails or screws.

ALTERNATE RAILING PLANS

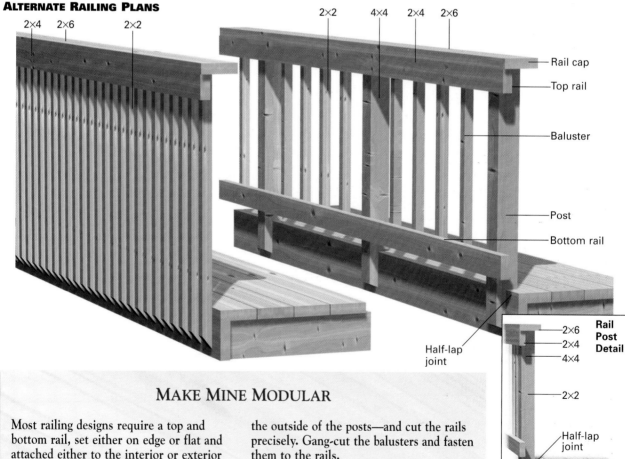

2×4   2×6   2×2

2×2   4×4   2×4   2×6

Rail cap

Top rail

Baluster

Post

Bottom rail

Half-lap joint

Rail Post Detail

2×6
2×4
4×4

2×2

Half-lap joint

MAKE MINE MODULAR

Most railing designs require a top and bottom rail, set either on edge or flat and attached either to the interior or exterior post faces.

Both styles lend themselves to modular construction: You build each section of rails and balusters separately, then install them.

In either case, measure the distance that the rails will span—either between or on the outside of the posts—and cut the rails precisely. Gang-cut the balusters and fasten them to the rails.

When it's time to install the sections, rest each end on a block of wood on top of the decking before you fasten them. Pieces of 4×4, or 2×4s set on edge, will provide a 3½-inch space beneath the bottom rail and the deck—a space that should comply with most building codes.

SIMPLE DECK EXTENSIONS

Your deck should be a place where family and friends enjoy the outdoors within easy reach of all the comforts of home. But if your deck is too small to accommodate the gatherings you'd like to host, don't reach for the wrecking bar just yet. A simple deck extension may be just the ticket.

Deck extensions are not difficult to build, nor do they need to be expensive. A modest investment can bring years of additional comfort and enjoyment. Use the same wood employed in the original structure, if possible. Creative use of finishes will help blend the new with the old (see "Finishes" on page 92). If your existing deck is structurally sound, your local codes will probably allow such an extension. Check with your local building department before you start planning.

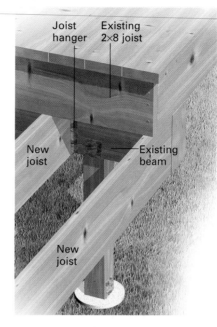

To add a new decking surface that is lower than the existing deck, tie the new joists to the beam with joist hangers. If the existing joists are 2×8s, you will have a comfortable 7¼-inch step down.

FRAMING FOR NEW DECK EXTENSION

To frame a new deck surface a step higher than the original, set the framing on top. In this case, 2×6 joists are ideal. With 1½ inch-thick decking on top of them, you will have a 7-inch step up.

TAKE STOCK OF YOUR SITE

Before you consider a deck extension, examine the existing structure closely to determine the best way to construct it. Most extensions—even tiered structures—can be added to an existing end joist, header, or beam and supported with posts along its exterior edges.

Study the examples illustrated on this page, then use the same construction techniques discussed in earlier pages of this book to add the space you need. Building an extension proceeds in the same order as building a new deck—posts first, then beams, then joists, decking, and finally, the railing.

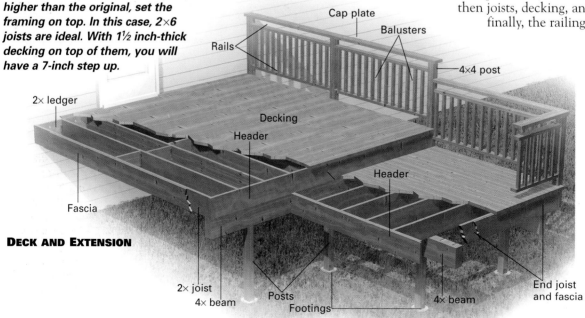

DECK AND EXTENSION

NEW RAILINGS FOR AN OLD DECK

The fundamental steps for adding railings are the same as for building railings from scratch. If you want to modify an existing railing, use these instructions to install the necessary additional railing parts.

INSTALLING POSTS

Some decks use a "through-post" design: The posts supporting the deck continue upward as part of the railing. Through-posts aren't necessary on an existing deck unless you add a new elevated section and need support from the ground up. Railing modifications, however, may require additional posts attached to the perimeter joists or fascia.

NOTCH THE DECKING: Place posts— as evenly spaced as possible—every 4 to 6 feet. Mark the side of the deck for each post. If the decking overhangs, cut a notch so that the post can rest flat against the perimeter joist or fascia. Use a circular saw to cut as much as possible, and use a saber saw to finish the cuts.

CUT AND NOTCH THE POSTS: Cut all the posts to the same length. This usually will be the height of the railing, less $1\frac{1}{2}$ inches (if you install a 2× cap on top of the posts), plus the width of the perimeter joist and the thickness of the decking.

A post does not have to be notched unless it needs to match existing posts. Notch the lower section of each post: half its thickness and the length of the joist plus decking. If your plan requires a post in the corner, cut notches for both directions, *below right*.

INSTALL THE POSTS: Attach posts to the side of the deck with two lag screws or carriage bolts. Use bolts (bolts provide more strength) where you have a clear space on the inside of the joist. Drill holes while a helper uses a level to make sure the post is plumb.

RAILS AND BALUSTERS

Whenever possible, purchase rail and cap pieces long enough so you will not have to splice them. Then cut the rail stock to the precise lengths required for your design and follow the steps shown on page 138 to install the rails, cap rail, and balusters.

You can change the posts and balusters from the style of the existing deck, but it's generally best to have the new design conform to the old one—unless the new space will be used for purposes completely different from the old space.

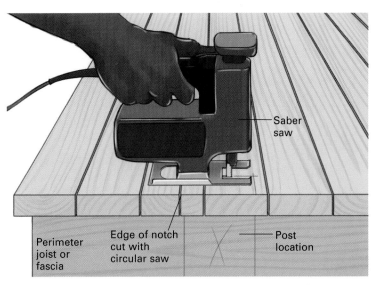

Perimeter joist or fascia

Edge of notch cut with circular saw

Post location

Saber saw

Use a circular saw and a saber saw to notch the old decking for each new post. Cut carefully so the post fits snugly in the notch.

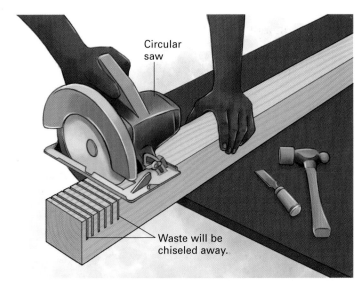

Circular saw

Waste will be chiseled away.

To notch a post, set a circular saw blade to a depth of $1\frac{3}{4}$ inches. Make a series of cuts spaced about $\frac{1}{4}$ inch apart, and chisel away the waste.

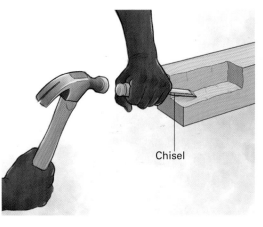

Chisel

A new post installed on the corner of a deck must be notched $1\frac{3}{4}$ inches along two adjacent sides. Start by cutting with a circular saw and finish with a chisel.

ADDING A SKIRT

The underside of a deck can offer some difficult design challenges. Large green-gray pressure-treated beams can be distracting, and the ground underneath may become muddy. Plantings of hedges or shrubs—chosen carefully so their mature height will not be higher than the deck—are an excellent solution.

You also can "skirt the issue." A well-built wood skirt may be the most visible feature of your deck. It will enhance the style of your deck and increase its utility by providing storage space. There are a number of different styles and material choices available for skirting a deck; installing latticework and solid 1× stock are two of the easiest.

The skirt should visually cover up what is unsightly, but be sure the design allows air to circulate freely under the deck surface. If rainwater that seeps through the decking is not able to evaporate quickly, it soon becomes standing water—a breeding ground for mosquitoes.

PROVIDING SUPPORT

Provide a nailing surface for all parts of the skirt—top, bottom, and sides. If the below-deck posts are near the edges of the deck, you may be able to use them as part of the framing by running horizontal 2×4s between them.

If there is no easy way to attach the skirt, build a frame like the one shown, below left.

BUILDING SIMPLE FRAMING: Screw vertical 2×4s to the outside of the perimeter deck joists down to about 2 inches above grade. If you want to install lattice panels (*see opposite left*), place the 2×4s where two sheets of lattice will meet; the edges need support. Next make a top and bottom frame. On the same outside face of the deck joist, fasten a 2×4 between the vertical supports with half its width exposed below the joist. Attach the bottom frame, toenailed to the vertical supports, plumbing the vertical members as you go.

REINFORCING THE FRAMING: A simple framing assembly is not very strong at the bottom. When you install the vertical 2×4s, place them next to a joist whenever possible. Joists on 16- and 24-inch centers should put the vertical supports at the lattice joints if you adjust the ends. Cut and miter (at 45 degrees) a 2×4 brace and screw it to the bottom of the vertical 2×4 and at the top to a joist or to the underside of the decking.

2×4 support

2×4 skirt framing

2×4 support

2×4

If the posts are spaced too far apart or are too short for framing, add framing below the deck for a surface to nail a skirt.

WATCH OUT FOR WEEDS

In some climates, almost no grass or weeds will grow in soil that is shaded by a deck. In climates where conditions encourage vegetation growth, many plants can spring up under—and even through—a deck.

First dig up and remove all the turf. Usually you can just spread landscape fabric over the area and shovel gravel on top to keep it in place.

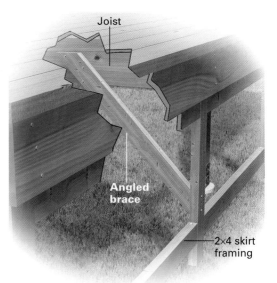

Joist

Angled brace

2×4 skirt framing

To provide support, install an angled brace that is attached to a joist. The bottom of unbraced skirt framing will not be strong enough.

INSTALLING A LATTICE SKIRT

Lattice makes an ideal skirt material because it is decorative and easy to install, and provides plenty of ventilation. Use sheets of lattice that are at least ¾ inch thick, made of either redwood or pressure-treated lumber.

CUT AND ATTACH THE LATTICE PANELS:

Cut the lattice so that all edges of the lattice panels will be supported by a framing member. Make sure the bottom of the lattice is about 1 inch above grade at all points (even pressure-treated lattice may rot if it sits in wet earth). Attach the lattice with 4d galvanized nails or 1¼-inch decking screws. If the lattice is brittle, drill pilot holes to prevent cracking it.

TRIM THE CORNERS AND JOINTS:

Apply trim to all exposed edges at outside corners and where the ends of sheets come together. At a corner, cut one piece of 1×2 and one piece of 1×3 to cover the lattice; install with galvanized screws or nails. Position the 1×2 edge to butt up against the 1×3, so the corner appears to be balanced.

INSTALLING A SOLID SKIRT

Vertical 1×8s or 1×6s, spaced at ¾-inch intervals, will hide the space under the deck more than lattice. They form a solid skirt that does not allow as much ventilation.

ATTACH THE BOARDS: Starting at a corner, drill pilot holes and drive 2-inch decking screws to attach the boards to the top and bottom framing pieces. Use the thickness of a board as a spacer, and check about every fifth board for plumb. You may want to trim the corners as described for the lattice skirt.

MAKING AN ACCESS DOOR

For storage or to provide access under the deck, make a door from three or four skirt boards. Tie the boards together with two horizontal nailers. Install flush hinges and an eyebolt latch.

To make a lattice door, cut a section of lattice to size and trim the edges with 1×4s on both sides. Drill pilot holes and drive 1⅝-inch screws every few inches in an alternating pattern. Attach the hinge to the face of the 1×4.

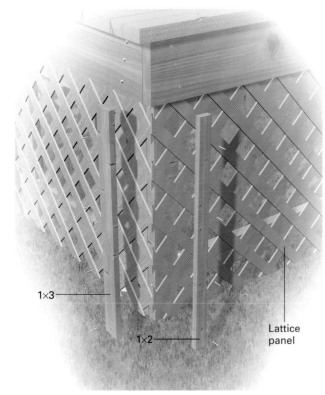

1×3

1×2

Lattice panel

Lattice skirting cuts easily and attaches quickly. If you don't like how exposed lattice edges look, trim the corners with 1×2 and 1×3 stock.

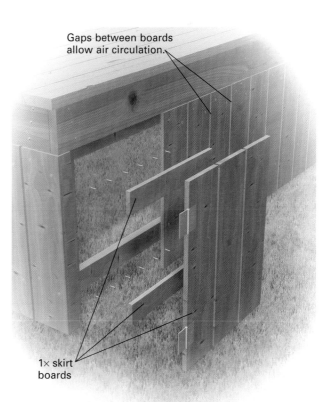

Gaps between boards allow air circulation.

1× skirt boards

To install a solid skirt, attach solid vertical 1× boards, leaving ¾-inch gaps between them for ventilation. Make an access door using the techniques shown on page 101.

RETAINING WALLS

Retaining walls can cut into slopes, freeing space otherwise unsuitable for a deck. Concrete block, brick, timber, natural stone, or precast decorative units are all suitable wall materials.

Because they hold back the pressure of the earth and water behind them, retaining walls must be designed with special considerations. First and foremost, they must allow a passage for water to drain out and away from them.

Dry-stacked materials must be arranged so that each course staggers backward into the slope. Staggering adds strength and keeps the wall from bowing or collapsing.

LAYING A BRICK WALL

Lay a brick wall on a concrete footing. Note the line stretched between wood corner blocks as a guide to keep the courses straight. Walls more than a foot high require a double thickness of bricks.

Line blocks along mason's line

DRAINAGE FOR A RETAINING WALL

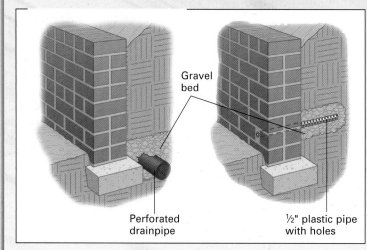

Gravel bed

Perforated drainpipe

½" plastic pipe with holes

Without adequate drainage, water pressure can build up behind a brick retaining wall and crack it. To avoid this, dig a trench at least 8 inches deep and wide behind the foundation. Shovel gravel into it, making one end higher than the other. Lay perforated drainpipe, holes facing down, on the gravel *(far left)*. The slope of the gravel directs water away from the wall.

Another approach is to place ½-inch perforated plastic pipe every 4 feet along the wall in the first above-grade course *(near left)*. Cut an inch off adjacent bricks to fit the pipe. Build up mortar under the pipe at the back of the wall so the pipe tilts up into the backfill. Surround the pipe with a few inches of gravel as you backfill.

MORTARED STONE

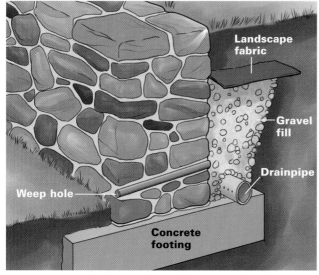

Landscape fabric

Gravel fill

Drainpipe

Weep hole

Concrete footing

Mortared stone is the most permanent material to use for a retaining wall. Pour a concrete footing as the base. A large drainpipe carries away most rainwater, and small drainpipes—called weep holes—let excess water through from the other side.

USING A BATTER GUIDE

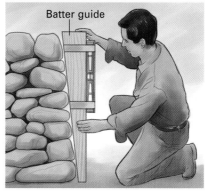

Batter guide

Make a batter guide from a board cut to the height of the wall, then cut at an angle along its length. Taper the guide 1 inch for every 2 feet of wall height. Tape a level to the straight side of the guide and use it to check the wall as you build it. When the bubble is centered, the angle is correct.

STONE TIPS (SO YOUR WALL WON'T)

■ Use large, flat stones for the base. Twist each stone and remove or add gravel until it sits solidly.
■ For all courses, use stones that are more flat than round.
■ Sort the stones into several piles so you can easily find small, medium, and large pieces as you need them.

DRY-STACKED STONE

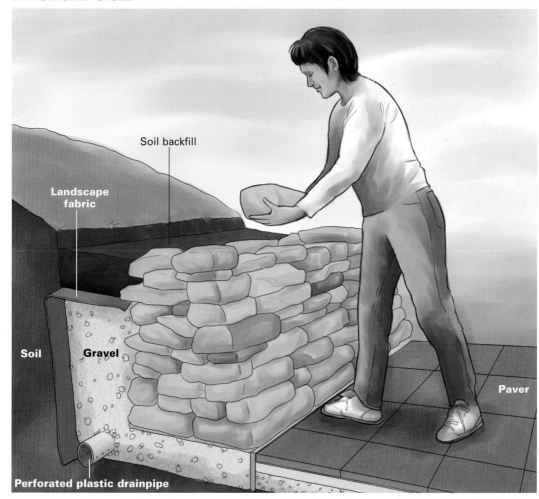

Soil backfill

Landscape fabric

Soil   Gravel

Paver

Perforated plastic drainpipe

To keep the weight of water runoff from collapsing your retaining wall, install a drainage system.

Lay perforated drainpipe in gravel so it can carry water away to a dry well or another area that will soak up the runoff.

Add more gravel, then landscape fabric.

As you build upward, fill the area behind the wall with gravel, and finish off the top with soil and sod or plantings.

RETAINING WALLS
continued

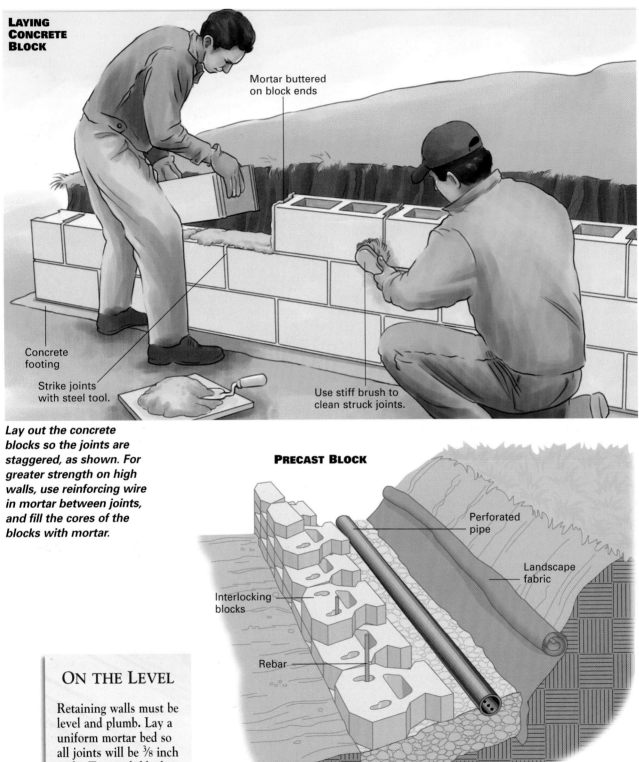

LAYING CONCRETE BLOCK

Mortar buttered on block ends

Concrete footing

Strike joints with steel tool.

Use stiff brush to clean struck joints.

Lay out the concrete blocks so the joints are staggered, as shown. For greater strength on high walls, use reinforcing wire in mortar between joints, and fill the cores of the blocks with mortar.

PRECAST BLOCK

Perforated pipe

Landscape fabric

Interlocking blocks

Rebar

Gravel

Sections of rebar or fiberglass anchoring pins help hold the blocks in place. Gravel and perforated pipe prevent damage from water pressure.

ON THE LEVEL

Retaining walls must be level and plumb. Lay a uniform mortar bed so all joints will be ⅜ inch wide. Test each block for level and plumb. As needed, tap the blocks with the trowel handle.

INTERLOCKING BLOCK

Some concrete blocks are self-battering—made with a ridge along the lower back edge that hooks against the block below it. These ridges also set each succeeding course back from the one below it. Interlocking blocks work best for walls that are no more than a few feet high.

GREEN WALLS

Blocks cast in the shape of oversized flower pots can be used to construct planted or "green" walls. Simply remove soil to position and level the blocks and fill the planting area with the soil. Stairstep your design up the slope face and plant flowers or ground cover.

Most blocks are manufactured for local consumption because of the shipping weight of these products. Look under "Concrete Products" in the Yellow Pages of your phone book to find a manufacturer in your area.

TIMBER WALLS

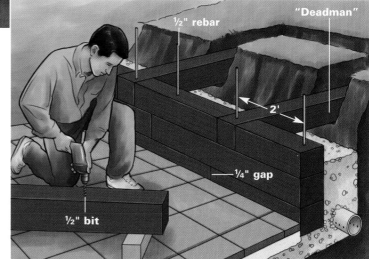

The first course of timbers will be at least partially below grade. Be sure it rests on a thick bed of gravel so water can drain away. Install perforated drainpipe to carry away additional runoff.

DEADMEN

If you're building a retaining wall more than 2 feet high, strengthen it with "deadmen"—perpendicular timbers attached to parallel timbers set in trenches in the slope.

Dig the trenches at the third or fourth course and about 6 feet back into the slope—at a depth that will make them even with the course they attach to.

Cut and lay 6-foot-long timbers in the trenches. Fasten the deadmen to the wall and rear timbers with 12-inch spikes or rebar driven through them.

POURED-CONCRETE WALLS

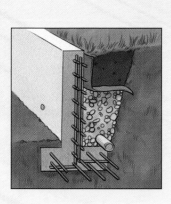

A poured-concrete retaining wall requires forming and placing a large amount of concrete, so consider hiring a contractor to build it.

The process involves inserting rebar horizontally in the concrete footing. It will help support the heavy wall. Other rebars are bent at a 90-degree angle and wired in place before the footing is poured. Then the vertical rebar are wired to horizontal rebar every 12 inches from the footing to the top of the wall. Forms are assembled at the front and back sides of the wall, and concrete is poured into the forms. When the concrete wall has cured, the forms are removed and gravel is poured into the space between the wall and the earth slope. A perforated drainpipe laid near the footing provides drainage behind the wall. The top foot of the wall is backfilled with soil.

Note that the footing is stabilized by earth fill on the front face and by the weight of gravel and earth on the back side of the wall.

If the wall is more than 3 feet high, the concrete forms need to be set so the base of the wall is thicker than the top, and the face of the wall slants back toward the sloped soil.

FOOTINGS FOR FENCES AND OVERHEADS

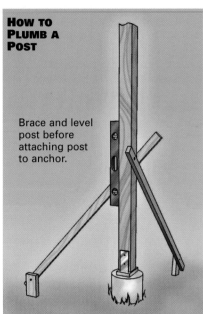

HOW TO PLUMB A POST

Brace and level post before attaching post to anchor.

Much of the privacy, shade, and ambience of a landscape comes from arbors, fences, gazebos, and other structures that use vertical posts. If the structure it to last, the posts need to be firmly anchored in the ground.

You have two techniques at your disposal: You can bury part of the post in the ground or fasten it above ground to a concrete pier and footing. In packed soil that is not sandy or moist, set the post in an earth and gravel base. In sandy, loose, or moist soil, set the pots in concrete.

LAYING OUT THE SITE

Using batter boards and mason's line, lay out the perimeter of your fence or other structure and square the corners with a 3-4-5 triangle. (See page 119 for more information.)

Many fences and overhead structures have posts spaced 8 feet apart; your site and design may require different spacing. Lumber is sold in even-numbered increments, so space the posts in even multiples of feet to avoid wasting material.

If you use factory-made panels, place the posts precisely. Measure carefully or lay the panels on the ground to determine post locations. (If you're using prefabricated panels, you can mark and dig postholes as you go. This method involves setting a post, holding a panel in place, marking the next hole, and digging it.)

DEPTH AND DIAMETERS

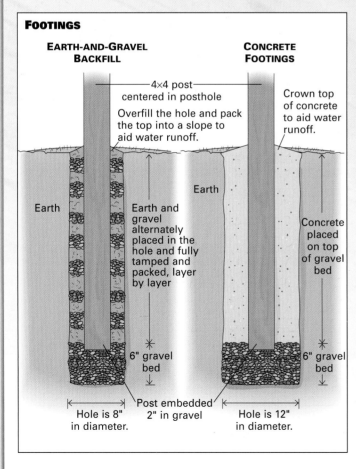

FOOTINGS

EARTH-AND-GRAVEL BACKFILL

CONCRETE FOOTINGS

4×4 post centered in posthole

Overfill the hole and pack the top into a slope to aid water runoff.

Crown top of concrete to aid water runoff.

Earth

Earth

Earth and gravel alternately placed in the hole and fully tamped and packed, layer by layer

Concrete placed on top of gravel bed

6" gravel bed

6" gravel bed

Post embedded 2" in gravel

Hole is 8" in diameter.

Hole is 12" in diameter.

Here are some guidelines for posthole dimensions. Consult your local building department for information specific to your area.

POSTHOLE DIAMETER:
The minimum diameter of the posthole depends on the footing:
■ **Earth-and-gravel backfill**: Make your posthole diameter at least twice the width of the post. A 4×4 requires an 8-inch diameter, a 6×6, a 12-inch diameter.
■ **Concrete footings**: Make the posthole diameter at least three times the width of the post. A 4×4 post requires a hole 12 inches in diameter; a 6×6 requires one 18 inches in diameter.

POSTHOLE DEPTH:
■ **Terminal posts**: As a general rule, one-third of the total post length should be below ground (at a minimum depth of 24 inches) and two-thirds above ground. Thus, a 6-foot terminal post should be 9 feet long, set in a 3-foot posthole.
■ **Line posts**: These can be set slightly less deep. Line posts for a 6-foot fence can be 8 feet long set in 2-foot holes. Local codes may require depths below the frost line.

SINKING A POST

■ Using a posthole digger, dig a hole that is three times as wide as the post and half of its exposed length.
■ Shovel in 4" of gravel and set the post in the hole.
■ Plumb the post and brace it.
■ Then shovel in 2 more inches of gravel.
■ Complete the earth and gravel installation, or fill the hole with concrete.

SETTING POSTS

Dadoed or mortised joints require posts cut to a precise height. With other styles, let the height run wild and cut the entire line later. Here's what to do:
■ Divide the actual size of your posts by 2 (a 6×6, for example, measures 5½ inches thick) and move your mason's lines this distance away from their original position. This new position will place the line in the plane of the outside post faces, as shown.
■ Stand an end post in its hole and twist its base into the gravel bed about 2 inches. On two adjacent sides and about two-thirds up the post, pivot 1×4 braces on a single duplex nail (its two heads make removal easy). Then plumb the post on two adjacent faces with a 4-foot carpenter's level or post level, keeping the post face just touching the mason's line. Stake the braces securely, attaching them to the post with a couple of box nails or screws. Repeat the process for the other end posts.
■ To help keep the intermediate posts straight, stretch another line between the end posts about 18 inches below their tops. Then set, align, and brace each successive intermediate post.
■ When all the posts are braced, shovel in the footing filler, either earth and gravel or concrete. Double-check each post for alignment and plumb. If you've installed concrete footings and you plan to fasten the rails and infill with screws, you can cut the posts and build the rest of your fence or overhead after the concrete sets. If you're going to nail your fence frame, wait until the concrete cures—three to seven days. In either case, leave the braces in place.

CUTTING POSTS

If you've set the posts with their heights wild, now's the time to cut them to length.
■ Measure one end post from the ground to the post height and mark it. If the grade is level, snap a level chalk line from that point to the other end post. That will mark all posts at the same height. If you're building a

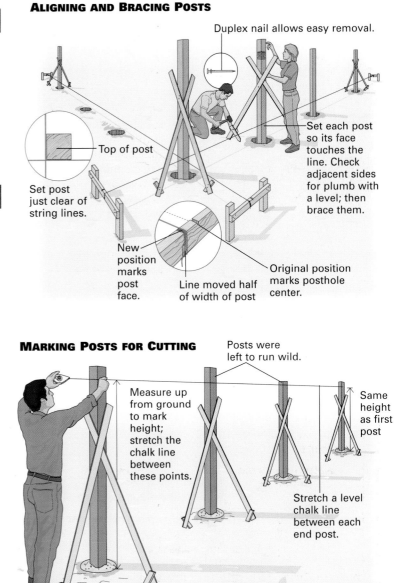

ALIGNING AND BRACING POSTS

Duplex nail allows easy removal.

Top of post

Set post just clear of string lines.

Set each post so its face touches the line. Check adjacent sides for plumb with a level; then brace them.

New position marks post face.

Line moved half of width of post

Original position marks posthole center.

MARKING POSTS FOR CUTTING

Posts were left to run wild.

Measure up from ground to mark height; stretch the chalk line between these points.

Same height as first post

Stretch a level chalk line between each end post.

contoured fence, measure the same distance up the other end post and snap the chalk line between them. Make sure all posts are marked, and resnap the line if necessary.
■ Carry the marks around each post with a try square. If you're building a contoured fence, you will cut at an angle. Carry the marks across the downslope and upslope faces first, then connect these lines on the fourth side.
■ Cut each post to height with a handsaw or a reciprocating saw. You'll be on a ladder, so be careful and, above all, patient. if you use a circular saw, start with it and finish the cut with a handsaw. Sharp blades make the job faster and safer.

BASIC FENCE BUILDING

Most fences are made with 4×4 posts sunk into the ground, with two or three horizontal 2×4 rails that support vertical or horizontal boards or panels (often called the infill). Use materials that resist rotting: pressure-treated lumber or naturally resistant species such as redwood, cedar, or cypress. Even if painted, untreated pine and fir won't last.

LAYING OUT AND SETTING POSTS

Using the procedures discussed on pages 118 and 119, lay out the site. If your fence runs downhill, refer to the illustrations *(right)* and cut the posts for a stepped or a sloped fence.

Start by stretching a taut line from one end or corner post to the other. If the ground is fairly level, or if you want the fence to follow the slope, attach the line at both ends at the same height from the ground (you can use a water level to make sure the height is the same). Mark all the posts at the line and cut them with a circular saw.

If you want a fence that steps down *(above right)*, use the same method to establish heights, but install fence sections that are plumb, then cut the posts.

FRAMING THE INFILL

INSTALL RAILS: Cut 2×4 rails to span the outside faces of the posts or to fit snugly between them. For inside rails, hold the rail in place and mark it. Attach the rails with rail hangers, or predrill pilot holes for galvanized nails or screws.

CUT AND ATTACH INFILL: Cut all the infill at the same time, and make a spacing jig to speed installation. If the infill stock is wider than 2 inches, attach it with two nails or screws at each joint.

STEPPED FENCE

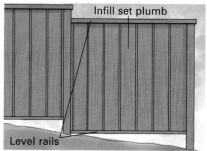

Install plumb posts on a sloped site as you would on a level site. For a stepped fence (above), attach level rails, then cut the posts. For a sloped fence (below), cut the posts and install the rails so they follow the slope of the ground. Install the infill plumb in both cases.

SLOPED FENCE

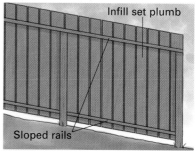

When the posts are set and cut, measure for inside rails. Use scrap wood to keep the bottom rail about 6 inches above the ground until you toenail it with 8d galvanized nails or use 2½-inch decking screws.

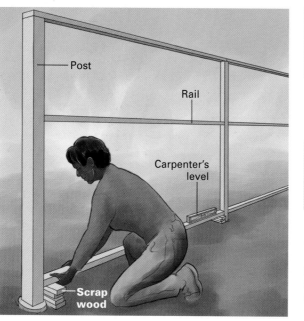

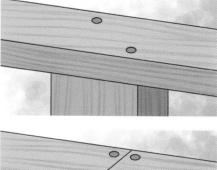

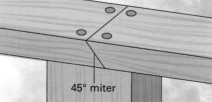

Fasten the top rail to the post in a diagonal pattern to avoid splitting the post. Miter adjoining pieces.

INFILL INSTALLATION TIPS

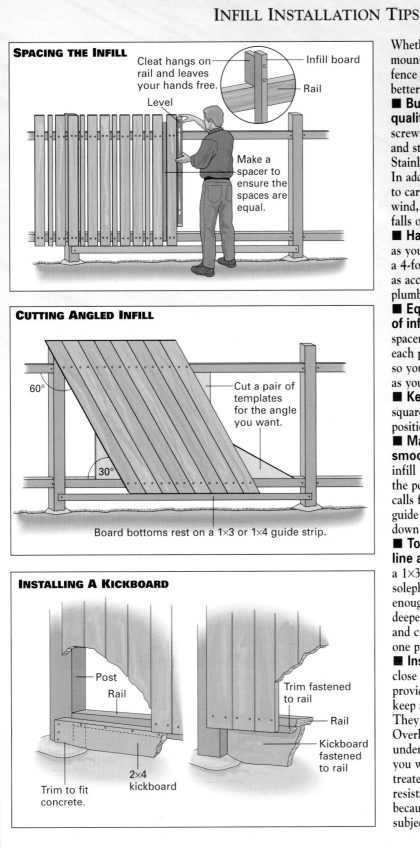

SPACING THE INFILL

Cleat hangs on rail and leaves your hands free.

Infill board

Rail

Level

Make a spacer to ensure the spaces are equal.

CUTTING ANGLED INFILL

60°

30°

Cut a pair of templates for the angle you want.

Board bottoms rest on a 1×3 or 1×4 guide strip.

INSTALLING A KICKBOARD

Post

Rail

2×4 kickboard

Trim to fit concrete.

Trim fastened to rail

Rail

Kickboard fastened to rail

Whether your fence incorporates surface-mounted or inset infill, these tips will make fence building easier and result in a sturdier, better-looking job.

■ **Buy enough fasteners, and of good quality:** Galvanized or treated nails or screws cost slightly more but will last longer and stain the fence less than plain steel. Stainless-steel fasteners are the best choice. In addition to their own weight, fences have to carry extra loads imposed by rain, snow, wind, and climbing kids. Much of this stress falls on the fasteners—use plenty of them.

■ **Hang boards plumb:** Check the infill as you go—every few feet at least—with a 4-foot level (smaller levels may not be as accurate). If the infill has gotten out of plumb, take your work apart and correct it.

■ **Equalize the spaces between pieces of infill:** Make them regular with a cleated spacer; it will save you from measuring for each piece. Hang the cleat on the top rail so you can free both hands to hold the infill as you fasten it.

■ **Keep angled infill even:** Use a bevel square, or make templates to properly position angled infill onto the frame.

■ **Make bottom edges flush and smooth:** Use guide boards to help place the infill (tack a 1×3 or 1×4 to the surface of the posts), unless your design intentionally calls for random lengths. Reposition the guide every few bays as you work your way down the line.

■ **To finish a wild-top edge, chalk a line at the cutting height.** Then tack a 1×3 or 1×4 guide so a circular saw's soleplate can ride on it. Set the blade deep enough to cut through the infill, but no deeper. Rest the saw on the cutting guide and cut the entire top of the fence in one pass.

■ **Install kickboards:** Kickboards will close the gap under the bottom rail, providing a more finished look, and will keep animals from crawling under the fence. They also keep flat rails from sagging. Overlay them on the posts or inset them under the bottom rail; trim with a 1×2 if you want. Make the kickboard of pressure-treated lumber, heartwood, or a decay-resistant species such as cedar or cypress, because the board touches the earth and is subject to rot.

BUILD A FRIENDLY FENCE

This lattice panel with a hanging basket enhances privacy and conceals unpleasant views but still admits sunlight and breezes. It lets you chat with the neighbors, yet keeps them at arm's length.

You can build this fence from scratch or work with an existing fence by replacing an existing section with lattice. Insert a new post if the existing section is 8 feet or longer.

BEFORE YOU BEGIN

■ Purchase prefabricated lattice panels to match or harmonize with the rest of your landscaping. Here, we show square lattice, but you can use diagonal lattice, which is more commonly available.

■ Inexpensive lattice panels may be only ½ inch thick. Consider building your own ¾-inch panel; it will be sturdier and last longer.

■ Use weather-resistant, pressure-treated wood or dark-colored heartwood of redwood or cedar to resist rot.

■ When buying the posts, factor in the depth of the postholes. If the holes will be 3 feet deep and the fence 6 feet high, for instance, you need 9-foot posts, so buy 10-footers.

■ Prime, stain, or apply water-repellent sealer to all pieces after cutting them. Give the fence a second coat after it's assembled.

For a friendly yet private screen, cut a window in a lattice panel to accommodate a hanging basket. Make just one panel for a small privacy screen. Or build an entire lattice fence, putting window panels near seating areas.

■ Use double-dipped decking screws or hot-dipped galvanized nails to avoid rust streaks.

BUILDING THE FENCE

LAY OUT THE SITE: Drive stakes at 4-foot intervals and stretch a line between them.
■ Dig postholes at least 30 inches deep or below your region's frost line.
■ Shovel a few inches of gravel into the bottom of each posthole, and insert the posts.
■ Use a post level to check for plumb, and temporarily brace the posts .

SET THE POSTS: Fill the holes with tamped earth or concrete.
Tamped earth-and-gravel setting.
■ Fill the hole about a quarter full, then tamp the soil with a 2×2 until it is firm. Add more soil and repeat until the hole is filled.
■ Mound the soil above grade and slope it so rainwater runs away from the post, then tamp the top firm with a 4×4.
Concrete setting.
■ Add concrete a little at a time and push a 2x2 up and down to consolidate it. Slope the top an inch above grade so rainwater runs off.
Both settings.
■ Using a combination square, mark the post height all the way around.
■ Cut posts with a reciprocating saw.

BUILD THE FRAME: Lay a 2×4 on top of the posts and attach it with two 3-inch decking screws.
■ Cut the 2×4 bottom rail to fit snugly between the posts. Drill angled pilot holes and attach the rail with 3-inch screws, 3 inches above grade.

INSTALL THE NAILERS: Measure the opening and cut the rear nailers.
■ Attach the nailers to the inside of the posts with 1⅝-inch decking screws driven every foot or so.

FIT THE PANEL: Measure the opening, mark the lattice panel, and cut with a circular saw.

MAKE THE CUTOUT: Using a framing square and a straight board, mark the cutout in the center of

the panel. Plan on a 20×30-inch cutout for a 12-inch basket. Cut the lattice with a circular saw.

■ Place the panel in the opening against the rear nailers.

■ Cut the front nailers and attach them as you did the rear nailers.

FRAME THE CUTOUT: Cut 1×2 front and rear frame pieces so they just cover the exposed ends of the lattice.

■ While a helper holds two framing pieces so they sandwich the lattice, drill pilot holes through the rear frame and lattice, and partway through the front framing wherever the frame and lattice cross.

■ Drive 2-inch screws through each pilot hole. (You may need shorter or longer screws, depending on the lattice thickness.)

APPLY THE FINISH: Paint, stain, or apply water repellent to the entire structure.

HANG THE BASKET: Drill a pilot hole in the rear of the top 2×4, centered above the opening; screw in a threaded eye hook and hang the basket from the hook.

MATERIALS

■ Lattice panel
■ Lumber: 4×4 posts, 1×2s for nailers and framing, 2×4s
■ Decking screws or galvanized nails
■ Concrete
■ Eye hook
■ Planter basket
■ Measuring tape
■ Posthole digger
■ Post level
■ Circular saw
■ Drill
■ Hammer
■ Framing square
■ Sawhorse

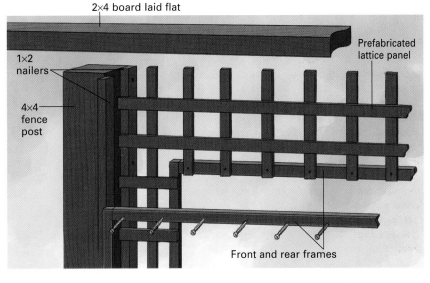

2×4 board laid flat

1×2 nailers

4×4 fence post

Prefabricated lattice panel

Front and rear frames

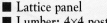

Hang the plant from the 2×4, not the lattice.

Lattice rests on the bottom ledger board.

After cutting the lattice, sandwich it between 1×2 nailers attached to the fence posts (above). Build two 1×2 frames for the front and rear of the opening, and screw them to the ends of the cut lattice. Top the structure with a 2×4 laid flat over the posts.

Support the lattice on 2×4s while cutting the opening.

OVERHEADS AND AMENITIES

Even the most stunning deck can feel incomplete without amenities—not only furnishings but overhead structures, which add both shade and a delightful architectural accent, and other elements that bring the comforts of home into natural surroundings.

Like all aspects of good design, these amenities should not look like "additions" to your landscape. They should appear as integral elements of the landscape theme, reflecting your sense of aesthetics and lifestyle.

Planning for amenities is not tricky, but it does require careful planning. Consider your lifestyle first—how you want to use your deck. Dining and food preparation areas are a must for frequent entertaining. Planters help separate one area of use from another. Outdoor lighting will extend the use of your space into the evening hours. An overhead structure or arbor will increase your enjoyment of the deck on sunny afternoons and also add a stunning design element to the entire space.

Inexpensive and practical, latticework provides shade and lets in gentle breezes. Here, it also tones down the massive character of this canopy. A canopy makes an ideal addition to a deck, providing privacy and partial shade.

This serene pool derives much of its appeal from the surrounding deck. Even poolside decks built with durable woods, such as the redwood used here, need special care and should be coated with a penetrating sealer.

Set just outside the kitchen door, this raised mini-platform deck provides an elevated view of the yard and adds an unusual architectural touch to the wider deck. The horseshoe-shaped railing helps set off the deck even more dramatically. A clear sealer preserves the natural wood tone of the deck and railing.

PRETTY ARBOR

Frame a private dining nook with an elegant arbor. The materials are inexpensive and its construction requires only basic do-it-yourself skills.

Build this neatly trimmed arbor on your deck and enhance its attractiveness by allowing vines to climb up and over it.

The lower rafters should span no more than 80 inches from beam to beam. For increased shade, top the arbor with lattice or 1×2s spaced 1½ inches apart. For less shade, space the rafters farther apart.

MATERIALS

- Wood: 6×6 posts, 2×10s, 2×2s
- Concrete mix
- Decking screws
- Measuring tape
- Posthole digger
- Carpenter's level
- Shovel
- Backsaw
- Miter saw
- Circular saw
- Clamps
- Drill
- Saber saw
- Chisel
- Hammer

GROUNDWORK

For a freestanding arbor, sink posts at least 3 feet into the ground. For example, an 8-foot-high arbor needs posts at least 11 feet long, so buy 12-footers. If possible, bolt some of the posts to existing deck posts or similar strong structural members.

Lay out the arbor location using the techniques shown on page 119 and square it with a 3-4-5 triangle.

POSTS: Using a clamshell digger or an auger, dig the postholes at least 30 inches deep, or to the depth required by local codes.

- Shovel several inches of gravel into each hole, and insert the posts. (You will cut them to height later.)

- Brace the posts temporarily so they are plumb (perfectly vertical). Use 3- to 4-foot 2×4s or 2×6s at the bottom, and 1×4 or 2×4 angle braces anchored to stakes (see illustration, *below opposite*). Getting the posts both plumb and placed the correct distance apart may require shifting, but if you are off an inch or so, it won't be readily visible.
- Combine water and bagged concrete mix and fill the postholes. Work the mix up and down with a stout stick to remove all air pockets. Overfill each hole so that rainwater will run away from the post.

FRAMING

The frame supporting the arbor roof consists of doubled 2×10 beams. Collar pieces add a decorative touch and help mark the position of the beams.

INSTALL THE COLLARS: Measure and mark the arbor height on one of the posts, then measure down 9½ inches.

- At this point, draw a line around the post using a small square.
- Miter the 2×2 collar pieces and attach them to the post, their top edges aligned with the lines you drew. Drill pilot holes and attach each collar piece with two 1⅝-inch decking screws.
- Working with a helper, place a level on top of a long, straight board (as long as the arbor), then place one end of the board on top of the 2×2 collar. Mark for the collar heights on the other posts. Install the other collars in the same way.

CUT THE POSTS: Set a short scrap of 2×10 on top of each collar piece; draw post cutoff lines. Cut the posts with a reciprocating saw.

INSTALL THE BEAMS: Measure the distances between the posts at the top, and miter-cut 2×10s for the outer beam pieces. (It's OK to bend the posts an inch or two if they are not equidistant.)

- Working with a helper, place each beam piece on top of the collar pieces at either end, and attach them by driving three 3-inch decking screws into each joint.
- Measure and cut the inside beam pieces, and laminate them to the outside beams using polyurethane glue and 1¼-inch decking screws driven every foot.

BUILDING THE ROOF

The arbor roof consists of notched 2×10 lower rafters set perpendicular to the upper rafters.

CUT THE RAFTERS: Cut all the 2×10 rafters to length. The lower rafters are 2 to 3 feet longer than the arbor's width, and the uppers are 2 to 3 feet longer than its length.

■ On a copier, enlarge the pattern illustration *below* until it measures 9½ inches tall. Use it as a pattern for the rafter ends. Cut one rafter end with a saber saw, and use it as a template to mark all the other rafter ends.

■ Also at this time, cut the decorative ends, which slip over the arbor frame.

NOTCH THE RAFTERS: Cut the notches as shown in the pattern below. For the lower rafters and decorative ends, notch the bottom of each end so they will fit over the beams. On top, cut a notch for the upper rafters to fit into. Cut notches on the bottom of the upper rafters for every lower rafter. Place rafter notches an equal distance apart.

To mark the notches, clamp the upper rafters and all the lower rafters together, and mark their top or bottom edges all at once.

■ Cut the notches first with a circular saw, then a saber saw. Clean out the corners with a handsaw and chisel. The notched rafters should fit tightly together.

SET THE RAFTERS: With a helper, set the lower rafters on top of the beams, spacing them evenly.

■ Slip the upper rafters onto the lowers, fitting the pieces together jigsawlike. This

requires jiggling and tapping with a hammer.

■ Once all the pieces are put together, drill angled pilot holes and drive 3-inch decking screws everywhere a rafter rests on a beam.

■ If the structure wobbles, stabilize it with angle braces as shown, *below left.*

APPLY THE FINISH: Apply two or more coats of stain, finish, or paint to the arbor.

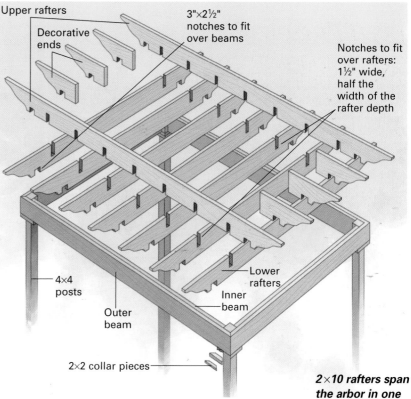

Upper rafters

Decorative ends

3"×2½" notches to fit over beams

Notches to fit over rafters: 1½" wide, half the width of the rafter depth

4×4 posts

Outer beam

2×2 collar pieces

Lower rafters

Inner beam

2×10 rafters span the arbor in one direction, tied together by two perpendicular rafters that slip into notches near the scalloped ends. Short, notched, decorative sections balance the design.

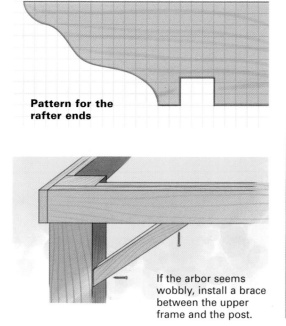

Pattern for the rafter ends

If the arbor seems wobbly, install a brace between the upper frame and the post.

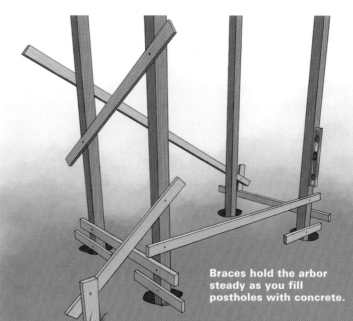

Braces hold the arbor steady as you fill postholes with concrete.

LOW-PROFILE ATTACHED OVERHEAD

You can build this overhead structure from the ground up or add it to an existing deck. If you're adding it to an existing structure, you'll have to provide the posts with adequate support, which may mean removing the decking and digging footings.

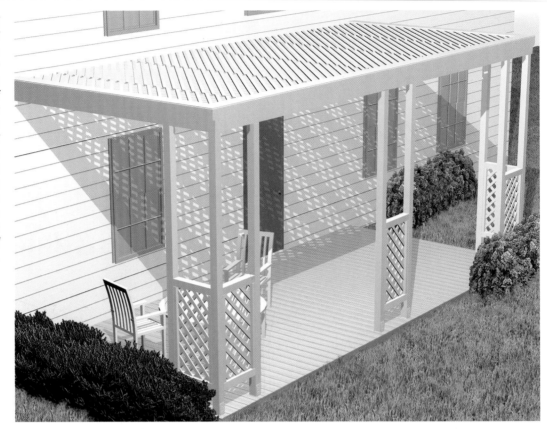

If a high overhead structure is impractical because it won't fit in the space between your first and second floors or below the roofline, this low-profile design may be ideal for your use.

MINIMUM MEASUREMENTS

To meet building code requirements in most municipalities, you will need at least a foot of unobstructed wall space above a door or window to attach the ledger board. Measure carefully before you set the final height of the supporting posts.

If you have a low roof overhang, you'll also need to make sure the joists will clear the bottom of the overhang. Mark the wall a couple of inches over a window or door (that's where the bottom edge of the ledger will go), then make another mark 7½ inches above the first to locate the top of the ledger. Run a level board out from the top mark past the edge of the overhang.

If your final level is below the overhang, you're ready to begin. If not, you may be able to trim the rafter tails or fascia without disturbing the sheathing or the roofing itself.

This design easily adapts to sites that have

different dimensions; but if you change the dimensions to fit your site, keep the overall size in increments of 2 feet.

LEDGER

Locate the ledger so that the bottom edge will be at least 2 inches above any doors or windows.

■ Measure and mark a point 3½ inches from each end of the ledger to leave space for the 4×8 beams.

■ Cut and bolt the ledger to the wall (see pages 116–117). Insert Z-flashing to keep moisture from collecting behind the ledger.

LAYOUT

Lay out the site with batter boards and mason's lines (see pages 118–119), and mark footing locations.

■ Set corner post faces so they're 2½ inches inside the mason's lines, the adjacent posts 24 inches on center; and the middle pair 19 inches on center.

■ Dig the footings, pour them, and install J bolts or piers. Let the concrete cure for three days to a week.

FRAMING PLAN

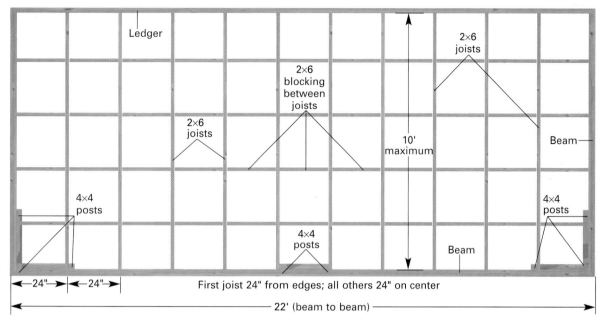

Ledger

2×6
joists

2×6
blocking
between
joists

2×6
joists

10'
maximum

Beam

4×4
posts

4×4
posts

4×4
posts

Beam

←24"→ ←24"→ First joist 24" from edges; all others 24" on center

22' (beam to beam)

If you're building on an existing slab that's at least 4 inches thick, local codes may allow you to install anchors directly on it. If you're building a new deck, use precast piers and fasten the deck beams to the posts.

POSTS AND BEAMS

Set the corner posts in post anchors and brace them plumb.

■ Mark the posts level with the top of the ledger, using a carpenter's level on a straight 2×4, or a water level.

■ Cut one corner post at the mark and notch it on two sides for the 4×8 beams.

■ Cut and notch the other corner post, brace both posts plumb, and attach them to the anchors.

■ Mark the heights of the remaining posts with a line from the corner posts, notch them, and install them with the notch facing out.

■ Measure the beams, allowing for mitered corners. Then cut and install the beams with coated or stainless lag screws or carriage bolts. Recess the holes for washers. Use angle brackets to attach the beams to the ledger.

WORKING ON TOP OF LATTICE

To work from above and not break through the lattice, use two 2-foot plywood squares. Kneel on one and place the other on the next square. Reposition the platforms as you move.

JOISTS AND BLOCKING

■ Mark the ledger and front beam at 24-inch intervals. Nail joist hangers at the marks.

■ Fit the joists and nail them to the hangers.

■ Snap chalk lines across the top of the joists on 24-inch centers. Cut blocking to length, and nail the top edges flush with the top of the beams.

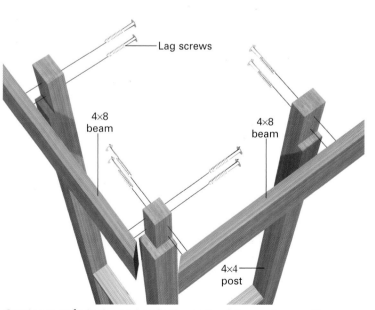

Lag screws

4×8
beam

4×8
beam

4×4
post

Cutting 1×7 ¼-inch notches in the ends of the posts provides a surface for the beams to rest on. Miter or butt-joint the beam ends at the corners. Fasten the beams to the posts with lag screws or carriage bolts.

LOW-PROFILE ATTACHED OVERHEAD
continued

LATTICE PANELS

Paint or stain the lattice panels, or buy them prepainted. Use full sheets wherever possible, making cuts so lattice ends are centered on a joist or block. If you need to cut a panel to fit, avoid running the saw over the staples holding the slats together. The saw will cut the staples, but the blade will wear out much sooner. Fasten the panels with 4d HDG nails.

Place 4×8-foot lattice panels on top of the joists and blocking. Center the panel edges on joists, blocking, and beams. Fasten the lattice with HDG 4d box nails. Nail 2×2-inch trim in 2-foot squares on top of the lattice.

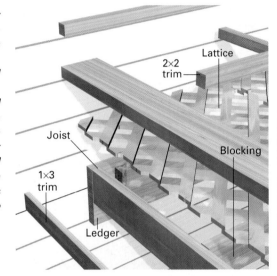

CANOPY AND TRIM

■ Set the inner edge of the 2×6 cap flush with the inside edge of each beam.
■ Install 2×2 trim over the joists and blocking to help secure the lattice panels.
■ Complete the canopy by nailing 1×3 trim under the overhanging cap. The trim hides the lattice edge and also serves as a molding.

RAILING PANELS

To make the decorative panels at the base of the posts, cut 2×4 rails (at any height that looks right to you) and toenail them to the posts. Make frames of 1×1 stops and install one of them on one side of the opening. Cut lattice and secure it with the second frame.

FREESTANDING ALTERNATIVE

If you don't have room to clear the roof and you can't trim it, you can build the overhead described here a few feet from the house. You will need to add rear posts and another beam to take the place of the ledger.

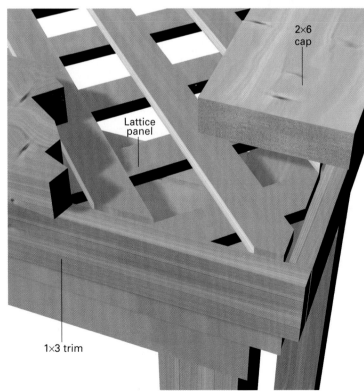

With the lattice panels in place, fasten pieces of 1×3 trim to the outside edges of the beams, flush with the top surface of the lattice. The trim will help support 2×6 caps laid flat on the beams.

To make lattice inserts, cut 2×4 rails to fit between the posts, and toenail them in place. Cut lattice panels and 1×1 frames to fit. Install one frame, insert a lattice panel, then install the other frame.

FINISHES AND MAINTENANCE

PAINTING: Choose a good-quality outdoor paint and apply an undercoat or primer. Always read and follow directions. Manufactured lattice often comes with an undercoat already applied. If you construct lattice yourself, paint the pieces before you assemble them, then touch up as needed after you install the lattice.

Paint beautifies and also keeps moisture from reaching and rotting the wood surface. Good paint may last 10 years. Check painted surfaces on an annual basis; when it's evident that the paint is no longer doing its job, avoid the urge to wait for one more year. It's easier and cheaper to repaint promptly than to replace rotted wood after it has been neglected.

STAINING: Stains penetrate wood instead of covering it. Semitransparent stains tint the surface and let the wood's natural grain show through; if you want to mask lower grades of lumber or want a covering with more pigment, choose a solid-color stain.

Rough or saw-textured lumber is a better candidate to stain than paint, but all stained lumber may need periodic restaining to counter the effects of weathering. The wood will last longer if you treat it with a clear water repellent after staining it. Follow the recommendations provided by the stain manufacturer.

WEATHERING: Woods with a natural resistance to decay—such as redwood, cedar, and cypress—weather beautifully and can be left in their natural state or treated only with a clear water repellent or other protective finish. These woods are more expensive than common structural woods, such as fir, pine, or larch. Remember that weathered wood may have more splinters than boards covered with paint or other types of finish. Finally, consider how the structure will look after the wood has aged. If it will seem out of place next to a neatly painted house, consider painting the wood instead.

MATERIALS FOR LOW-PROFILE, ATTACHED OVERHEAD

Description	Material/Size	Quantity
Ledger	2×8 lumber, 12'	2
Footings (if used)	Poured concrete, 4–5 cu. ft.*	3
Posts	4×4 lumber, 8' minimum	8
Perimeter beams	4×8 lumber, 12'	4
Joists	2×6 lumber, 10'	10
Blocking	2×6 lumber	88 lin. ft.
Lattice	4×8 sheets wood or vinyl lattice	8
Trim	2×6 lumber, 12'	4
	2×2 lumber	190 lin. ft.
	1×3 lumber, 12'	4
	2×4 lumber, 16'	1
	1×1 lumber	80–90 lin. ft.
Lag screws and washers	Coated or stainless, ½"×5"	32
Post anchors	To hold 4×4 posts	8
Bolts for post anchors	As required; usually 2 each	16
Beam brackets	To hold 4×8 beam	8
Bolts for beam brackets	As required, usually 2 each	16
Joist hangers	To hold 2×6 joists and blocking	108
Angle brackets	To attach end beams to ledger	6
Nails for joist hangers	1½" hanger nails	2 lbs.
Nails for 2×6 lumber	16d HDG	5 lbs.
Nails for light trim	8d HDG	1 lb.
Nails for lattice panels	4d HDG	2 lbs.

*Average amount; will vary by site

GEOMETRIC OVERHEAD

With squared ends and a strictly rectangular shape, this overhead is simple to build. Traditional homes look best with a pressure-treated wood structure that is painted. For contemporary homes, use unfinished or stained redwood or cedar.

The rectangular grid of this overhead structure will cast a louverlike, slatted pattern on the deck below. If you want nearly square shadows, space the 2×6 rafters and the 1×3 top pieces 12 inches on center. For less shade and a lower material cost, space them at 16 or 24 inches on center.

START WITH THE LEDGER

■ Cut a 2×8 ledger and a 2×2 nailer to length (as shown here, 10 feet long). The nailer helps support the 2×6 rafters so you don't have to use unattractive joist hangers.
■ Attach the nailer flush with the bottom edge of the ledger with glue and 6d galvanized box nails or 2-inch decking screws.
■ Cut the two 2×10 beams to the same length as the ledger.
■ On both the ledger and the top of one of the beams, draw layout lines for rafters at 12, 16, or 24 inches on center, depending on the amount of shade you want. Be sure the beam is crown side up.
■ Mark a level line on the house, at least 7 feet above the patio or deck (here, 8 feet).
■ With helpers and steady ladders, lift the ledger and attach it to the house. (See

instructions for installing the ledger to different surfaces on pages 116–117.) This ledger does not need to be as strong as a deck ledger, but you'll need at least two fasteners every 16 inches to keep it from warping.

CLAD AND INSTALL THE POSTS

The 4×4 posts get their decorative interest from simple 1×4 and 1×8 cladding attached to opposite faces.

At the rear of the deck, measure from the decking to the top of the 2×2 nailer and cut the 4×4 posts to that length.
■ Cut the 1×4 and 1×8 trim to the same length, and nail them to the posts with 6d galvanized casing nails, overlapping the 1×8s.
■ On the front of the deck, mark the post locations. (Use the methods described on pages 118–122 for squaring the post sites.)
■ With a helper, raise each post, plumb it on two adjacent sides, and brace it temporarily with staked 1×4s.
■ Anchor the posts to the decking with pre-drilled 3-inch decking screws.
■ Dig holes and shovel in 4 inches of gravel.
■ Set the posts straight in the holes, leaving them uncut. You'll cut them to height later.

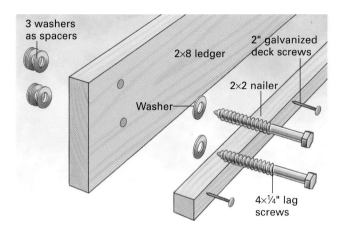

3 washers as spacers

Washer

2×8 ledger

2" galvanized deck screws

2×2 nailer

4×¼" lag screws

Attach a 2×2 to the bottom edge of the ledger, then attach the ledger using this or any of the other methods shown on pages 116–117.

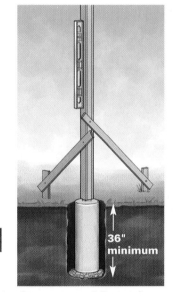

1×8 4×4 1×4

3" galvanized decking screws

6d galvanized casing nail

Adding 1× to a post bulks it up and covers knots and cracks. This treatment adds a crisp, professional-looking touch to the project.

■ Mark the posts about an inch above grade for positioning the bottom edge of the cladding.

■ Remove each post, install the cladding, and reposition the posts, then brace them securely and plumb on adjacent sides.

■ Fill each hole with concrete, sloping the surface so water drains from it. Let the concrete cure for three days to a week.

■ With a helper, use a water level to mark the posts at the same height as the top of the 2×2 nailer. Transfer the cut line to all four faces of the post, and cut the cladding and post with a circular saw and a handsaw.

INSTALL THE "CEILING"

Three components—a double beam, rafters, and top pieces—complete the project and provide its distinctive character.

BEAMS: Determine how far you want the beams to extend beyond the posts, and mark and cut them to that size.

■ With a helper on a ladder at one post and you at the other, set the first beam flush with the top of the post, centered on the structure.

■ Tack the beam in place with duplex nails then raise the second beam and tack it also.

■ Drill two holes centered on the posts and evenly spaced on the beams, then fasten the beams with ⁵⁄₁₆×8-inch carriage bolts. Remove the duplex nails.

RAFTERS: Cut the rafters so they will overhang the front beam by 2 to 3 inches.

■ Set the rafters on the 2×2 nailer and attach them to the ledger and beams at the marks you made earlier.

36" minimum

Set posts equidistant from the house (see page 119 for squaring corners). Then brace and plumb them.

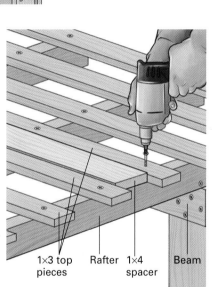

1×3 top pieces Rafter 1×4 spacer Beam

Decking screws provide enough holding power to attach beams to posts. Drive angled screws to hold rafters; one screw is enough for the top pieces.

■ Use 2-inch decking screws driven at an angle into predrilled pilot holes. Then snap a chalk line at evenly spaced intervals across the tops of the rafters.

TOP PIECES: Cut the 1×3 top pieces to the same length as the beams.

■ Using the chalk lines on the top of the rafters, position the top slats and attach them with a single 2½-inch galvanized or coated decking screw at each point the pieces intersect a rafter. Predrill the holes to avoid splitting the wood, especially at the ends.

DECK-SIDE ARBOR

This narrow overhead—with its cantilevered, slatted roof—may provide just the shade you need in a particular spot. Encourage vines to climb up and over the arbor to increase the shade and add to its charm.

With its long, narrow profile, this overhead offers a number of practical and aesthetic solutions to difficult outdoor design problems. For example, use it to provide partial shade on a section of a deck or to shelter a lounging area from the afternoon sun. Or use it to make shade with a slim profile for an above-the-deck planter, keeping the plants cool and the soil from drying out.

Enlist a helper or two to build it. Eight-foot ladders make the job easier and safer.

The 2×6 beams should span no more than 8 feet between posts. Make the 4×4 rafters 4 feet long. Pairs of rafters spaced 6 inches apart should be placed 30 to 36 inches between each pair.

INSTALLING THE POSTS

These posts are attached to a deck railing and are supported by below-deck posts set in the ground. Dig holes at least 10 inches in diameter and at least 42 inches deep. Then set the support posts in concrete or tamped earth and gravel. Cut the posts to the proper height after you've set them.

Attach the posts to railing posts if possible, with one set in the ground at an outside corner and one fastened to the house. How you attach each post will depend on how your railing is put together. You will need a flush nailing surface for the support post. Fastening a vertical 1×6 or 2×6 to the rail post will usually fill the space. Cut this spacer to fit between the top and bottom rail.

When the 1×6s or 2×6s are attached to the post, measure and cut 6×6 posts to the proper height.

■ While a helper holds the post and plumbs it in both directions, drill pilot holes and drive 4×¼-inch lag screws through the top and bottom rail and into the post.

■ Drive two or three screws through each rail, offsetting them to reduce the risk of cracking a rail.

■ Attach the bottom of each post to the deck with at least two 4-inch angle brackets and screws.

FASTENING THE TOP FRAME

Use screws instead of nails to attach the upper frame so you won't shake the posts while you work. Once in place, the upper frame will strengthen the overall structure. Make sure the concrete has cured for three to seven days before attaching the upper frame of an overhead at the edge of a patio.

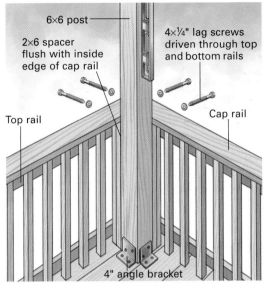

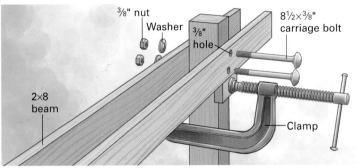

Clamped scraps of wood allow you to rest the beams while you work. Make a firm "sandwich" of post and beams with carriage bolts, nuts, and washers.

Choose a solid rail post—preferably one at a corner—and attach the new post to the railing top and bottom rails or directly to the railing post. You will probably need to add vertical 1×6s or 2×6s to fill the space between the rails and the new post to make the connection firm.

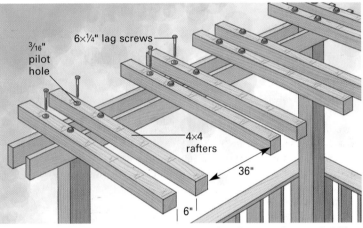

Before installing the rafters, mark them for the top slats and drill plumb pilot holes. When planning slat spacing, remember that you can't attach them over rafter screws.

CUT AND ATTACH THE BEAMS: Cut two 2×8 beams to the length of the overhead, plus a foot or two of overhang on each end. Set them next to each other—crown edge up—and mark the positions for the 4×4 rafters.

■ Measure 9 inches from the top of each post and clamp a piece of scrap on both sides.

■ With a helper on a ladder at one post and you at the other, raise one beam and rest it on the scrap ledges.

■ Center the beam between the posts and angle-drive a 2-inch decking screw at the top edge of the beam to hold it on the posts. Do the same with the other beam.

■ Drill holes—centered and evenly spaced, and countersunk for washers and nuts—and fasten the beams to the posts with two 8½×⅜-inch carriage bolts, washers, and nuts. If you use longer bolts, cut the ends off after tightening the nuts.

THE RAFTERS: Cut all the 4×4 rafters to the same length—about 4 feet. Set them next to one another on a flat surface—crown side down—and mark the top edges where the 2×2 slats will be attached.

■ Using a framing square, mark where screws will attach the rafters to the beams.

■ Drill pilot holes carefully; if necessary, use a drill jig to ensure well-plumbed holes. Use a drill bit that is at least 6 inches long.

■ With a helper on a ladder, raise the rafters and lay them on the beams at the layout lines. Drill ³⁄₁₆-inch pilot holes through the

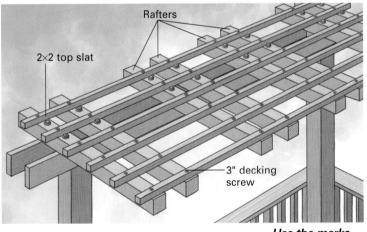

rafters and into the beams. Drive a 6×¼-inch lag screw (with a washer) into each joint.

TOP SLATS: Cut all the 2×2 slats to the proper length. In this installation, we have spaced them 8 inches on center. Space them closer together if you want more shade. Set the 2×2s on the layout lines, drill pilot holes, and drive a 3-inch decking screw into each hole.

Use the marks on the rafters to fasten the slats evenly. Predrill the stock and attach the slats with screws.

ATTACHED BENCHES

Versatility is the key to these bench designs—even though they're permanent. You can adapt the backless bench, *below*, to a patio by anchoring it to 4×4 posts sunk in the ground. The backed-bench design, *opposite*, uses existing deck posts for support and provides a useful substitute for a railing section.

Here are some general rules for benches:
■ The seat height should be comfortable—15 to 18 inches from the surface.
■ The view from the bench should be pleasant.
■ Its location should encourage conversation.

Because its supports are partly hidden by the overhanging slats, this backless bench appears to float above the deck.

■ Make the benches safe. The back of an attached bench—used instead of a railing—usually needs to be at least 42 inches high and cannot have open spaces wider than 4 inches (check with your local building department for bench-design requirements).

A BACKLESS BENCH

Use a backless bench on a low-lying platform deck or as a transition on a multilevel deck. The bench, *left*, with its support partially hidden, appears to float above the surface.

We've mounted it to the edge of a deck. You can bolt the posts to interior joists after removing the decking, notching it, and replacing it. This design uses decking screws as fasteners; carriage bolts and lag screws will provide stronger joints. They require additional drilling, however, and may not work if your deck construction won't allow you to get a wrench on them.

CUT POSTS AND FRAMING PIECES: Construct enough supports to install one every 4 to 5 feet.
■ For each bench, cut a 4×6 post, 2×6 front support, and seat cleats. Make sure the front support is long enough to reach from the bottom of the deck joist to a height of 15 to 18 inches.
■ Miter the ends of the seat cleats at 22½ degrees. (For a freestanding modification, cut the posts at 15 to 18 inches and bolt 2×6 feet to both sides.)

ASSEMBLE THE SUPPORTS: Fasten the two post sections—flush at the tops—with six or seven 3-inch decking screws driven into predrilled pilot holes.

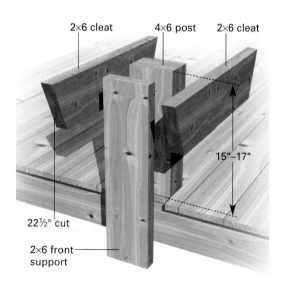

2×6 cleat   4×6 post   2×6 cleat

15"–17"

22½° cut

2×6 front support

Assemble each support from a 4×6 post and three 2×6s. Notch the decking so the front support can be attached to the deck joist or fascia.

Clamp 2×2s as an overhang guide; use ½-inch plywood for spacers. Adjust the spacing before attaching the last slats.

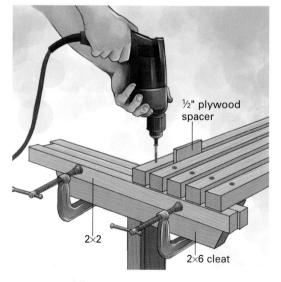

½" plywood spacer

2×2

2×6 cleat

■ Center one cleat on the laminated post, flush at the top, and fasten it with four 3-inch decking screws through predrilled pilot holes. Attach the other 2×6 cleat in the same way.

FASTEN THE SUPPORTS: The front support needs to be snug against the deck joist, so notch the decking if necessary.
■ Use a post level to plumb the post in both directions (see page 122).
■ Predrill pilot holes at an angle through the 4×6 and through the face of the 2×6 beam, then drive 3-inch decking screws through the post and front support.

INSTALL THE SEAT SLATS: Cut twelve 2×2s to a length that will overhang each cleat by 3 inches. To keep the overhang consistent, clamp two 2×2s to the side of the cleat.
■ Lay the slats on a flat surface and mark pilot holes so the slats will be centered on the cleats.
■ Start the first slat with a ¼-inch overhang on the front of the cleats and fasten it with 3-inch decking screws at each support.
■ Fasten the remaining seat slats, using scraps of ½-inch plywood as spacers.

Anchor this seat to the rail posts for support. Use 2×4s for the back and 2×6s for seat slats. Place the bench where it can be part of a conversation area or where it faces a pleasant view.

SEAT WITH BACK

This design uses existing rail posts for part of the framing. You can attach the bench without altering balusters or rails with most rail designs. However, the seat may look better if you remove all the balusters (building codes permitting, of course). If the rail posts are spaced more than 6 feet apart, install intervening posts (see pages 137–141).

INSTALL THE SEAT SUPPORTS:
Each support requires two 25-inch 2×4 cleats—mitered on one end at 22½ degrees—and one 15-inch 4×4 seat post.
■ Cut the pieces and mark both sides of the rail post 15 inches above the decking.
■ Have a helper hold a 2×4 level at the mark while you drill pilot holes and drive three 3-inch deck screws.
■ Attach the other 2×4 to the other side of the post. Fasten the 4×4 post with two screws on each side plus angled screws to the deck.

CUT AND INSTALL THE BACK BRACE:
Use a circular saw to cut a 4×4 to the dimensions shown. Attach the back support to the rail post with several screws.

INSTALL THE SEAT AND BACK SLATS:
Cut three 2×4s for the back and three 2×6s for the seat to the length of the bench (overhanging them 3 inches, if possible). Space them evenly and attach them to the 2×4s with two 3-inch screws driven into each joint.

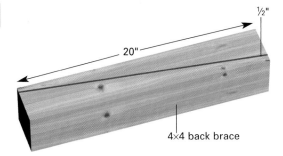

½"
20"
4×4 back brace

Use a chalk line or straightedge to mark the angled rip cut for the back brace. Mark both sides and make the cut with a circular saw. This cut is difficult; practice on a scrap first.

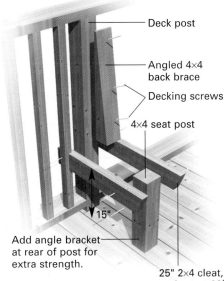

Deck post
Angled 4×4 back brace
Decking screws
4×4 seat post
15"
Add angle bracket at rear of post for extra strength.
25" 2×4 cleat, end cut at 22½°

Mark the deck post 15 inches from the decking, and attach the cleats at the mark. Level and attach the seat post between the 2×4s and to the decking. Install the back brace with its bottom edge flush with the top of the cleats. Then fasten the back and seat slats.

FREESTANDING BENCHES

This bench, with its wide slats, provides plenty of sturdy comfort and can easily be moved around the deck.

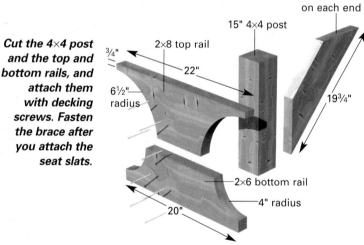

Cut the 4×4 post and the top and bottom rails, and attach them with decking screws. Fasten the brace after you attach the seat slats.

2×6 brace, cut at 45° on each end

15" 4×4 post

2×8 top rail

3/4"

22"

6½" radius

19¾"

2×6 bottom rail

4" radius

20"

B enches made of dimensional lumber will not be lightweight, but they will be stable. And you'll be surprised how easily you can move them about your deck or patio to respond to changing shade patterns or entertainment needs.

"PICNIC-STYLE" BENCH

With its wide slats and cross-braced legs, this bench is reminiscent of a picnic table, and its design allows versatility, too. Make the bench permanent by attaching it to joists below the decking, or by setting posts in footings next to a platform deck or patio.

In a permanent installation, you can dispense with the bottom rails and braces. Choose any length, and install a support every 4 feet.

CUT THE SCALLOPED RAILS: Each support requires a 22-inch 2×8 top rail and a 20-inch 2×6 bottom rail. (For more strength, install two rails on each side of the posts.)
■ Cut the pieces to the proper length.
■ Mark and cut each end of one top and one bottom rail. For the top rail, set a compass at 6½ inches and—with the compass point just at the corner of the board—mark the scallop outline on both ends as shown below.
■ Use the same technique to mark the bottom rail, setting the compass at 4 inches.
■ Make all the cuts with a saber saw, then sand the curved cuts smooth.
■ Use the first pieces as templates for marking the others.

CUT THE POSTS AND BRACES: For each support, cut a 15-inch 4×4 post and a

BUYING FACTORY-MADE WOODEN OUTDOOR FURNITURE

You may find wooden benches and picnic tables at a local deck yard priced only slightly higher than the cost of materials to build your own. Carefully check out the quality of the lumber and the fasteners; they may be wanting. You may be able to make a flimsy piece solid by strategically drilling pilot holes and driving a few screws. Avoid pieces that have warped or cracked wood. You may be able to beautify and make untreated lumber rot-resistant by applying a stain or sealer.

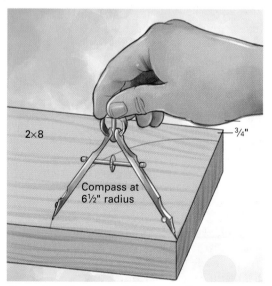

2×8

3/4"

Compass at 6½" radius

To scallop the top and bottom rails, set a compass just at the corner of the board and draw the arc.

19¾-inch 2×6 brace. Miter each end of the brace at 45 degrees.

ASSEMBLE THE SUPPORTS: Assemble the 2×8 top rails so they form a **T** flush with the top of the post and overhang by 9¼ inches on each side.
■ Drill pilot holes and drive four 3-inch decking screws.
■ Attach the bottom rail in the same fashion, flush with the bottom edge of the post and overhanging it by 8¼ inches.

CUT AND ATTACH THE SEAT SLATS: Cut the three 2×8 slats to length. Then set your compass at 7¼ inches.
■ Center the point of the compass on the width of one slat with the pencil just touching the end of the slat.
■ Mark the curve on the corners, and cut the curves with a saber saw.
■ Lay the seat slats on the support assemblies. (Have a helper keep things from toppling over.)
■ Attach them at ¼-inch intervals with three 3-inch decking screws.

ATTACH THE BRACES: Turn the bench upside down and have a helper check each support for square as you position the angle-cut braces.
■ Drill pilot holes and drive decking screws through the braces into the posts.
■ Make sure each brace is centered on the middle seat slat, then fasten the braces with screws driven through the slat.

BUTCHER-BLOCK BENCH

This design adapts butcher-block-table construction to create a multipurpose addition to your deck or patio. Increase the impact by building a companion coffee table using the same design and shortening the legs.

CHOOSE A LAMINATING METHOD: The seat slats and the legs are made by laminating 2×4s side by side with glue and predrilled 2¾-inch screws. Before you start, stack the slats in position and mark the sides of each pair for the screws. Stagger the marks so you won't drive screws on top of each other.
■ Cut the legs (one 15-inch and one 11½-inch 2×4 for each leg) and predrill them every 6 inches in a

zigzag pattern so the screws won't split the wood along a grain line.
■ Spread a thin layer of glue and drive the screws.
■ Then laminate two legs, notch side down, to a 48-inch slat, with a 41-inch slat between the legs.
■ Laminate the rest of the 48-inch slats until you have only one left.
■ Then fasten the remaining pair of legs, notch up, with a 41-inch slat between them.
■ Finish the bench with the final 48-inch slat. When the glue has dried completely, sand the surfaces smooth.
■ Use a belt sander to get the surface smooth and level. (Be careful—a belt sander can remove a lot of wood quickly.)

Take the time to sand the top of the bench smooth. Apply several coats of sealer, with no spaces between the slats; water may puddle.

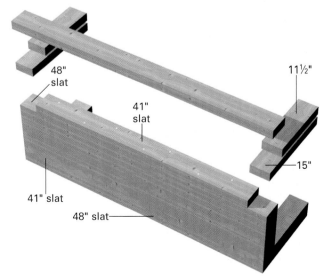

Start with a 48-inch slat, leg pieces, and a 41-inch slat. Align each slat carefully— flush at the top—and mark the positions; then laminate them with glue and screws. Stagger the screws to avoid splitting the wood.

GARDEN BENCH

This sturdy bench can be easily moved for the best possible view. Five-quarter lumber would reduce the weight and lighten its appearance.

This bench has the look of crafted furniture, but, in fact, its construction does not require fancy joinery. It does, however, require precise cuts. Rent or buy a power miter box (also called a chop saw), which makes perfectly square cuts with ease.

Use top-grade wood that won't warp, shrink, or splinter. Kiln-dried clear or B-grade redwood is an excellent choice; cedar heartwood is another. Choose boards with close, straight grain.

The design calls for ⁵⁄₄ (five-quarter) lumber, which is actually 1 inch thick. Standard 1× stock would be too thin; you can use 2× lumber, but the bench will be heavy and less graceful. You may be able to find ⁵⁄₄×6 decking; you'll probably need to have the ⁵⁄₄×8 stock for the backrest specially milled. If milling costs are a problem, make the backrest from a 2×8.

CUT THE BACK- AND ARMRESTS

Use a circular saw or table saw to cut the three pieces to the dimensions shown at left, tapering the outer edge of the armrest from 5½ inches to 2¾ inches.
■ Cut the 2-inch rounded notch at the top of the seat back with a saber saw.
■ Use a sanding block to round all slightly so they won't be sharp.

If you use different designs for the armrest and backrest, make them complementary. For example, if you round the front corners of the armrests, also round the end corners of the backrest.

Make an angled rip cut along the outside edge of the armrest. Clamp the boards securely before making long cuts such as these; practice on scrap pieces if you're not sure you can cut straight lines.

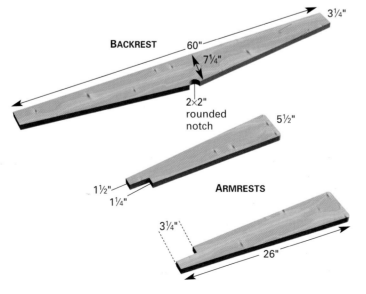

BACKREST 60" 3¼"

7¼"

2×2" rounded notch

1½"
1¼"

5½"

ARMRESTS

3¼"

26"

BUILD THE FRAME

Use ⁵⁄₄ lumber for the horizontal framing members and 2×4s for the posts.

■ Cut the rear posts to 32 inches and the front posts to 23 inches.

■ Cut notches ³⁄₈ inch deep and 1 inch high in the two rear posts for the notched end of the armrests. The armrests need to fit snugly, so make precise cuts.

■ With a helper, assemble the frame on a flat surface. Check each joint for square before drilling pilot holes and driving 2½-inch decking screws.

■ First attach the side rails to the posts with the edges flush at front and rear; then attach the front and back rails. Notice that the top back rail is cut shorter than the front rail and is fastened inside the rear posts.

■ Finally, measure the distance between the front and rear rails and cut and install the center block between the rails.

ADD THE SEAT SLATS, ARMRESTS, AND BACKREST

Cut the seat slats so they overhang the frame by an inch on both sides. Notch both ends of the front slat so it fits around the front posts. Lay the slats on the frame evenly spaced, and attach them by drilling pilot holes and driving 2½-inch decking screws.

■ Have a helper hold the backrest so it overhangs the posts by the same amount on each side. Make sure the bottom is level.

■ Drill pilot holes and drive two 2½-inch decking screws through the backrest into the posts.

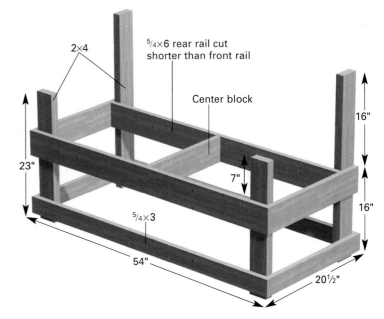

Before you attach the armrest, fit each one into the grooves in the rear post—positioned exactly as they will be when fastened.

■ Drill two pilot holes in the front of the armrest into the posts and one pilot hole in the thin side of the rear notch, *below.*

■ To attach each armrest, spread polyurethane glue into the grooves in the rear posts and on the top of the front posts.

■ Slip the notched end of the armrest into the groove.

■ Drive 2½-inch decking screws through the pilot holes.

■ Sand all sharp edges to prevent splintering.

■ Apply a stain and sealer, or two or three coats of exterior enamel paint.

This design calls for ⁵⁄₄ (five-quarter) lumber for horizontal framing members. If you use 2×6s and 2×3s instead, increase the length of the fasteners.

Position the seat slats so they overhang 1 inch on each side and in front, and so the gaps between them are equal. Before attaching the backrest, make sure it is centered and that the bottom edge is level.

Attach the armrests with polyurethane glue and carefully placed screws. The notches must be cut precisely to support the armrests.

PLANTERS

This bench and planter combination is large enough to hold small trees as well as flowers. The gaps between the bench slats permit water to run through, reducing the possibility of rot.

Planters put gardening within easy reach and help separate one part of your deck from another. Make them small enough so you can easily reach all of the soil and high enough so you don't strain your back.

These planters are designed to hold soil, but you can use them for flowerpots as well. Put your showiest flowers in prominent places and arrange potted foliage around them. Size the planters so your pots can fit snugly inside.

You can build several planters in a day with a circular saw, drill, and basic carpentry skills.

PLANTER-BENCH

A combination planter and bench lets you tend your plants while comfortably seated or is simply a pleasant spot to enjoy the foliage.

If you want a longer unit, build three or more boxes of the same size, and position them either in a row or form a right-angle corner. Install seat slats between them.

START THE BOXES: For each box, cut nineteen 2×4s to the same length; 24 inches is recommended. Working on a flat surface, make square frames with lapped ends, *opposite*. Fasten the lapped ends with two 3-inch decking screws at each joint.

Next make a bottom with 1×4s. Cut the pieces to fit, and fasten them to one of the 2×4 frames, with ⅛-inch gaps for drainage.

Stack two courses of 2×4 frames on the one to which the bottom is attached, and fasten a 16-inch length of 2×2 to all the frame corners by driving 2½-inch screws into predrilled holes. Build the other box(es) to the third course using the same techniques.

BUILD THE BENCH: This design requires spacers to separate the bench slats. Cut eighteen ¼- to ½-inch by 3½-inch-square spacers from exterior plywood. Then cut seven 2×4 bench slats to the length you want the bench. Set the first slat on the third course of each box, and attach it to the 2×2 corner brace. Fasten the remaining slats to each other by driving 3-inch screws through the spacers inserted between the slats.

FINISH THE PLANTERS: When the bench is completed, cut 2×4 fillers to fit between the last bench slat and the box corner. Screw them to the corner brace and to the bench slat. Then complete each box by attaching the last 2×4 frames to the corner braces.

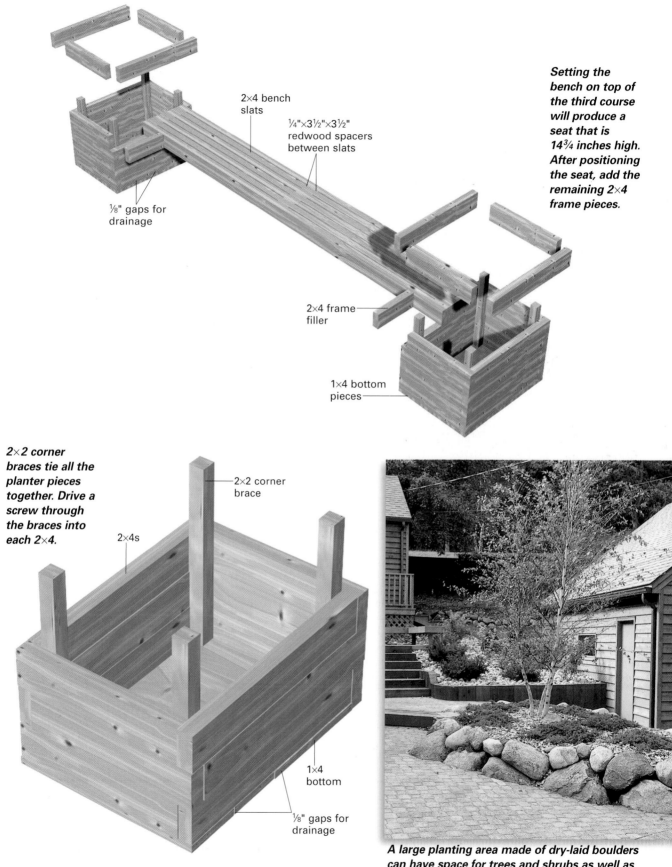

2×4 bench slats

¼"×3½"×3½" redwood spacers between slats

⅛" gaps for drainage

Setting the bench on top of the third course will produce a seat that is 14¾ inches high. After positioning the seat, add the remaining 2×4 frame pieces.

2×4 frame filler

1×4 bottom pieces

2×2 corner braces tie all the planter pieces together. Drive a screw through the braces into each 2×4.

2×2 corner brace

2×4s

1×4 bottom

⅛" gaps for drainage

A large planting area made of dry-laid boulders can have space for trees and shrubs as well as smaller plants. Gravel surrounding the plants harmonizes with the boulders and cuts down on the need to weed. Boulders this large must be installed with earth-moving machinery.

PLANTERS
continued

Fill this planter with soil or place potted plants in it. The legs allow air to circulate under the planter so there is less chance of damage to the deck or patio surface.

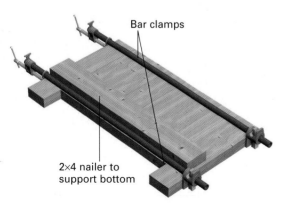

Practice clamping and gluing so that you know just how much glue to apply. There should be a small amount of squeezed-out glue; allow it to partially dry, then scrape it away. You can add 2×4 nailers (before the glue sets) on the interior for increased strength.

PLANTER WITH LEGS

This planter partially relies on glue to hold the pieces together. Use polyurethane glue; it keeps boards fused together even in climates with severe winters.

These dimensions produce a planter that will stand 3 inches off the deck or patio surface. Change the length of the corner pieces if you want shorter or longer legs.

MAKE THE SIDES: Cut five 14-inch 2×4s for each side and two 17-inch 2×4s for each leg. Working on a flat surface covered with a drop cloth, spread glue along the edges of the boards. Clamp the sides with two pipe clamps or bar clamps. Make sure the tops and bottoms are flush, and allow them to dry. Scrape away squeezed-out glue when it is partially dry. Do the same for the other sides.

ASSEMBLE THE PIECES: Stand the sides up and nail or screw them together at the corners. At the bottom inside edge of each side, attach 2×4 nailers by drilling pilot holes and driving two 2½-inch decking screws into each joint. Cut a piece of ¾-inch pressure-treated plywood to fit in the bottom. Drill a grid of ⅜-inch holes for drainage, and set it in the bottom. Attach the bottom with screws driven from the outside of the box.

Show off your attractive clay pots and move your foliage at will. Wall-hung containers embellish an otherwise plain surface with splashes of color.

PLANTER WITH GROOVE DESIGN

A simple geometric design takes less than an hour to build and adds style to a plain planter. It's made by cutting grooves in the finished surface, or you can attach molding or 1×2s symmetrically to the outside of the planter.

MAKE THE PLANTER: Miter-cut four pieces of 2×12 to the same length; 18 inches is recommended. Attach the corners by drilling pilot holes and driving 12d casing nails. Cut 1×4s for the bottom—½ inch shorter than the width of the box—and attach them with nails or screws so they are recessed ¼ inch all around. (Lay out the 1×4s on the box before you attach them; you may have to rip the end pieces for the recess.)

CUT THE GROOVES: Use a framing square to draw cut lines for parallel and perpendicular grooves. In our example, the grooves are ⅜ inch wide and are spaced 3 inches from the edges of the planter in both directions.

Set a circular saw to the desired depth (in this case, ⅜ inch), and use a speed square as a guide to make straight cuts along the lines. It will take three or more passes with the saw blade to produce a groove that is ⅜ inch wide.

Although it may appear complicated, this planter can be quickly built with common carpentry tools. If you are unsure of your ability to make precise 45-degree corner miters, practice on scrap.

Placed in front of ground-level windows filled with glass block, this mortared tile planter enlivens a drab spot with a splash of color. The tiles cover a cement-block wall. Flowers planted in the block recesses add pleasant contrasts.

Draw lines to mark the sides of each groove. Carefully set the blade of a circular saw to the correct depth. Cut the grooves. Each groove requires several passes.

OUTDOOR TABLES

This outdoor table design can be adjusted for multiple duties. Lengthen the legs and build it as a food preparation counter. Shorten the legs to construct a coffee table.

When the temperature is right and the sky is clear, eating outdoors is a rustic joy—all the more so if your outdoor dining area is as convenient as the one you use indoors.

Here's a table that fits the bill—large enough for small groups and sturdy enough to stand up to the rough treatment of the elements and outdoor use.

Construct the tabletop with lumber that is smooth and nearly free of knots; choose boards with a close grain so that the top will be easy to wipe and won't splinter. Use a naturally rot-resistant species of wood, or stain pressure-treated lumber to improve its looks.

DINING TABLE

If the benches or chairs you'll use have seats 16 to 17 inches high, make your table 29 to 30 inches high—the standard for indoor dining. If your benches are lower, adjust the table height accordingly. (If in doubt, make it higher; you can always trim the legs later.) Four to six diners can use a table that is 44 inches wide and 62 inches long.

Make each support from 4×4s and 2×4s fastened with lag screws and washers. The more precisely you cut the framing pieces, the tighter and stronger the joints will be.

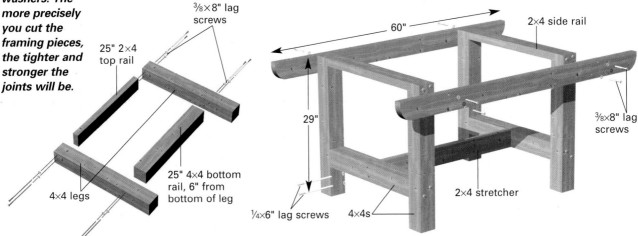

⅜×8" lag screws

25" 2×4 top rail

4×4 legs

25" 4×4 bottom rail, 6" from bottom of leg

60"

2×4 side rail

⅜×8" lag screws

29"

¼×6" lag screws

4×4s

2×4 stretcher

CUT THE LEG ASSEMBLIES: All the framing pieces must butt together tightly to make strong joints, so cut them precisely. If you will be cutting with a circular saw, practice cutting scrap 4×4s until you can produce cuts that are square all around.

For each of the two leg assemblies, cut a 2×4 top rail and a 4×4 bottom rail, each to 25 inches. Cut two 4×4 legs to the height of the table less 1½ inches.

ASSEMBLE THE LEGS: Lay the pieces on a flat surface and clamp the four assemblies together with a long bar clamp or pipe clamp. Check for square before you start drilling.

Position the top rail flush with the tops of the legs, and the bottom rail 6 inches from the bottom of the legs. Drill pilot holes and attach the legs to the rails with ⅜×8-inch lag screws and washers.

BUILD THE TABLE FRAME: Cut a 2×4 stretcher 27 inches shorter than the overall length of the table—35 inches for a table that will be 62 inches long. Stand the two leg assemblies up, and attach the stretcher between them with two ¼×6-inch lag screws at each end.

Next miter at 45 degrees two 2×4 side rails 2 inches shorter than the length of the table, and attach them to the posts with two lag screws at each joint. The side rails should run past the legs by 10 inches on each side. Now you're ready for the tabletop.

ATTACH THE TOP: Cut all the 2×6 top pieces to length (44 inches in this design), and attach them centered on the side rails with 3-inch decking screws or 16d galvanized nails. Sand the edges smooth.

OUTDOOR WORKTABLE

An outdoor worktable such as the one shown on this page can be a great timesaver for potting and other gardening chores—even for preparing outdoor meals. The shelf below is large enough for buckets or bags. Rounded corners on the front of the backsplash add a small, effective decorative detail.

A worktable countertop should be 35 to 37 inches high. Even if you will be using it for rough gardening work, use wood that is smooth and free of large knots so you can wipe it easily.

CONSTRUCT THE FRAME: Cut 2×4 legs to the height of the table minus ¾ inch, and cut

2×4 crossbraces for the top and bottom. Assemble the frame on a flat surface with two 3-inch decking screws into each joint.

ADD THE TOP, SHELF, AND BACK: For both the table and the shelf, cut 1×6s or 1×8s to fit; attach them with 8d galvanized nails or 2-inch decking screws. Use a saber saw to cut the rounded edges of the 1×10 backsplash, and attach it to the top rails with the same-size nails or screws.

A practical table with a shelf beneath can serve a multitude of purposes. If you like, add another shelf in the middle.

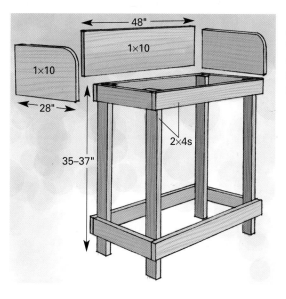

The framing is simple. Take the time to check each joint for square before fastening.

BARBECUE CABINET AND COUNTERTOP

Place a barbecue cabinet where you can easily tap into your home's electrical and plumbing lines. Consider the location of the grill first. Most propane grills must be at least 1 foot from combustible surfaces.

This versatile outdoor kitchen setup will make outdoor cooking easier, so you'll probably do more of it. A counter next to the grill makes preparation easier and gets the cook out of the kitchen and into the open air. Guests and family members will have more fun helping with the food preparation.

PROVIDE PLUMBING AND ELECTRICAL SERVICE

With its sink and refrigerator, this cabinet brings kitchen convenience outdoors so you won't have to make as many trips inside. You can wash vegetables in the 15-inch-square bar sink. The wiring and electrical work can be complex, so plan carefully or hire a professional.

If you install the cabinet on a deck extension, you can run the utility lines underground. Good design and planning will save time and money later.

PLUMBING: Connect copper water lines for the sink by tapping into interior pipes that run on an outside wall of the house.

Install a separate shut-off valve for each line so you can easily turn the water off from inside. Where winters are severe, make sure you drain the outside lines so the pipes won't freeze and burst.

Connecting the drain line into the house drainage system can be complicated. Check with local codes, and be sure the drain line is properly vented (this usually requires the sink to be within 5 feet of a vented stack and the installation of a vent loop).

If you will use the sink only occasionally, you may want to have the drainpipe empty into the yard. If so, use only biodegradable soap when you wash. Or have the drainpipe lead to a dry well—a hole in the ground that is below the level of the sink, about 2 feet in diameter and 4 feet deep, filled with gravel and covered with landscape fabric and sod.

ELECTRICAL: Install a GFCI receptacle inside the cabinet for the refrigerator, and another one above the cabinet so you can plug in small appliances. (See page 60 for information on adding an outdoor receptacle.)

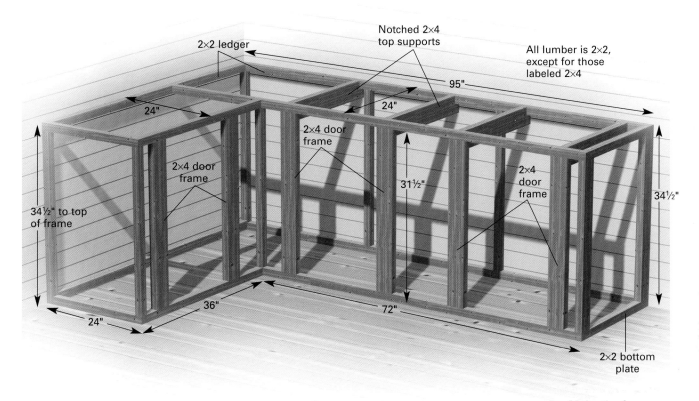

2×2 ledger

Notched 2×4 top supports

All lumber is 2×2, except for those labeled 2×4

95"

24"

24"

2×4 door frame

31½"

2×4 door frame

34½" to top of frame

2×4 door frame

34½"

24"

36"

72"

2×2 bottom plate

Make the frame with 2×2s and 2×4s. The deck or patio will serve as the cabinet floor. Use vertical 2×4s to frame each side of the door openings, then attach horizontal 2×4 headers.

FRAME THE CABINET

Before you start the cabinet framing, make sure you know the opening size for the refrigerator. You should be able to easily slip the unit into place.

Construct the cabinet framing out of 2×2s, with 2×4s for the door frames. (The 2×2s may seem spindly, but when the tongue-and-groove siding is installed, the structure will be strong.)

For a standard-size cabinet, the frame should be 34½ inches high and 24 inches deep. When measuring, always factor in the 1½-inch thickness of the framing members. For instance, the vertical 2×2s and 2×4s are cut to 31½ inches; the added thicknesses of the 2×2 top and bottom plates produce a total framing height of 34½ inches.

Sketch out a design, using this plan as a reference, and include dimensions for the framing members and openings. Choose pressure-treated stock that is straight and free of cracks. Drill pilot holes for each fastener to avoid splitting the wood.

Start by constructing the back wall framing.
■ Cut the 2×2 ledger and framing pieces to the proper length, and assemble each wall section on the deck.
■ Attach the assembly to the house with 3-inch decking screws driven into the studs (find the studs by locating the nail lines in the siding). If the siding is brick, drill holes in the brick first, and use masonry anchors. Make sure the frame remains square as you fasten it.
■ Assemble the remaining frames. With a helper, position the sides, check them for square and level, and attach them to each other and to the decking with screws driven through predrilled holes.
■ After the entire framing is complete, cut and notch the 2×4 countertop supports so they fit under the ledger, flush with the house and flush with the top of the framing, *above*.
■ Then cut horizontal 2×4 headers to fit between the 2×4 door frames, and attach them to the door frames with screws driven at an angle.

BARBECUE CABINET AND COUNTERTOP
continued

Plan for the placement of tongue-and-groove pieces on each side of the doors so they will be even at the corners. Mark the position of the pattern across the opening.

INSTALL SIDING AND DOORS

The cabinet facing should complement the overall look of your deck and house. You can face the cabinet with the same materials as the house, but you may need to compromise if things don't look compatible with the deck.

Grooved T1-11 or other sheet siding will be the easiest to install: Just cut the sheets to fit and attach them with decking screws or nails.

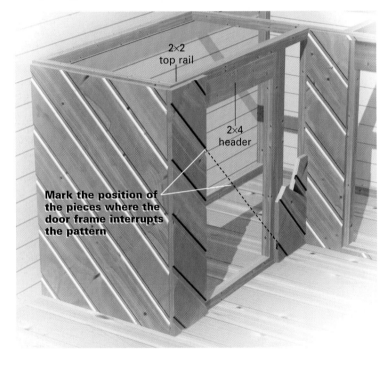

2×2 top rail

2×4 header

Mark the position of the pieces where the door frame interrupts the pattern

CABINET DOOR

Join the tongue-and-groove pieces together with polyurethane glue. Before the glue dries, attach a frame of 1×2s on the face, then 1×2s around the perimeter.

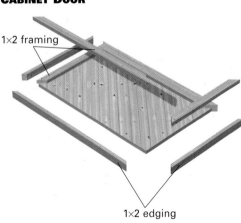

1×2 framing

1×2 edging

INSTALLING 1×4 OR 1×6 TONGUE-AND-GROOVE SIDING: Place a strip of ¼-inch plywood on the deck next to the framing to keep the bottom of the siding slightly raised above the deck or patio.

You can make the 45-degree miters with a circular saw, but it will be easier with a power miter saw or radial arm saw. As you cut each piece of siding, use it as a template to mark the next piece before installing it. Attach the boards by drilling pilot holes and driving 4d casing nails at an angle through the base of the tongue and into the framing. Install the pieces tongue-side up.
■ Cut a triangular corner piece first. Nail it in place as described above.
■ Cut and install the remaining pieces on the rest of the framing.
■ Where a doorway interrupts a board, *left*, use a straight board to mark the positions of the pieces on the other side of the door so the pattern will be consistent across the opening.

TRIM OUT: When the paneling is installed, attach a 1×2 filler across the doorway opening, then trim the corners, the top edge, and the door frames with 1×2 stock to cover all exposed siding ends (*see page 84*). When trimming the door openings, miter the trim corners.

MAKE THE DOORS: Cut pieces for the door facing at a 45-degree angle so when they are fitted together they produce a rectangle that is 1³/₄ inches less than both dimensions of the door opening. (When you add the 1×2 door edging to the tongue-and-groove paneling, the door will be shorter by ¼ inch all around—just right for clearance.)
■ Assemble the pieces temporarily (but tightly), and measure the door panel.
■ Cut and miter four 1×2s for the face frame and four more for the perimeter edging.
■ Working on a flat surface, apply a bead of glue on each tongue and press the pieces together.
■ Adjust the pieces for square, then attach the face and perimeter frames with glue and 3d casing nails or screws, keeping edges and corners flush.

INSTALL THE DOORS: Use nails as spacers at the bottom to position the doors in the opening, leaving ⅛-inch gaps all around. Install hinges and catches.

MAKE THE COUNTERTOP

Ask your supplier for vitreous or impervious tiles that have proven themselves durable for outdoor use in your climate.

BUILD THE SUBSTRATE: Cut pieces of ¾-inch pressure-treated plywood so the edges overhang the framing by about an inch all around. Attach it with screws. Cut out the opening for the sink with a saber saw. Cut pieces of ½-inch cement backer board to fit exactly on top of the plywood. Attach it to the plywood with a grid pattern of 1¼-inch decking screws spaced 4 to 6 inches apart.

DRY-RUN: Set most of the tiles in place on top of the countertop with plastic spacers between them. This allows you to make adjustments, if necessary; you may avoid cutting some tiles by adjusting the layout. Avoid using slivers of tiles. Use a snap cutter to cut the tiles so your pattern is complete before you begin setting the tiles.

SET THE TILES: Mix thin-set mortar, using liquid latex additive.
■ Remove a section of dry-laid tiles about 3 feet square. Apply the thin-set to the backer board with a notched trowel, and set the tiles in it. Push each tile into place with a very slight twist; do not slide the tiles around.
■ Once a section is laid, use a beater board (a scrap of 2×6 wrapped with carpeting) and a hammer to tap all the tiles down.

GROUT AND CLEAN: Wait at least a day for the mortar to dry.
■ Mix sanded grout with latex additive, and apply it with a laminated grout float (one that has a squeegee-like, hard rubber face).
■ First, hold the float nearly flat as you push the grout into the joints with sweeping motions in several directions.
■ Then tilt the float up and scrape away as much excess grout as possible.
■ Wipe the grouted surface immediately with a damp sponge, making sure that the grout lines look the same. You can use the handle of a toothbrush to scrape each joint.
■ Rinse and wipe several times.
■ Allow the grout to dry, then buff the surface to a shine with a dry cloth.

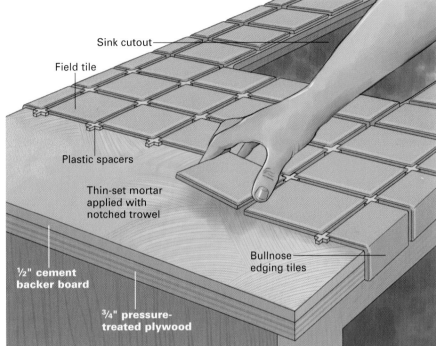

Sink cutout

Field tile

Plastic spacers

Thin-set mortar applied with notched trowel

Bullnose edging tiles

½" cement backer board

¾" pressure-treated plywood

Position the tiles in a dry run—so you know exactly where each tile will go—before setting the tiles in thin-set.

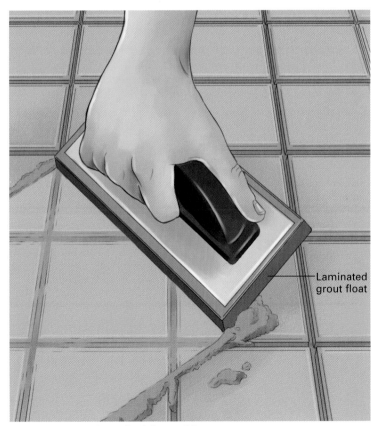

Laminated grout float

Press the grout into the joints with a grout float, then wipe it away. Sponge off the excess.

A STORAGE HATCHWAY

Make this large storage bin to hold a hose, garden tools, or kids' toys. The holes in the bottom ensure that water will drain and items will stay dry. The joist through the center of this storage opening will not get in the way of most storage items.

Cut two lines in the decking along the inside edges of joists. A straight board tacked to the decking serves as a cutting guide.

If your deck is at least 2 feet above the ground, you have plenty of potential storage space right below your feet. Make an access door to unlock that potential.

If all you need is periodic access to an under-the-deck hose bib, simply cut out and make the door. But for a usable compartment, build a storage box to keep equipment dry.

The compartment design at left is two joists wide (32 or 48 inches, depending on the spacing of the joists) with an uncut joist between them. This middle joist will not get in the way of most storage items. A pressure-treated plywood box will resist rotting; a grid of holes provides drainage for rainwater.

FRAME THE OPENING

Make the opening about 3 feet by 4 feet—larger than that and lifting it will take too much effort. Use a framing square to draw lines on the decking for the center.

CUT THE OPENING: To make this plunge cut, set the blade of a circular saw at the thickness of the decking.
- Retract the blade guard and rest the front edge of the base plate on the deck a few inches away from a corner of the opening.
- Set the blade just above the line, pull the trigger, and lower the blade slowly, holding the saw firmly so it does not skip away.
- When the blade has cut through and the saw is resting on the deck surface, stop the blade. Press a straight board against the side of the base plate and tack it to the deck.
- Using the board as a guide, cut each line, stopping short of the corners. Be careful not to nick adjacent boards.
- Finish the cuts with a saber saw. Set the decking aside; you'll use it to make the door.

ATTACH THE FRAMING: The door will get walked on, so build a strong support under it.
- Cut 2×8 blocks (which will support the front and rear edges of the door) to fit between the joists.
- Fasten them flush to the joists with predrilled screws or nails at an angle. Cut 2×2s to fit between the 2×8s and attach them to the sides of the joists.

MAKE AND SUPPORT THE BOX

If you want access just to the area under the deck, you can skip this part. If the box will be shallow and won't hold anything heavy, you can simply build it and attach it to the 2×8s and the joists. For a stronger box, first install a footing, post, and beam.

BUILD A SUPPORT: Use a plumb bob to locate and mark a spot on the ground directly beneath the center of the opening.
■ Dig a hole at this spot and pour concrete for a footing. Depending on the distance between the ground and the deck, you may need to install a post anchor and post, or a beam anchor for a beam that will rest directly on top of the footing.
■ Make a beam several inches longer than the opening by laminating two 2×6s together.
■ Attach it to the footing or post.

BUILD THE BOX: Build the box, then slide it into position from below. Build it with ¾-inch exterior-grade plywood, cut to fit between the 2×8 blocking and the joists.
■ In the center of two of the sides, cut a notch 2 inches wide and a little deeper than the depth of your joist. When the box is assembled, the notches will allow the sides to fit around the center joist.
■ Cut and assemble the four sides and attach them with 2-inch decking screws.
■ Screw 2×2 support strips to the corners and at the bottom on all four sides.
■ Cut a bottom to fit, with cutouts at each corner to fit around the 2×2s.
■ Drill a series of 1-inch holes for drainage.
■ Drop the bottom plate in from the top of the box and screw through the 2×2 support strips to attach it.
■ Slide the box into place from below the deck opening. It should fit snugly against the 2×2s. If you need to make up space, insert a flat-laid 2×4 between the bottom and the beam, and drive screws into the 2×4 through the bottom of the box.

BUILD THE DOOR

■ Lay out the pieces cut from the opening with the same spacing as the decking. Anchor the cutouts with scrap tacked to the deck and positioned snugly against the door pieces.
■ Cut two 2×6 or 2×8 braces—4 inches shorter than the door—and attach them with two 2½-inch coated screws at each joint. Use a drill and a saber saw to cut an oval hand hole about 2 inches by 4 inches.
■ Set the door in the opening. If necessary, cut one or two sides so the gap is even all around. Sand the edges of the door and the decking. Attach the door to the decking with two or three 1½×3-inch utility hinges.

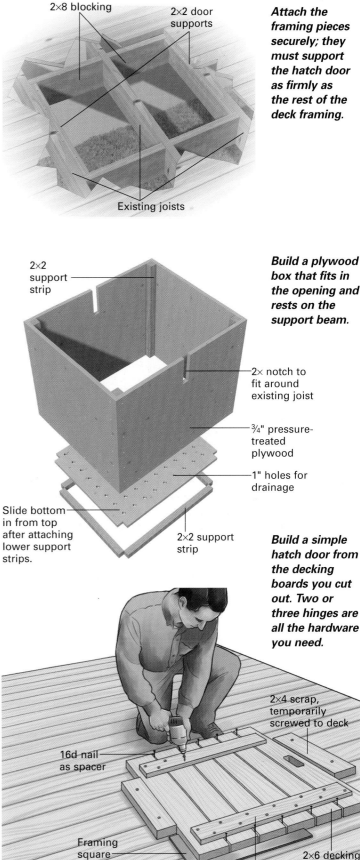

2×8 blocking
2×2 door supports
Existing joists

Attach the framing pieces securely; they must support the hatch door as firmly as the rest of the deck framing.

2×2 support strip
2× notch to fit around existing joist
¾" pressure-treated plywood
1" holes for drainage
Slide bottom in from top after attaching lower support strips.
2×2 support strip

Build a plywood box that fits in the opening and rests on the support beam.

Build a simple hatch door from the decking boards you cut out. Two or three hinges are all the hardware you need.

2×4 scrap, temporarily screwed to deck
16d nail as spacer
Framing square
2×6 brace
2×6 decking

LIGHTING

With a low-voltage lighting system, you can match the deck lamps with others along walkways or in the landscaping, creating a unified look all the way from the house to the gate.

The small accent lights mounted under the steps and along the skirt of this deck show off its redwood tones and make the stairs easier and safer to use at night. The lamps are mounted directly to the surface, with only a small hole drilled for wiring.

If you need to run wire through areas that receive heavy foot traffic, bury the wiring in conduit for safety and convenience. Dig a trench to the depth specified by local codes, and join runs of conduit only with connectors designed for underground use.

Adding lights to a deck takes planning, but it's not difficult. Choose the system you prefer—either line-voltage or low-voltage systems—review the installation guidelines, and prepare to enjoy your deck day and night.

LINE-VOLTAGE LIGHTING

A line-voltage system uses the 120-volt AC power in your house. Working with line voltage is easy enough for homeowners with experience doing their own electrical work. Most outdoor line-voltage wiring requires approval from a building inspector, however.

LAYOUT: Using wooden stakes, mark the location of lights, switches, junction boxes, and receptacles.
■ Tie colored lines between the stakes to show where to dig trenches for wiring.
■ Run the line to the power source.

CONDUIT: Cut away the sod for wiring trenches. Then cut conduit to length and lay sections in place. Attach fittings as you work.
■ Avoid making sharp bends in the conduit. The wire inside should be able to slide through it smoothly.
■ Wherever the conduit will attach to a junction box or fixture, mount the junction box securely—to the side of the house, for example. Attach fittings to the conduit.

WIRING: Using a tool called a fish tape, pull wire through the conduit to each box and receptacle. Pull out several inches of wire at each location for making the connections.
■ Run wire from the beginning of the circuit to the house wiring. Leave it unconnected at this time.
■ If you're uncomfortable finishing the wiring yourself, have an electrician complete the job. Otherwise, wire the switches first, followed by the junction boxes, receptacles, and fixtures.
■ Make sure all outdoor circuits have GFCI protection, and use waterproof gaskets on all exposed components. Point the open ends of all wire connectors downward so they don't collect water.

FINAL CONNECTIONS: Turn off the power at the main service panel. With all other parts of the system wired, connect it to the circuit you have chosen. Turn the power on.
■ Turn on each fixture to test the bulbs, and replace the ones that don't work. If any fixtures are not getting power, turn off the

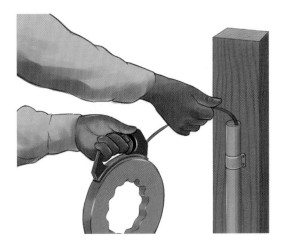

When the conduit is in place, you may have trouble pushing wire through it. To work around bends and over long distances, use a fish tape and pulling lubricant.

Tie the fixtures to the electrical supply lines with approved wire connectors. Turn on the power at the source to test the bulbs.

electricity at the main service panel and check the fixtures with a multitester. When all the fixtures work, adjust the lights at night to create the look you want.

CLEANUP: When you are satisfied with the placement of your outdoor lighting, fill in the trenches and cover them with sod. Secure any conduit and wires that extend above ground.

INSTALLING A LOW-VOLTAGE SYSTEM

Low voltage is safe, easy to install, and inexpensive to operate. The easiest way to install a low-voltage system is to buy a low-voltage lighting kit, which includes cable, lights, and a transformer that lowers voltage so it is safe to the touch. Purchase a kit with a timer or a photovoltaic switch to turn the lights on automatically when it gets dark.

■ Mount the transformer near an outdoor receptacle where it won't be damaged.

■ Lay out the light fixtures and poke the mounting stakes into the ground. Dig a shallow trench for the cable, lay it in, and cover it. Plug in the transformer.

■ If you want to place lights on a railing or a fence, run the cable where it is out of the way, and fasten it with cable staples about every foot, so it won't dangle. Use mounting plates that are designed for installing light fixtures on a horizontal surface.

■ Connect the parts of a low-voltage system to the transformer, and then plug it in. Check each connection in the circuit to be sure everything is finished. Then turn the power back on.

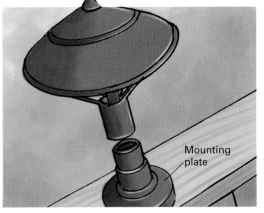

Mounting plate

To install low-voltage lights on a railing, purchase a kit with mounting plates. Drill the hole, then install the plate with the screws provided.

Low-voltage system transformer

GFCI outdoor receptacle

Cable staples

Run low-voltage cable alongside posts and under rails, or wherever it will be least visible. Fasten it with round-topped cable staples; standard square-topped staples may cut the cable.

BUILD A FOUNTAIN

Complete this quick fountain project in an afternoon. Inexpensive and easy to assemble, the fountain brings the cooling sound of water to your patio.

STEP 1: Locate the fountain within reach of a garden hose and an outdoor electrical outlet. That will show it to its best advantage; it will be the focal point of your patio. If the outlet isn't protected, have a GFCI outlet installed. For safety, install metal conduit or PVC pipe between the outlet and the fountain to run the electrical cord through.

STEP 2: Dig a hole for the bucket. The bucket should fit snugly with its lip rising just above the surface of the soil. Cut a ½-inch-wide slit in the lip of the bucket with a handsaw for the pump's cord to pass through.

STEP 3: Mark the center of the saucer on its back by measuring across the saucer horizontally and vertically, drawing a light line along the ruler. The center of the saucer is located where the lines cross. Drill a hole for the tubing to go through at this point using a ¾-inch masonry bit. Next, drill several drainage holes around the saucer. If drainage holes in the pots are too small for the tubing to pass through, enlarge them with the drill and masonry bit. Also, drill additional drainage holes in the pots.

STEP 4: Rinse pots, saucer, and rock to remove dust that might clog the pump. Set the pump on a brick in the bucket, threading its electrical cord through the slit.

STEP 5: Thread the flexible tubing through the saucer, leaving just enough tubing underneath to reach the pump. Attach the tubing to the pump. Fill the bucket with water and place the inverted saucer on top of it.

STEP 6: Thread tubing through the center hole of the largest pot. Set the pot on the saucer and fill it with river rock. The rock holds the tube upright. Thread the remaining tubing through the drainage hole of the top pot; then set it on the river rock.

STEP 7: Pull the remaining tubing up (don't stretch it) and fill around it with river rock. Cut the tubing so that the fountain spout is even with the rim of the pot. Attach the fountain nozzle to the end of the tubing.

STEP 8: Wipe dust from the fountain; then turn on the pump. Because soil around the fountain may become damp, plant this area with water-loving plants.

NOTES:
- All pot dimensions refer to diameter.
- Always wear eye protection when drilling.
- If there is a chance of a small child pulling the fountain over, use PVC pipe instead of flexible tubing. Anchor the fountain with bricks in the bucket. Always supervise children near water features.
- In cold climates, store your fountain indoors to prevent the pots from cracking. Store the pump submerged in water so its seals won't dry out and shrink over the winter.

MATERIALS

- 5-gallon bucket
- Submersible pump
- Flexible water garden tubing long enough to run from the pump to the fountain
- Fountain nozzle
- River rocks
- 12" to 14" saucer
- 12" to 14" pot
- 10" to 12" pot
- 6" pot
- Metal conduit wide enough to admit pump plug
- Drill with ¾-inch masonry bit
- Shovel
- Knife or saw

This do-it-yourself fountain can add a splash to any outdoor room.

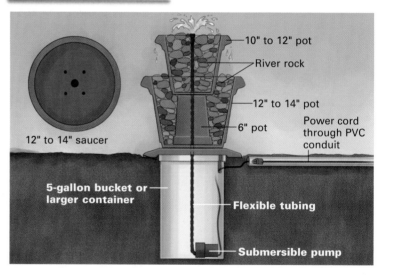

12" to 14" saucer

10" to 12" pot

River rock

12" to 14" pot

6" pot

Power cord through PVC conduit

5-gallon bucket or larger container

Flexible tubing

Submersible pump

SELECTING A PUMP

Submersible pumps come in various sizes for pumping different amounts of water. The size of pump you choose depends on how much water your water feature holds. Most small fountains and ponds require the simplest submersible pump, designed to recirculate 50 gallons or less. Larger ponds with waterfalls necessitate heftier pumps. Most pumps run economically, costing pennies per day. They require little maintenance.

PONDS

Ponds can make a big splash next to, or as part of your patio. A garden pond also adds sparkle to your overall landscape, showcases goldfish and aquatic plants, and lures birds and other wildlife to your yard. Having a pond near your patio can be soothing, fascinating, and fun.

MATERIALS: Flexible pond liners have revolutionized the use of water in home landscaping. The liner is a low-cost, easy-to-install, custom-fit alternative to concrete or molded forms. Molded fiberglass ponds come in many sizes and shapes, but expect to pay extra for fanciful custom designs.

LAYOUT AND EXCAVATION: Outline the pond shape on the lawn with a garden hose.
■ With the hose in place, remove the sod within and excavate to a depth of 9 inches, sloping the sides at about a 20-degree angle. Leave a ledge—a shelf for aquatic plants—then dig again to a total pond depth of 18 inches. Slope this final excavation also. Your garden-supply center can help you select attractive plants for the ledge.

LEVELING THE EDGE: Level the edge of the pool along its entire perimeter.
■ Center a post in the excavation area and extend a leveled 1×4 from the post to the edge. Mark a horizontal line where the 1×4 intersects the grade.
■ Dig to this depth around the perimeter of the pond, repositioning the board as you go. Your edging should be at least 2 inches above the patio or lawn grade to prevent any runoff from contaminating pond water.

LINING THE POOL: Line the pool bottom with damp sand and spread the liner over the excavation. Press the liner down and add 4 to 6 inches of water. The weight of the water will form the liner to the pool.
■ Adjust the liner to prevent wrinkles, and fill in increments, adjusting as you go.
■ Fill the pond, lay flagstone or pavers on the pond edge, and cut away the excess liner.
■ Install a GFCI outlet to provide power to a submersible pump, which circulates and aerates the water.

A vinyl liner keeps this pond full and clear; use rocks or patio blocks to conceal the edges. Garden centers also carry rigid plastic pools in various sizes and shapes.

INSTALLING A POND LINER

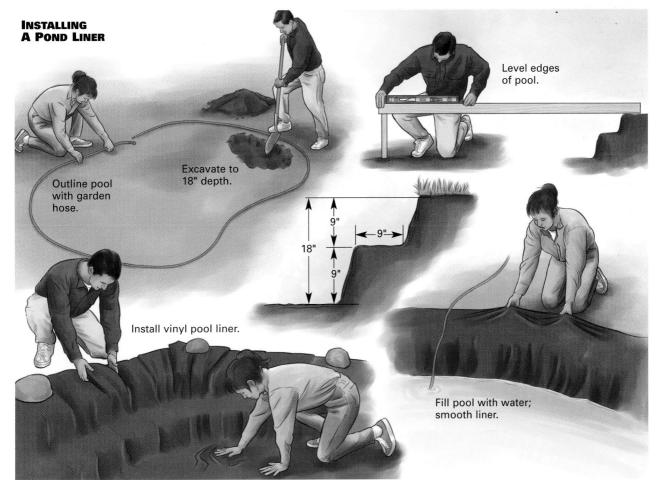

Outline pool with garden hose.

Excavate to 18" depth.

Level edges of pool.

9"

9"

18"

9"

Install vinyl pool liner.

Fill pool with water; smooth liner.

DECK PLANS

This chapter features plans for eight decks, progressing from low ground-huggers to more complex structures. Each plan is complete and ready to build and includes a full materials list. The construction details conform to most municipal building codes, but you should check with your local building department and get proper permits before starting any work.

Each deck is designed for a specific site, but you can adapt any one of them to fit your site. Even if you do not plan to build any of the designs on the following pages, you'll still find it worthwhile to take a look at the drawings. You may find the details useful for adapting another plan or even designing your own deck.

The plans are arranged with the easier ones first and progress to more elaborate projects. The techniques and details presented for the simpler designs make the more complex designs easier to understand. The plans will help you see how footings, structural components, decking surfaces, railings, stairs, benches, and trim come together to make a complete deck.

The simple shapes of this deck blend well with the unadorned style of the house and fence. Its horizontal benches provide pleasant contrast to the vertical lines in the siding of the house and fencing.

HOW TO ADAPT A PLAN FROM THIS BOOK

Whether you are looking through this book for ideas and inspiration to design your own deck, or you intend to use one of the plans with little or no alteration, you are more apt to find a deck just right for you if you know exactly what you are looking for. Use the design principles described earlier in this book to help you identify your goals and priorities.

After you've selected a plan, you may find you need to adapt it. The following general principles list most of the changes you may want to make.They can be applied to any deck. No matter what changes you make, treat your design as if you were starting from the ground up. Draw plans to scale on paper before starting construction.

TO CHANGE SIZE

EXPANDING: If you want to expand the deck outward from the house, the easiest way is to lengthen the joists. You can safely extend them beyond the beam (this extension is called a cantilever) as long as the length of the cantilevered section is no more than one-fifth the total span of the joist. If you need to extend the deck farther, you can add a second beam or move the first beam out and make all the joists larger.

To expand the deck along the length of the house, simply lengthen the ledger and beam and add more joists. The longer beam will require an additional post or two, or you can enlarge the beam and increase the spacing between posts. In addition to the structural changes, you will also have to increase the number or length of decking boards and make railings or benches proportionately longer.

TO MAKE A DECK SMALLER: To shorten a deck along its length, reduce the number of joists and use shorter decking boards. The beam and ledger must also be shortened accordingly. If you want the deck narrower, move the beam closer to the house and use shorter joists. You will also need fewer decking boards.

ALTERING THE SPANS

Remember that any alteration of the spans in a deck structure may require changing the size of the lumber.

TO CHANGE SHAPE

The easiest changes involve variations on a basic rectangle. For instance, wrapping a deck around a corner of the house or adding an extension will change the deck from a rectangle to an L. Structurally, this change involves the same principles as enlarging a deck, except that you are lengthening some of the joists instead of all of them, and adding a short beam under the new addition instead of under the entire deck.

ADDING LEGS: Another approach to varying the basic rectangle is to think of an L, or a T, or a Z, as separate decks joined together. Design the main platform, following the plan you are using, then design the additional leg as a separate deck to be joined to it. You may also be able to use parts of two different plans.

TO CHANGE HEIGHT

You can raise or lower a deck by changing the heights of its posts. If you are adapting a ground-level deck plan for higher floor levels, be aware than most codes specify a maximum deck height (usually 30 inches above the ground) allowed before a railing is required. If your proposed height is greater than 5 feet, you should add diagonal cross-bracing.

MINIMUMS: If you are lowering a deck to the ground, you can change its structure so that the joists are nailed into the face of the beam, rather than sitting on top of it. You may need to excavate in order to maintain at least an 8-inch clearance between earth and wood. In addition, use heart redwood or pressure-treated material for decks close to the ground to resist rot and termite damage.

NEW LEVELS: For a one-step change in level, design the main platform as in the existing plan. If the smaller platform is to be raised, run joists under it just as though the deck were all one level. However, instead of laying decking boards on the joists where the platform is to be raised, run another set of joists crosswise on top of the first ones. Their depth should be the same as the desired height of the step, usually 7 inches. With this method, the decking on the raised platform will run perpendicular to the main decking, making the change in level more obvious and less hazardous.

If the second level is lower than the main platform or separated by several steps, it is easiest to design it as a separate deck system and join it to the main platform. Footings will usually be in the same places, as though the deck were all one level, but posts under the secondary section of deck will be lower or higher than the main platform. Where the two decks meet, the same posts can support both levels; just attach a stringer to the sides of the posts for the lower deck, and place a beam on top of it.

OTHER ALTERATIONS

FOOTINGS: Some areas may require deeper or larger footings than those used in the plan you have selected. The structure of the deck can remain the same. All you have to do is redesign the footings and piers. For steep sites, local codes may require drilled footings or footings connected by concrete grade beams. Consult your local building officials to see what is required.

You may need to change the number or location of footings—to minimize digging, to avoid utility lines, or to take advantage of existing footings from an old deck. Such changes generally require redesigning the structure of the deck to reflect new joist and beam spans. The span charts on pages 84–85 can help you select appropriate sizes as you redesign such structural modifications.

RAILINGS: You may need to change the height of a railing to comply with local codes. Simply change the height of each post accordingly, and add or delete rails or alter the spacing to make up the difference. Other simple changes include varying the location of openings. Make sure the new design has posts wherever railing terminates or changes direction. Then move other posts, if necessary, to maintain uniform spacing between all the posts. If you change the post spacing on one side of the deck, lay out the opposite side to match.

The easiest way to change the style of the railing is to keep the post arrangement called for by the plan and alter the size or configuration of the other railing members. Because almost all railing systems begin with posts spaced 3 to 6 feet apart, put these in place, then attach rails and stringers. If you choose a railing design that has a different post arrangement from the one in the plan, you can bolt posts to the deck's band joist or a 2-by fascia.

STEPS OR STAIRS: You'll almost certainly have to adapt any stairs between the deck and the ground to suit your own site. Make sure that all steps in a flight of stairs are exactly the same height, and that riser and tread dimensions comply with local codes.

Steps between deck levels or between the house and the deck will probably be the same dimensions as those in the plan. However, you can vary the design by using different types of tread lumber, different sizes of boards, or different size overhangs. You can also add risers or kickboards, if they are not included in the plan, to produce a more finished look.

TRIM DETAILS: There is no limit to the decorative touches— planters, fascia boards, and trim—that you can add to your deck. In most cases they require no structural changes. The only limitations are aesthetic— be sure that these details harmonize with the house and yard, that they are not excessive, that they do not call undue attention to themselves, and that they maintain proportions in keeping with those of the rest of the deck.

VARY THE PATTERN OF DECKING BOARDS

The easiest variation is to use different size decking boards—for instance, 2 by 4s instead of 2 by 6s—or to alternate decking boards of different sizes. If you want to use smaller boards than those in the plan, make sure the boards will safely span the distance between joists.

In some cases you can also change the direction of the decking boards. For example, if the plan shows them running perpendicular to the joists, you can easily run them diagonally. The joists will have to be closer together—close enough that the diagonal measurement from joist to joist still will be within the acceptable span for your decking. If the plan shows diagonal decking boards, you can run them perpendicular to the original diagonal direction. You could also run them perpendicular to the joists— and increase the joist spacing to match the span tables. You cannot run the decking boards parallel to the joists without changing the entire structural system.

A QUICK DECK

Here is a simple deck made of sections you can lay directly on the ground or on a level surface such as a patio, a concrete pool skirt, or even a rooftop. Construction is as easy as it gets. Boards called sleepers sit on an existing firm surface.

Two-by-four cleats run across the sleepers and 2×4s nailed across the cleats create the walking surface. You can change the deck's shape and size by rearranging the sections.

CONSTRUCTION

Because the sections have no structural system tying them together, they require a level area that is stable and uniformly flat. Nevertheless you may find that, over time, the sections shift in relationship to one another. This problem can usually be solved by leveling the sections periodically, by toenailing the sections together, or by installing the deck over long sleepers. Be sure to check with local building officials to make sure that what you have in mind is allowed.

MATERIALS LIST

For 12 sections, set on sleepers

	Quantity	Material	Size
Base	198 sq ft	landscape fabric (for weed control)	
	1 cu. yd.	gravel	
Sleepers	2	2×4s	12'
	2	2×6s	12'
Decking and Cleats	38	2×4s	12' (cut into 35½" pieces)
Screws	10 lbs	#8×2" deck screws, HDG (hot-dipped, galvanized)	

THE 3×3 DECK SECTIONS: You can build the sections for your deck in almost any size or shape. The basis for this deck is a 3-foot-square section. This size is large enough to cover a good-sized area quickly, yet light enough to be easily carried and installed. Each 3-foot section also goes together quickly. If you make the sections much smaller, it will take much more sawing and assembly to finish your deck. Larger sections may be too heavy to lift comfortably.

ASSEMBLY: To construct each section, cut the 2×4s into 35½-inch lengths. Build a simple spacing jig as shown.
■ Place nine of the 2×4s inside the jig, with their best faces down.
■ Lay the two cleats on top, flush with the ends of the decking boards, and screw the pieces together, pre-drilling the holes.
■ After assembling the sections, nail spacers to the cleats, as shown, to provide uniform spacing between sections. Some sections will not need spacers, so you may wait to attach the scraps until you decide on a final configuration.

A wood deck that is placed directly on the ground will not last indefinitely, even under ideal conditions. But if you follow the methods outlined here, you should get years of service from your deck.

SITE PREPARATION: The most important feature of this design is the surface it rests on. Choose a site that drains well. Your deck won't last long if it sits on ground that stays damp for extended periods of time. Excavate a shallow depression and fill it with a 3-inch layer of gravel or crushed rock. To control weeds, line the excavation with a layer of landscaping fabric before putting down the gravel.

INSTALLATION: The sections are attached to a series of eight sleepers, which lie directly on the gravel. The sleepers help keep the sections in line and level to one another.
■ Lay out mason's lines to guide placement of the sleepers and sections. Because work will proceed from the center outward, lay out the middle first rather than the edges.

■ Level the bed as best you can with a rake.
■ Place the sleepers, as shown, and add or remove gravel as necessary to level them.
■ Set the assembled sections on sleepers, starting in the center. The spacers attached to the edge of the cleats will help maintain consistent gaps between the sections.
■ For extra rigidity, toenail the sections to the sleepers.

CONSTRUCTING 3×3 MODULES

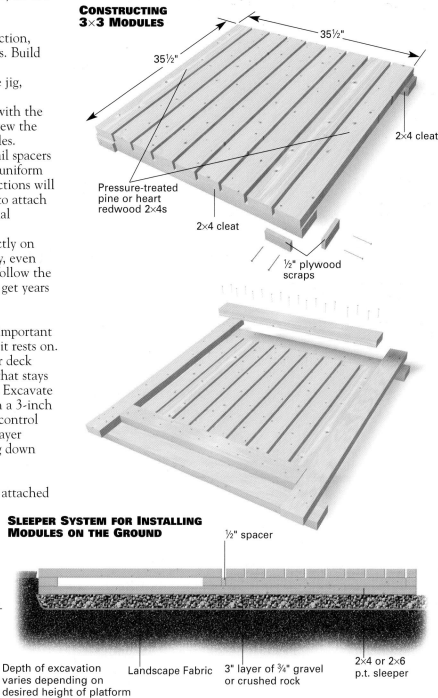

35½"

35½"

2×4 cleat

Pressure-treated pine or heart redwood 2×4s

2×4 cleat

½" plywood scraps

SLEEPER SYSTEM FOR INSTALLING MODULES ON THE GROUND

½" spacer

4"+/-

Depth of excavation varies depending on desired height of platform

Landscape Fabric

3" layer of ¾" gravel or crushed rock

2×4 or 2×6 p.t. sleeper

A SIMPLE GARDEN PLATFORM

PLAN VIEW

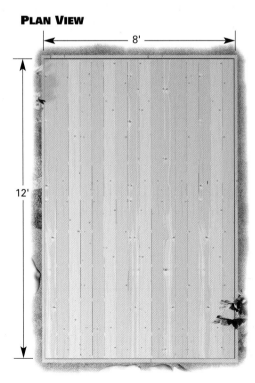

8'

12'

This freestanding deck is a permanent, raised platform that can be installed anywhere in a level yard. It offers an ideal solution for a problem area, such as a drab corner where nothing seems to grow. Use it as a retreat, dining area, or fantasy platform for children's play.

CONSTRUCTION NOTES

Because it is a simple rectangle, this deck will look more attractive if you locate it along an existing visual axis. You can soften its edges with plantings or with other natural decorative accents.

The deck's low profile is maintained by hanging the joists between rather than on top of the beams and by using fairly small structural members (2×6s). This limits the width of the deck to about 8 feet, but you can increase the span by adding a third beam.

LAYOUT AND FOOTINGS: When you lay out your site, note that the outside edges of the piers are flush with the outside edges of the beams and that the piers are poured after the footings. You can use pre-cast piers as an alternative.

■ Set up your batterboards as shown on page 118 and tie layout lines to mark the outside edge of the pier.

■ Dig the holes and pour the footings.

■ While the concrete is still wet, set form tubes for the piers with their inside edges tangent to the layout lines. Level the tubes carefully, because the beams bear directly on top of the piers.

■ Pour the piers, and while the concrete is still wet, set anchor bolts about 2 inches from the outside edge, leaving 5½ inches of the bolt exposed.

BEAMS AND JOISTS: Because this deck will be installed just above grade, the wood for the joists and beams should be either naturally resistant species, such as redwood, or pressure-treated lumber rated for ground contact. All hardware should be galvanized.

■ Hold the beams in place on top of the piers and mark them for the anchor bolt holes.

■ Drill a recess in the beam to hold a washer and nut, then drill bolt holes slightly oversize with a 9/16-inch bit.

■ Bolt the beams in place and nail on the joist hangers as shown in the framing plan.

■ Cut the joists to length and install them in the joist hangers. Note: The end joists are 7 inches longer than the others and are nailed directly to the beam ends.

DECKING, FASCIA, AND FINISH

When installing the decking, make sure its edges are flush with the outside of the beams. If you're building a smaller platform, you can let the decking lengths extend over the edge —"run wild," as the builders say—then trim it all in a single pass with a circular saw.

■ Screw the decking to the joists. Use two screws per joist in each board.

■ Miter the ends of the 2×10 fascia boards and nail the boards to the outside of the platform, creating an attractive skirt that keeps out debris.

■ If your design results in a surface more than 10 inches above grade, provide a step.

■ Finish the deck with stain or paint, or let it weather naturally.

MATERIALS LIST

	Quantity	Material	Size
Footings	18 cu ft	concrete (for 6 piers 10" dia. × 36" and 6 footings 18" dia. × 8")	
	6	½" anchor bolts	
Framing			
Beams	2	4×6s	12'
Joists	10	2×6s	8'
Decking	17	2×6s	12'
Fascia	2	2×10s	8'
	2	2×10s	12'
Nails	2 lbs	joist hanger nails	
	5 lbs	16d HDG common	
Screws	7 lbs	#8×3½" decking screws	

FRAMING PLAN

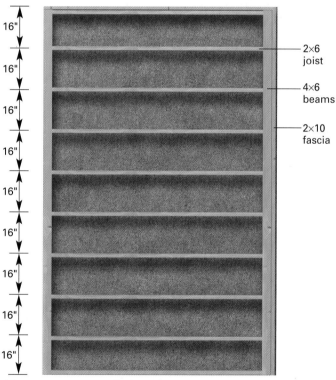

2×6 joist

4×6 beams

2×10 fascia

16" 16" 16" 16" 16" 16" 16" 16" 16"

Measurements are made from the center of each joist or are "on center"

SECTION

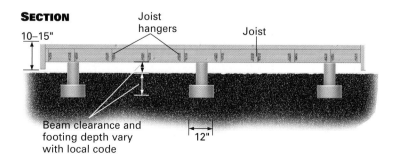

10–15"

Joist hangers

Joist

Beam clearance and footing depth vary with local code

12"

A GROUND-LEVEL DECK

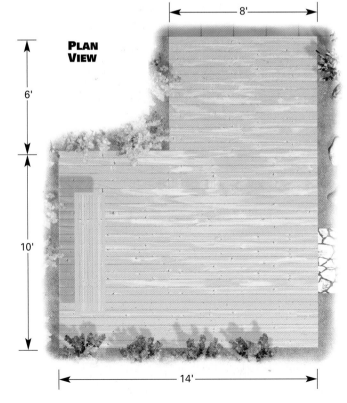

PLAN VIEW

8'

6'

10'

14'

This simple ground-level deck can be adapted to a variety of settings, including installations directly on the ground or over an existing patio. Sleepers run the entire length of the deck and decking runs across them for the entire width.

CONSTRUCTION NOTES

Despite its simplicity, this L-shaped deck makes an ideal transition area between the house and lawn. It provides a usable space away from the main traffic corridor, where a table or a pair of lounge chairs invite casual relaxing.

By building the deck in a shallow excavation and edging it with a masonry or concrete border, you can add a touch of elegance. A wood surface that is level with the ground creates a dignified and dramatic landscape element.

BUILDING THE DECK

This deck was designed to be built directly on or slightly below grade. For a long lasting structure, choose a site that drains well, and use pressure-treated wood that is rated for ground contact. You can alter the size and shape of this deck very easily by changing the length of the decking boards and the length and spacing of the sleepers.

SITE PREPARATION: Lay out the perimeter of the deck and excavate. For a deck surface that is flush with the surrounding grade, dig down 8 inches, and pour a concrete retaining border. For a deck that sits slightly above grade, a 3-inch excavation is plenty. After excavating, lay down landscape fabric to control weeds, and spread a 3-inch-thick layer of gravel.

CONSTRUCTION: The sleeper spacing on this deck is 42 inches, a span that requires 2×6 decking. If you use smaller decking boards, add more sleepers.
■ Cut the 4×4 sleepers to length and lay them on the gravel bed. Space sleepers for 2×4 decking no more than 24 inches apart; for 1-inch decking, space the sleepers no more than 16 inches apart.
■ Screw the decking to the sleepers with #8×2½-inch decking screws, two per sleeper. A layout line strung above each sleeper will help maintain a straight line of screws.

TRIM AND FINISH: For a flush deck, place the border before building the deck. With an above-grade deck, you can add a wooden fascia as a finishing touch. After all the construction is finished, stain or paint the deck to suit your taste.

MATERIALS LIST

Element	Quantity	Material	Length
Base	200 sq ft	landscape fabric (for weed control)	
	1.75 cu yd	¾" gravel	
Sleepers	2	4×4s	10'
	3	4×4s	16'
Decking	12	2×6s	8'
	20	2×6s	16'
Screws	10 lbs	#8×2½" deck screws, HDG (hot-dipped, galvanized)	
Border options			
A. Fascia	2	2×4s	6'
	1	2×4	10'
	1	2×4	14'
	1	2×4	16'
	1	2×4	18'
B. Concrete	1 cu yd	concrete	
	120'	1×8 (for forms)	
C. Brick	½ cu yd	concrete	
	360	paver bricks	
		mortar	

OPTIONS FOR BORDERS

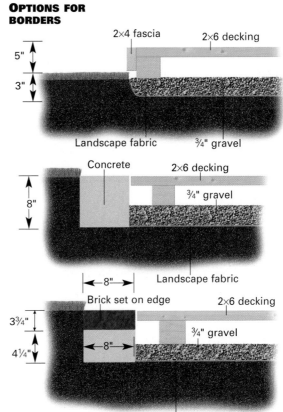

LAYING OUT SLEEPERS

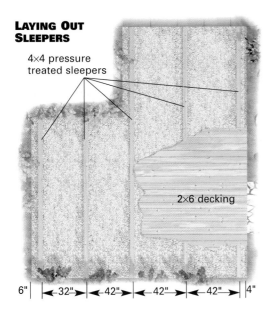

4×4 pressure treated sleepers

2×6 decking

6" 32" 42" 42" 42" 4"

REFURBISHING AN OLD PATIO

MATERIALS LIST

	Quantity	Material	Size
Footings	23 cu ft	concrete (for 8 piers 10" dia. × 36" and 8 footings 18" dia. × 8")	
	8	metal post anchors	
	16	⅜"×4½" carriage bolts with nuts and washers	
Sleepers	2	4×4s	8'
	4	4×4s	16'
		assorted shims and scrap blocks	
	1 tube	exterior construction adhesive	
Decking	16	2×6s	14'
	18	2×6s	10'
Fascia	2	2×8s	8'
	1	2×8	14'
Screws	10 lbs	#8×3½" decking screws	
Nails	1 lb	12d HDG common	

Although patios can be a useful and pleasing element in most landscapes, many are too small to be of much use. If you'd like to expand your patio—or replace an aging one—consider covering it with a larger deck. It's far easier and faster.

The deck featured in this plan is for a condominium with a small yard and a correspondingly small patio. By expanding the outdoor living area, the deck makes the limited space much more usable and enjoyable. It also provides a strong focal point for the yard and creates an inviting transition between outside and inside.

PREPARATION

A concrete or masonry patio is an excellent base for a deck, and it requires no special preparation, even if it is in marginal condition. If you want to extend your deck beyond the patio, however, you must provide support for the outside edge of the deck. If the patio is fairly level, you may be able to prepare a gravel bed beyond the patio and lay sleepers directly on it.

More likely, the patio slopes significantly (more than ¼ inch or so per foot) away from house, making it difficult to level the sleepers. In this case, you'll need concrete piers and footings. (See pages 120–121.)

Lay out the piers, dig the holes, then form and pour the piers. Because the sleepers will bear directly on the piers, with no posts, it is critical that all of the piers are level with one another. The easiest way to ensure this is to form and pour your own piers, rather than installing precast units.

BUILDING

SLEEPERS: This plan uses 4×4 sleepers, which function as beams. Make them from pressure-treated or naturally durable stock such as redwood or cedar. Note that when placing sleepers on a sloped patio, the sleepers must run parallel with the slope so that they don't become dams that trap water.

■ Lay out the sleepers as shown in the framing plan at right.

■ Level each sleeper periodically with shims, nailing the shims to the bottom.

■ Attach the sleepers to the patio with exterior construction adhesive.

FASCIA AND DECKING: It is best to lay out all the decking first so you can get the spacing just right.

■ Nail 2×8 fascia boards to the exposed sides and ends of the sleepers to give the deck a finished appearance.

■ Screw the decking to the sleepers with #8×3½-inch decking screws. Drive two screws per board into each sleeper.

FRAMING PLAN

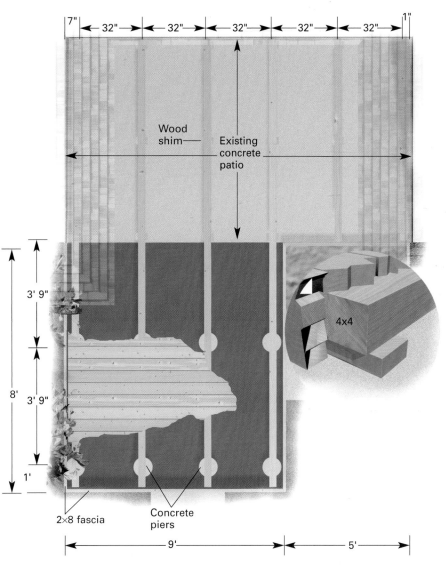

7" | 32" | 32" | 32" | 32" | 32" | 1"

Wood shim

Existing concrete patio

4x4

3' 9"

8'

3' 9"

1'

2×8 fascia

Concrete piers

9'   5'

SECTION

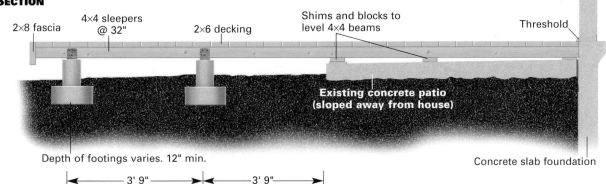

2×8 fascia

4×4 sleepers @ 32"

2×6 decking

Shims and blocks to level 4×4 beams

Threshold

Existing concrete patio (sloped away from house)

Depth of footings varies. 12" min.

Concrete slab foundation

3' 9"   3' 9"

A HILLSIDE DECK

This deck features an extremely versatile and widely used construction system. Its foundation, like that for many of the decks in this book, consists of poured concrete piers, sunk in the ground below frost level. Metal brackets, cast into the top of the piers, anchor wooden posts that rise to support wooden beams. The beams then carry the floor joists and decking. By varying the size and spacing of the posts, beams, and/or joists, you can design almost any size deck that will still carry the necessary loads.

CONSTRUCTION NOTES

This design is appropriate for flat sites as well as slopes. Because the posts are easily cut, the piers don't have to be absolutely level.

The deck featured here is freestanding—that is, it doesn't rely on another structure for support, although you could easily adapt it to do so. Building a freestanding deck is often easier, because you don't have to tie it to an existing building. The built-in bench featured in this plan is very sturdy and gives a simple, clean look to the deck.

PLAN VIEW

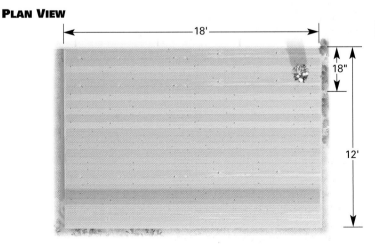

18'

18"

12'

ADAPTING FOR SLOPES

The illustration on the opposite page shows the deck constructed on a gentle slope, but the structure could easily be adapted for steeper slopes by lengthening the posts and increasing the footing depths.

Railings are required along any side of the deck that is more than 30 inches above the ground (check your local building code for the exact requirements). For gentle slopes, a bench may be sufficient protection.

LAYOUT AND FOOTINGS

You'll need four mason's lines to lay out this deck—one to mark one end of the deck and the others to represent an edge of each beam. The steeper the slope, the more difficult the layout will be because all measurements have to be made along a horizontal plane rather than along the slope. For more information on laying out a site, see pages 118–119.

■ Set batter boards and stretch mason's line between them to make the layout.
■ Measure along the beam lines to locate the footings.
■ Drive stakes to mark the holes, then temporarily remove the lines so you can excavate. When excavating for footings on a slope, measure the depth of the hole from the downhill edge.
■ Place the forms in the holes and pour the footings and piers.
■ As you set the forms, make sure that all the forms are level and that the metal post

brackets are in line. Restring your layout lines and use them to position the anchors in the wet concrete.

POSTS, BEAMS, AND JOISTS

If the posts are not made of pressure-treated lumber, you should soak their ends in a preservative first.
■ Cut the posts about 6 inches longer than necessary and bolt them to the top of the piers. Plumb them and brace them with diagonal 2×4s.
■ Mark the top of the uppermost posts and cut them to length.
■ Use these posts as a reference to mark the remaining posts and cut them.
■ Bolt the beams to the posts, aligning the beam ends with the layout line that marks the end of the deck.
■ Toenail the 2×6 joists to the beams and nail blocking between the joists along the center beam.
■ Snap chalk lines along both ends of the joists to mark the long edges of the deck.

DECKING AND FASCIA

Before attaching the decking, bolt the 2×8 bench uprights to the joists as shown on page 203. When you install the uprights, be sure they're level and equidistant from the joists.
■ Mark each upright exactly 18 inches from the top end, and align this mark along the top edge of the joist when bolting it.
■ Clamp the uprights to the joists to hold

A HILLSIDE DECK
continued

them in place as you drill the bolt holes.
■ Provide support for the decking under the bench by nailing a wood cleat onto the side of each upright opposite the joist.
■ Screw the deck boards to the joists using two screws at the end of each board.
■ When you reach the 2×8 bench uprights, either notch a long deck board to fit around them or cut short lengths of decking to fit in between.
■ Once the decking is in place, nail the fascia around the outside edge of the deck, keeping the fascia's top edge flush with the deck surface. Miter the corners for a more finished look.

BENCH DETAILS

After the decking is in place, assemble the rest of the bench.
■ Cut off the corners of the cleats so the ends will be hidden behind the 2×4 trim as shown.
■ Bolt the cleats in place so they are centered on the 2×8 upright and level.
■ Nail the 2×2s to the cleats to make the seats.
■ Toenail the pieces in place so the nails don't show. You may find it necessary to predrill the holes to keep the pieces from splitting.
■ When all the 2×2s are in place, trim their ends.
■ Install the 2×4 trim boards around the bench's perimeter, mitering the corners for a more finished look.

MATERIALS LIST

	Quantity	Material	Size
Footings	11 cu ft	concrete (for 9 piers 8" dia. × 36" and 9 footings 18" dia. × 8")	
	9	metal post anchors	
		18⅜"×4½" carriage bolts with nuts and washers	
Framing			
Posts	1	4×4	8' (for 6 short posts)
Beams	3	4×6s	18'
Joists	10	2×6s	12'
Blocking	2	2×6s	10' (cut into 9 22½" pieces)
	9	metal post/beam connectors	
	18	⅜" x 4½" carriage bolts with nuts and washers	
Decking	24	2×6s	8'
	24	2×6s	10'
Fascia	2	2×8s	12'
	2	2×8s	10'
	2	2×8s	8'
Bench			
Uprights	2	2×8s	10' (cut into 10 23½" pieces)
Upper & Lower Cleats	4	2×4s	8' (cut into 20 15" pieces)
Seat	21	2×2s	8'
Trim	4	2×4s	10'
Bolts	20	⅜"×5" carriage bolts w/ nuts and washers	
	20	⅜"×3½" carriage bolts w/ nuts and washers	
Nails	5 lbs	8d HDG finish nails (for bench)	
	7 lbs	16d HDG common nails	
Screws	10 lbs	3½" decking screws	

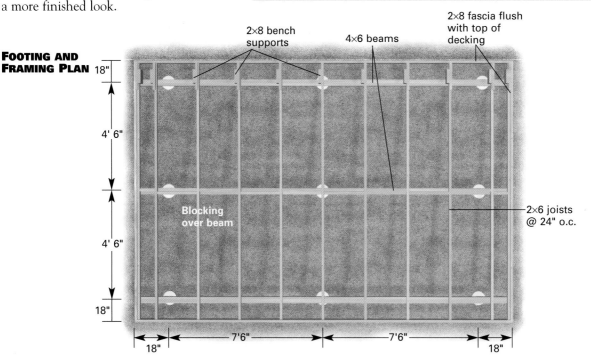

FOOTING AND FRAMING PLAN

2×8 bench supports

4×6 beams

2×8 fascia flush with top of decking

18"

4' 6"

Blocking over beam

4' 6"

18"

2×6 joists @ 24" o.c.

18"   7'6"   7'6"   18"

END VIEW

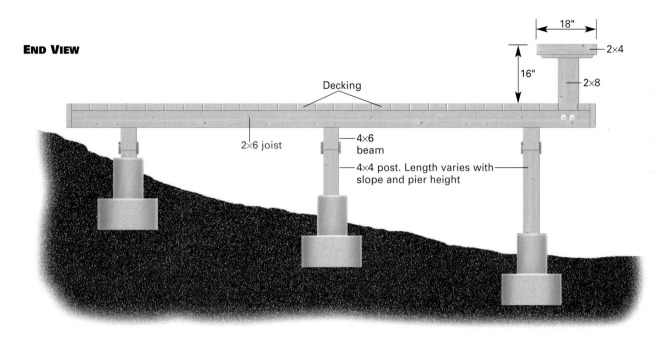

18"

16"

2×4

2×8

Decking

2×6 joist

4×6 beam

4×4 post. Length varies with slope and pier height

DOWNHILL SIDE

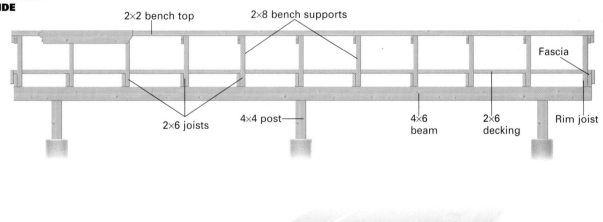

2×2 bench top

2×8 bench supports

Fascia

2×6 joists

4×4 post

4×6 beam

2×6 decking

Rim joist

BENCH DETAIL

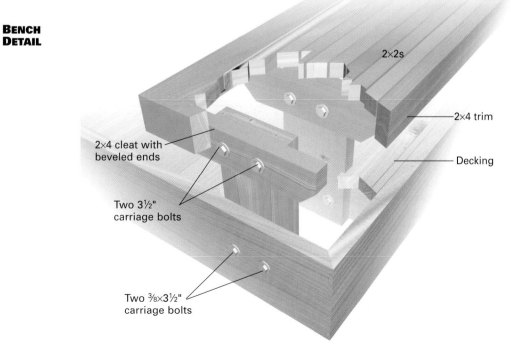

2×2s

2×4 trim

2×4 cleat with beveled ends

Decking

Two 3½" carriage bolts

Two ⅜×3½" carriage bolts

A MULTILEVEL DECK

A deck that follows the contours of slope offers several advantages. First, its stepped design minimizes the amount of grading the must be done to accommodate the structure. And, if the slope is not too steep, you can keep all parts of the deck close to enough to the ground to eliminate the need for railings. Multiple levels can also help define areas of the deck for specific uses such as dining or socializing.

CONSTRUCTION NOTES

In order to keep the deck as low to the ground as possible, this design combines two different structural systems. On the lower platform, the decking is supported directly by 4×6 beams which rest on poured concrete piers. Because there are no posts between the beams and the piers, the piers must all be level with one another. Note that you can alter the design to include posts if such a

modification better suits your site. the piers in this plan are poured separately after their footings, but you can modify your installation by using poured in place piers or precast piers.

The upper platform is supported by a beam-and-joist structure. Posts on piers raise the platform to a height approximately 28 to 30 inches above grade—generally the maximum height allowed for decks without requiring railings.

The two levels and the intermediate step are all tied together structurally. Not only does this provide an economic use of materials, it also makes it easier to keep all the elements level with each other. The vertical spacing between the levels is also planned with standard framing lumber in mind. The rise of each step is 7½"—the actual width of a 2×8.

To keep the lower platform as close to the ground as possible, you can excavate shallow trenches between the piers that will carry the low beams. Sloping these trenches will also improve the ability of the soil under the deck to drain effectively.

This design calls for spans that are near the maximum for the size of lumber specified. Lower grades of lumber will necessitate reducing the spans.

LAYOUT AND FOOTINGS

Start your layout with batterboards and mason's line. For information about how to make batter boards and to get additional layout tips, see page 118.

■ Set one pair of batter boards and stretch a line to indicate the center of the long beam (shown at the left edge of the Footing and Beam Plan on page 206).

■ Set another pair of batter boards and stretch a second line for the piers that will carry the ends of the short beams (those across the bottom of the drawing.)

The lines should cross directly over the center of the corner pier and should be perpendicular to each other.

■ Measure from the intersection point to lay out the positions of the various piers along the two lines, using the dimensions shown in the Footing and Beam Plan.

■ Drop a plumb bob from the lines to mark the center of the holes, and drive a stake into the ground to mark each pier.

■ Set a third pair of batter boards and stretch a line for the second long beam, making sure it is perpendicular to the line you used to mark the bottom row of piers.

■ Stake the pier centers along this line as you did for the others.

■ Finally, set batter boards and lines for the remaining three sets of piers (those perpendicular to the long beams). Measure and stake as before.

■ Take down the lines but leave the batter boards in place for now.

■ Dig the holes for the footings, put the forms in place, and fill them with concrete.

SAFETY NOTE

There is an important safety consideration to keep in mind when designing a multilevel deck. Changes in level can be difficult to see, especially in dim light. Then, too, the parallel pattern of the decking can also camouflage changes in level, even under a bright sun.

You can solve this problem with lighting for night time use or by altering the pattern on the deck.

PLAN VIEW

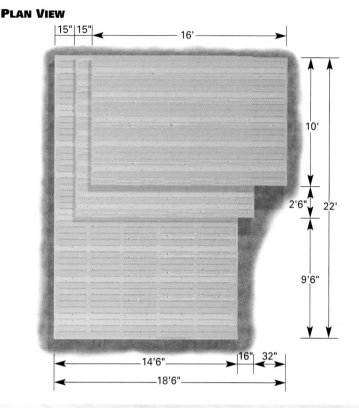

MATERIALS LIST

Element	Quantity	Material	Size
Footings	2 cu yards	concrete (for 20 piers 8" dia. × 36" and 20 footings 18" dia. × 8")	
	20	metal post anchors	
	40	3/8"×4½" carriage bolts with nuts and washers	
Framing			
Posts	1	4×4	4' (for 4 short posts)
Beams	2	4×6s	8'
	4	4×6s	10'
	2	4×6s	14'
	2	4×8s	16'
Joists	1	2×6	16'
	2	2×6s	8' (for six 30" joists)
	9	2×8s	10'
	2	2×8s	12' (for six 48" joists)
	2	2×8s	14'
	3	2×8s	16'
Blocking	1	2×6	12' (for five 28½" pieces)
	2	2×8s	8' (for eight 22½" pieces)
Joist hangers	10	2×6s	
	13	2×8s	
Decking	47	4×6s	16'
Fascia	2	2×4s	10'
	2	2×4s	12'
	4	2×4s	16'
Nails	4 lbs	joist hanger nails	
	10 lbs	16d HDG common nails	
Screws	20 lbs	#8×3½" decking screws	

A MULTILEVEL DECK

continued

■ When the footings harden, restring the lines and center the forms for the piers directly under the lines.

■ Double-check to make sure the distance between the piers is correct, and level the tops of the piers, trimming the tops of the forms if necessary.

■ Fill the forms with concrete, and set post anchors into the wet concrete, centered under the layout lines. Measure to make sure the distance from anchor to anchor is correct.

FOOTING AND BEAM PLAN

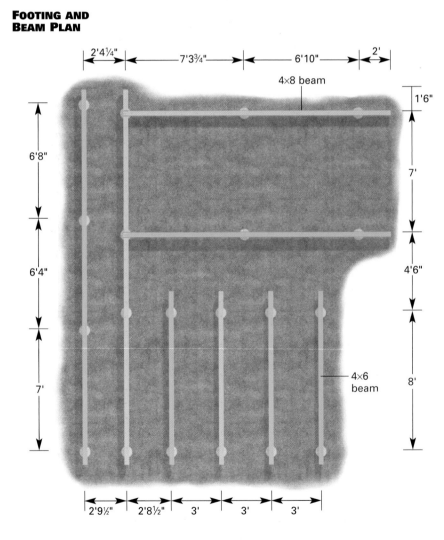

FRAMING

Install the 4×6 beams first, drilling and bolting them in place.

■ Cut posts to support the 4×8 beams and bolt them to the remaining four piers.

■ Install the 4×8 beams on top of these posts. Note: One end of each 4×8 beam rests on one of the 4×6 beams.

LOWER DECK: The narrow part of the lower deck is framed with short 2×6 joists hung between the beams on joist hangers.

■ For air circulation, cut the joists about ¼-inch short to provide a gap at each end.

■ Nail the joist hangers to the joists first. Hold them in place and nail the hangers to the beam or stringer. This way you can be sure the top of the joist will be flush with the top of the beam.

■ To frame the step, hang short 2×8 joists from the side of one of the 4×8 beams with joist hangers.

■ Attach the other ends to the rim joist, which rests on the ends of the short 4×6 beams.

Two long 2×8 joists resting on the short 2×6 joists you installed previously complete the stair framing.

■ Frame the upper deck by toenailing the 2×8 joists to the 4×8 beams.

■ Nail a rim joist to both ends of the joists. Because the rim joist surfaces will be visible, be careful not to mar them.

■ Install blocking between the upper deck joists and the short, lower deck joists.

DECKING AND FASCIA

Start the decking flush at the end and work toward the step, ripping the last board to fit, if necessary.

■ Start the step and platform from the edge closest to the lower platform, the first board flush with the rim joist.

■ Nail the fascia to the edges of the two decks and the steps as shown in the illustration labeled "Section Through Side Steps" on page 208. Miter the corners.

FOOTING AND FRAMING PLAN

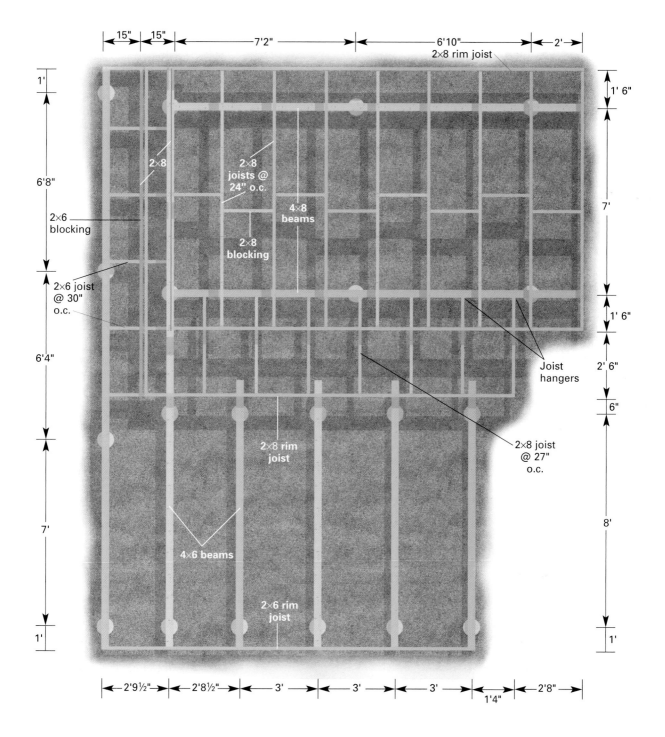

15" 15" 7'2" 6'10" 2'

2×8 rim joist

1' 1' 6"

6'8" 7'

2×8

2×8 joists @ 24" o.c.

4×8 beams

2×6 blocking

2×8 blocking

2×6 joist @ 30" o.c.

1' 6"

2' 6"

Joist hangers

6'4" 6"

2×8 joist @ 27" o.c.

2×8 rim joist

7' 8'

4×6 beams

2×6 rim joist

1' 1'

2'9½" 2'8½" 3' 3' 3' 2'8"

1'4"

A MULTILEVEL DECK
continued

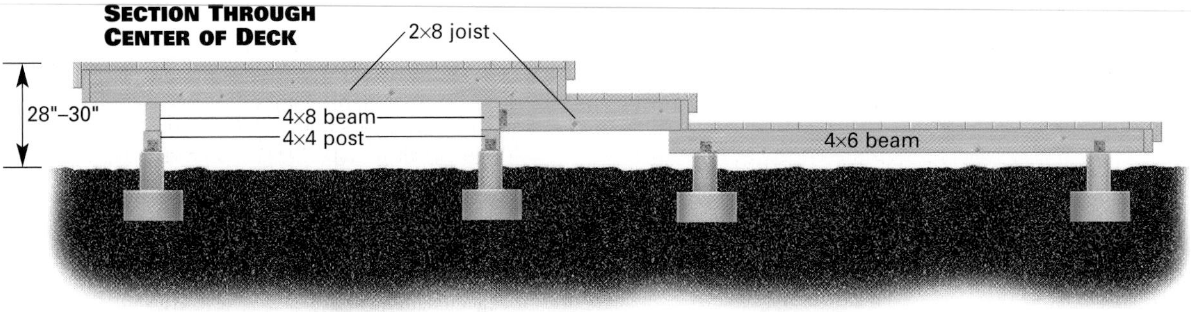

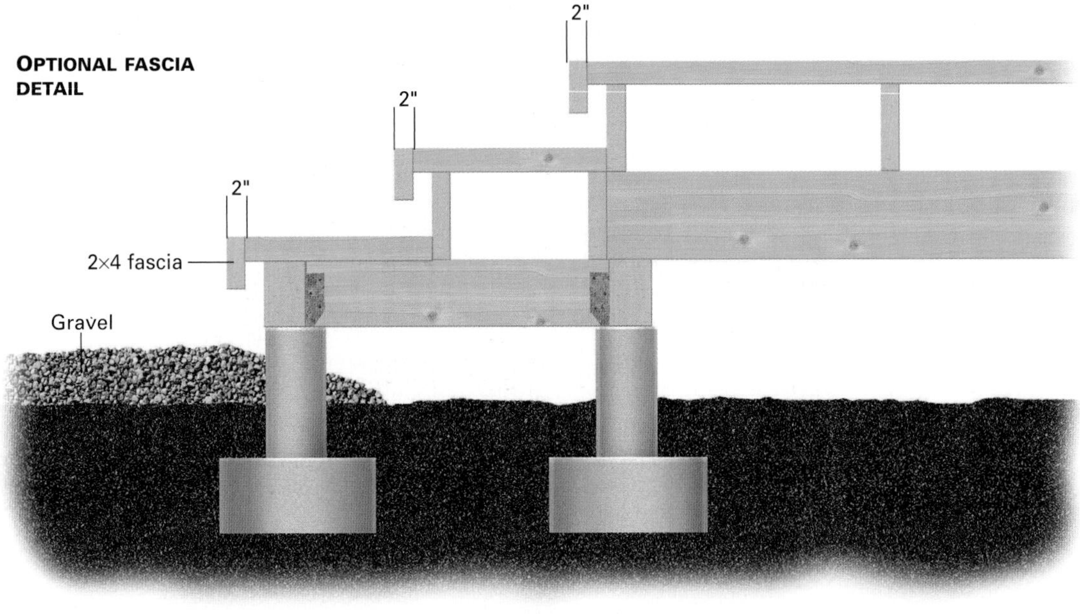

SECTION THROUGH CENTER OF DECK

2×8 joist

28"–30"

4×8 beam
4×4 post
4×6 beam

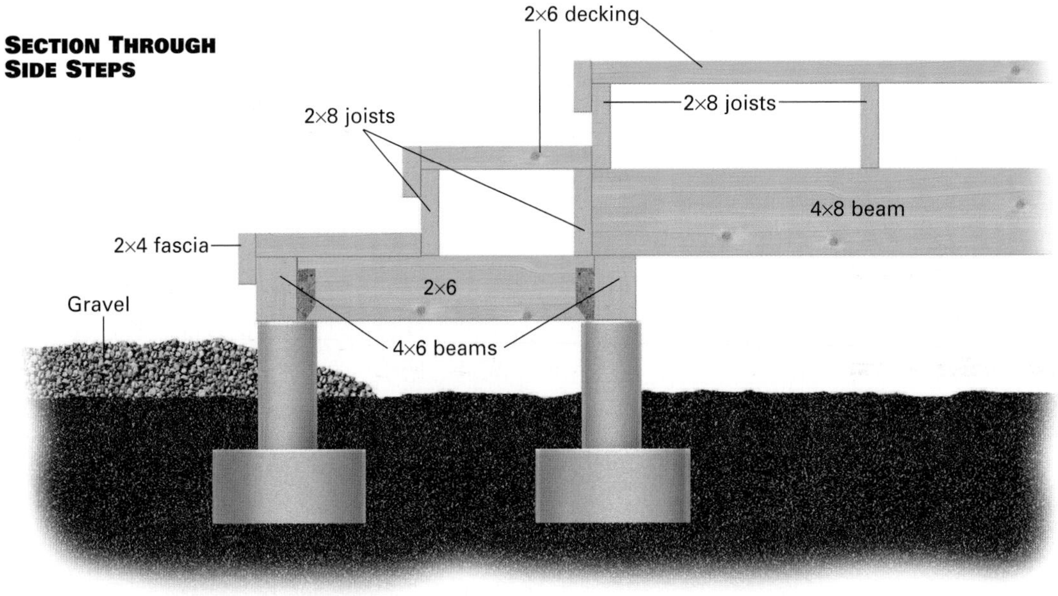

SECTION THROUGH SIDE STEPS

2×6 decking

2×8 joists

2×8 joists

4×8 beam

2×4 fascia

Gravel

2×6

4×6 beams

OPTIONAL FASCIA DETAIL

2"

2"

2"

2×4 fascia

Gravel

DECK PATTERN VARIATION

If you have longer decking boards, you may want to alter the pattern of the decking. The variation with the border shown here results in a more formal appearance. The Footing and Framing Plan for Variation (below) shows the same footing locations, beam structure, and upper platform joists as the plan on page 204. The major changes are the addition of short joists between the outer beams of the lower platform and between the joists along the left side of the upper step.

MULTILEVEL DECK VARIATION

Dimensions do not include fascia.

FOOTING AND FRAMING PLAN FOR VARIATION

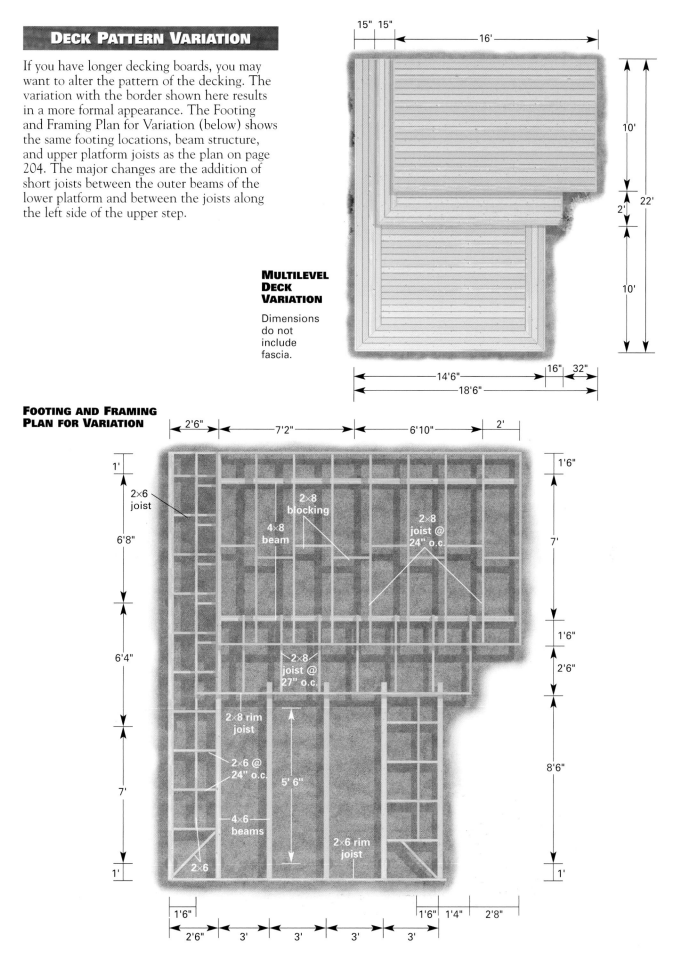

A PLATFORM DECK WITH STEPS

For a home with a first floor that is several steps above ground level, this multilevel deck can make the perfect transition between house and yard. The design features a series of steps and platforms that cascade away from the doorway to the garden below. Because the height of this deck averages 20 to 30 inches above grade, it won't require railings in most localities, but it does use benches to help define individual areas. Check with your building code officials to make sure you design conforms to local specifications.

CONSTRUCTION NOTES

The deck itself is free standing, supported on concrete piers. Four by four posts rise from the piers to carry 4×8 beams, which in turn support the joists and decking. Each of the two platforms uses two beams.

A fifth beam, located where the platforms meet, carries some of the weight of each section. This fifth beam shares oversize posts with beams for the upper platform. The two beams are bolted together for added stability.

Steps lead off both sides of the lower platform to the ground below. Depending on the drop, a simple box step (as shown on the right hand side of the deck illustration, above) may be enough, or you can build a conventional stairway (shown on the left side, above) with stringers and treads.

Two wide steps run the full length of the upper deck, to provide seating and leading traffic into the house. These stairs are the only part of the deck actually connected to the house. They are supported by a series of short joists, one end of which bears on the deck, the other hung from a ledger bolted to the house.

LAYOUT AND FOOTINGS

Start your layout with batter boards and mason's lines.
■ Stretch lines to represent the center of the two beams for the upper platform. Use the house as a reference from which to measure.

PLAN VIEW

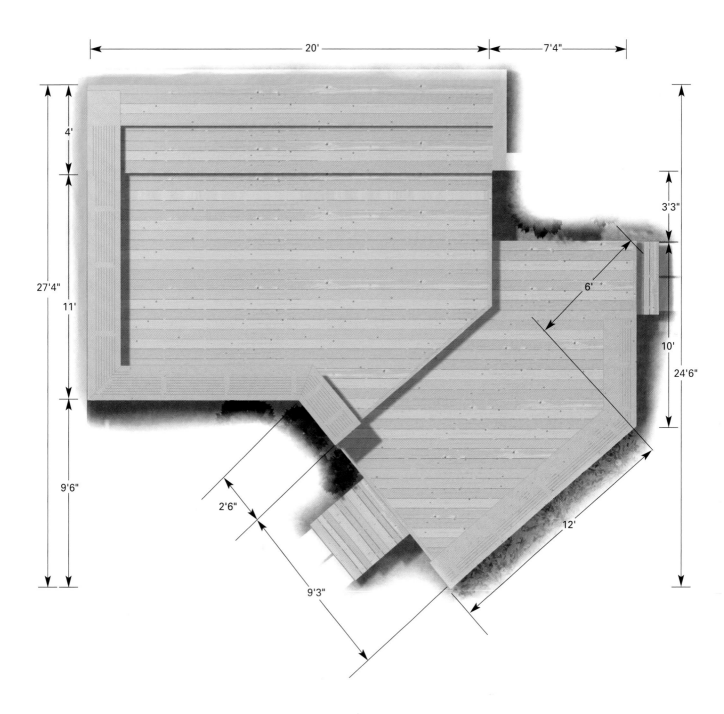

■ Once you have them in place, set these lines for the remaining beams at the proper angle (130 degrees), using the steps outlined on the following pages.

■ Begin by tying a new line—for the shared beam—to batter boards about 2 feet beyond where you think each end of the beam will be. The point where the new string crosses the others is where two beams come together.

■ Adjust the new line until the intersection is properly situated.

A PLATFORM DECK WITH STEPS

continued

■ Mark both lines at this point.
■ Make another mark—on either of the lines—6 feet from where they cross.
■ Mark the other line 8 feet from where they cross.
■ Adjust the angle of the new line until the distance between the marks equals 12 feet-9 inches. (See the opposite page for an illustration of this technique.)

As you adjust the lines, make sure they continue to cross at the proper place.
■ Stretch the lines for the other beams parallel to the one you've just positioned.
■ Mark the ground for the footing holes, then remove the strings. Dig the holes, set the forms, and pour the footings.
■ Put the lines back on the batter boards to help locate the pier forms.
■ Pour the piers and set metal post anchors in the wet concrete.

FRAMING

LEDGER: Locate the top of the ledger for the steps leading into the house 10 inches below floor level. This allows for rise of the stair plus 1½-inch thick stair treads and a 1-inch drop outside the door for weather protection. Attach the ledger with any of the methods shown on pages 116–117.

POSTS: The deck's height is set by the length of the posts.
■ Cut the posts 3 inches too long and bolt them to the piers.
■ With a transit or a water level, mark them at the proper level, using the top of the ledger as a reference.
■ Mark the tops of the posts for the upper platform 15 inches below the top of the ledger. Mark those for the lower platform 22½ inches below the ledger.

BEAMS AND JOISTS: After the posts are cut, bolt the beams in place.
■ Install the joists and rim joists, starting with the lower platform and working your way up.

MATERIALS LIST

	Quantity	Material	Sizes
Footings	1 cu yd	concrete for 11 piers (8" dia. × 36") and 11 footings (18" dia. × 8")	
	11	metal post anchors	
	22	⅜"×4½" carriage bolts with nuts and washers	
Framing			
Ledger	2	2×8s	10'
Posts		4×4s	(varies with site)
	1	4×8	(length varies with site)
Beams	1	4×8	8'
	3	4×8s	10'
	2	4×8s	12'
	1	4×8	14'
Joists	11	2×8s	8'
	5	2×8s	10'
	10	2×8s	12'
	1	2×8	14'
	3	2×6s	8'
	1	2×6	10'
	8	2×6s	12'
Blocking	1	2×8	8' (cut into 22½" +/- pieces)
	1	2×8	10' (cut into 22½" +/- pieces)
	2	2×6s	8' (cut into 22½" +/- pieces)
Joist hangers	6	2×6s	
	11	2×8s	
Corner joist hangers	2	2×8	
	1	2×6	
Post to Beam Connectors	10	4×4	
	1	4×8	
Bolts	18	½" dia. × 5" lag bolts with 90 washers	
	44	⅜" dia. × 4½" carriage bolts with nuts and washers	
	6	½"×4" carriage bolts and washers	
	2	⅝"×10 carriage bolts with nuts	
Decking	42	2×6s	8'
	54	2×6s	10'
Fascia	2	2×4s	8'
	6	2×4s	10'
	2	2×4s	12'
	1	2×4	14'
Bench			
Uprights	3	2×12s	10' (cut into 24 14½" pieces)
Cleats	2	2×4s	12' (cut into 24 11¼" pieces)
Aprons	2	2×4s	16'
	5	2×4s	12'
	1	2×4	8"
Seat	2	2×4s	16'
	5	2×4s	12'
	1	2×4	8"
Stairs			
Stringer	1	2×12	12'
Treads	3	2×6s	12'
	3	2×4s	12'
Nails	3 lbs	joist hanger nails	
	25 lbs	16d HDG common nails	
Screws	30 lbs	#8×3½" deck screws	

FOOTING AND FRAMING PLAN

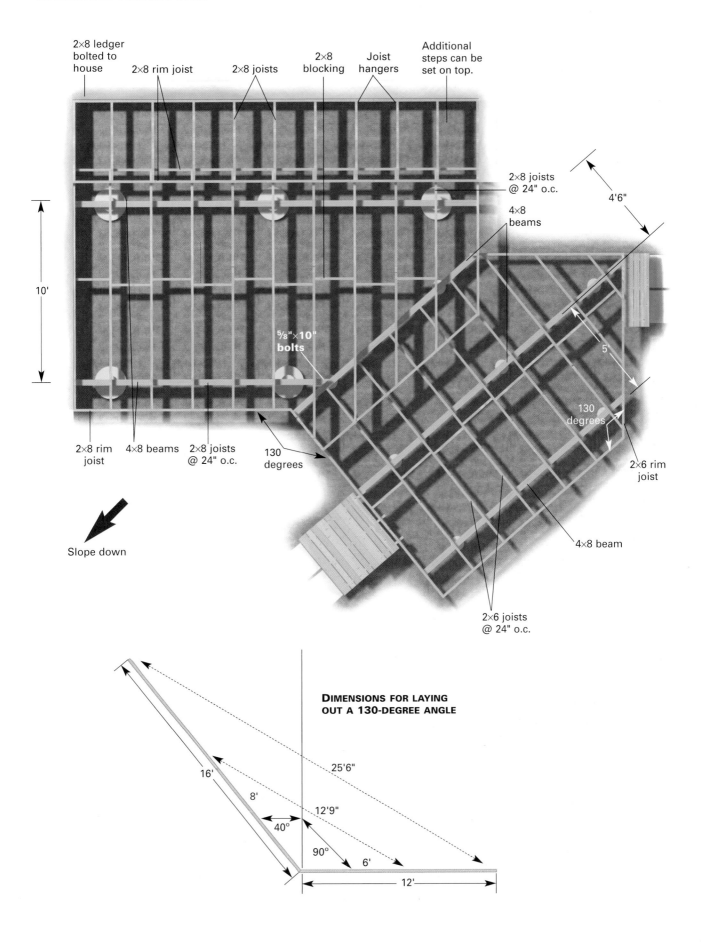

2×8 ledger bolted to house

2×8 rim joist

2×8 joists

2×8 blocking

Joist hangers

Additional steps can be set on top.

2×8 joists @ 24" o.c.

4×8 beams

4'6"

5

130 degrees

2×6 rim joist

2×8 rim joist

4×8 beams

2×8 joists @ 24" o.c.

130 degrees

$^5/_8$"×10" bolts

10'

Slope down

4×8 beam

2×6 joists @ 24" o.c.

DIMENSIONS FOR LAYING OUT A 130-DEGREE ANGLE

16'

8'

40°

90°

6'

25'6"

12'9"

12'

A PLATFORM DECK WITH STEPS
continued

■ Screw the decking boards to the joists, two screws per board per joist. Add the fascia to finish the process.

FRAMING DETAIL

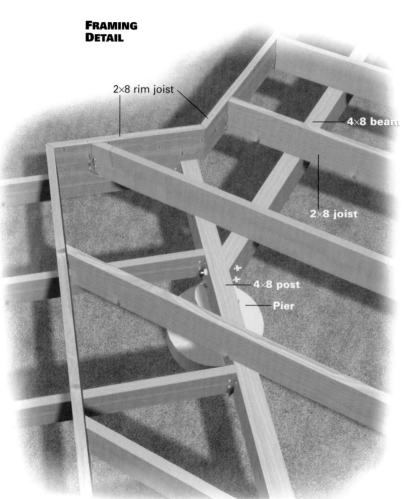

2×8 rim joist

4×8 beam

2×8 joist

4×8 post

Pier

BENCHES

The benches on this deck are built in place.
■ Start by cutting the pieces to size, then bolt the 2×4 cleats to all the uprights.
■ Lay out the location of each upright on the deck. Predrill the uprights. To make sure each upright is aligned properly, square it against the edge of the deck with a framing square and then toenail it in place. Set the nails carefully for a neat appearance.
■ After the uprights are in place, plumb them.
■ Then screw the apron pieces to either side, using two screws per apron per upright.
   Note: The apron runs up onto the stair at the top of the deck and can be toenailed in place.
■ Nail a line of 2×4s to the cleats along the outside edge to start forming the seat.
■ Fill in the middle of the seat with 2×2s. Use nails as spacers to maintain an even gap between the pieces.
■ You can toenail the pieces through their sides to keep the nails from showing if you want to.
■ Stagger the end joints and miter the pieces at the corners.

ACCESS STAIRS

Build stairs after the deck is finished, following the illustrations in this sections and using the techniques discussed on pages 130–133.

SECTION

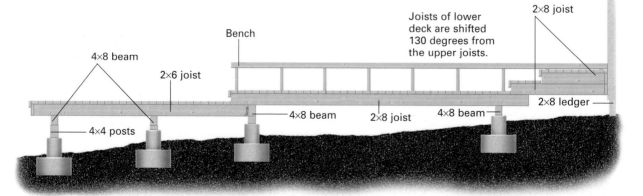

Bench

Joists of lower deck are shifted 130 degrees from the upper joists.

2×8 joist

4×8 beam

2×6 joist

4×4 posts

4×8 beam

2×8 joist

4×8 beam

2×8 ledger

**STAIR AND
BENCH DETAILS**

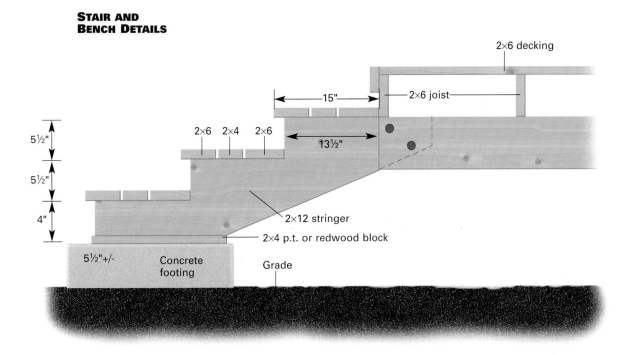

2×6 decking

15"

2×6 joist

2×6   2×4   2×6

13½"

5½"

5½"

4"

2×12 stringer

2×4 p.t. or redwood block

5½"+/-

Concrete footing

Grade

BENCH DETAIL

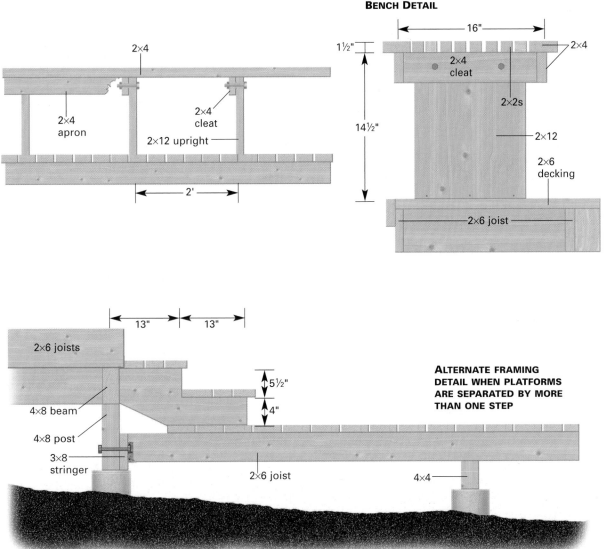

2×4

2×4 apron

2×4 cleat

2×12 upright

2'

16"

1½"

2×4

2×4 cleat

2×2s

2×12

2×6 decking

14½"

2×6 joist

13"   13"

2×6 joists

5½"

4"

**ALTERNATE FRAMING
DETAIL WHEN PLATFORMS
ARE SEPARATED BY MORE
THAN ONE STEP**

4×8 beam

4×8 post

3×8 stringer

2×6 joist

4×4

A WRAPAROUND DECK

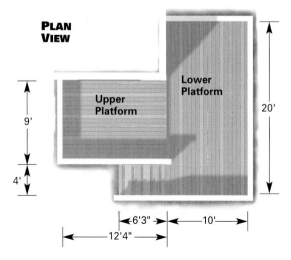

PLAN VIEW

Upper Platform

Lower Platform

9'

4'

20'

6'3"

10'

12'4"

Despite its grand appearance, this deck is actually a simple two-level platform. Wrapped around a corner of the house, it combines privacy and style. Trim and siding integrate the design with the architecture of the home.

GROUNDWORK

POSITION: After clearing and preparing the building site, set up batter boards and mason's lines to establish the ledger and footing locations. Take care that the lines intersect at the outside edges of the posts.

Mark the locations for the footings and

piers, remove the mason's lines, and dig footing holes. Follow local building codes for hole depth and width. Reset the lines.

CONCRETE: Set and level the concrete forms in the footing holes and pour the footings. Set post anchors in the wet concrete, with the outer edge flush with the mason's lines.

LEDGERS AND POSTS

Each level of the deck is held up on one side by its own 2×10 ledger bolted to the house. The lower ledger starts as a single 2×10 and becomes doubled where it extends past the house.

■ Snap a line 2½ inches below floor level on the house to indicate the top of the ledger.

■ Mark a line for the lower ledger on the adjacent wall, 7½ inches below the first line.

■ Using the procedures on pages 116–117, remove the siding with a circular saw and bolt the upper ledger in place.

■ Cut the pieces of the lower ledger and assemble them with 8d nails or 3-inch decking screws every 16 inches.

■ Set the far post in its anchor and brace it.

■ Brace the lower ledger and bolt it to the house and to the far post.

POUR LANDING WITH PIERS

To save time, pour the stairway landing at the same time as the footings or piers.

Dig a hole 8 inches deep, 42 inches wide, and 60 inches long. Level 4 inches of gravel in the hole. Build a form for the landing with 2×10 lumber.

Fill the form with concrete and, before the concrete hardens, set anchor bolts for attaching the stringers at the bottom of the stairs.

MATERIALS LIST

	Quantity	Material	Size
Footings	1 cu yd	concrete for 12 piers (8" dia. × 36") and 12 footings (18" dia. × 8")	
	12	metal post anchors	
	24	⅜"×4½" carriage bolts with nuts and washers	
Stair Landing	.25 cu yd	concrete (7 cu ft) for 6"×36"×54" slab	
	2	anchor bolts for 2×4 cleat	
Framing			
Posts	15	4×4s	8'
Ledger	1	2×10	12'
Ledger/Beam	1	2×10	14'
	1	2×10	20'
Beams	2	2×8s	12'
	4	2×8s	10'
Joists	18	2×8s	10'
Blocking	4	2×8s	8' lengths
Ledger bolts	18	½" × 6" lag bolts with 90 washers	
Post bolts	8	½" × 8" lag bolts and washers	
Beam bolts	16	½" × 7" carriage bolts with nuts and washers	
	10	½" × 6" carriage bolts with nuts and washers	
	2	½" × 11" carriage bolts with nuts and washers	
Joist hangers	2×8s	39	
Decking	40	2×6s	10'
	18	2×6s	12'
Stair Treads	2×6s	4	10' (for 5 steps)
	2×2s	2	10' (for 5 steps)
Railing and Skirts (68 lineal feet)			
Frame	27	2×4s	8'
	7	2×4s	10'
	2	2×4s	12'
	1	2×4	16'
Cap rail	1	2×6	8'
	5	2×6s	10'
	1	2×6	12'
Siding		Sheathing and/or siding material to cover 700 sq ft (460 on outside of deck, 210 on inside of railings + 5% waste)	
Trim	2	1×4s	8'
	10	1×4s	10'
	2	1×4s	12'
Flashing			6" wide by 68' long
Nails	15 lbs	16d HDG common nails	
	5 lbs.	Joist hanger nails	
		Nails for siding and/or sheathing, depending on material used.	
Screws	17 lbs	#8×3½" deck screws	

A WRAPAROUND DECK
continued

■ Brace and plumb the remaining posts in their anchors, but do not cut them. You'll cut them when the deck platform is finished.
■ Mark posts level with the ledgers they face.

BEAMS

■ Nail the 2×8s for the beams together with two 8d nails or screws driven every 16 inches.
■ Prop the beams in place so their top is flush with the mark on each post.
■ Drill holes and bolt the beams to the post.

JOISTS AND DECKING

■ Install joists 24 inches on center, hanging them between the ledger and beams with joist hangers.
■ Install blocking for both levels.
■ Install the decking boards so their edges are tight against the posts.
■ Trim the single step with 2×4 fascia.

**SECTION THROUGH
BOTH PLATFORMS**

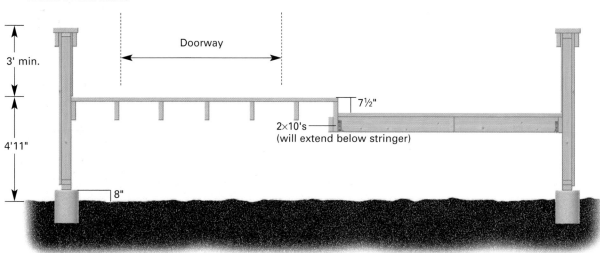

Doorway

3' min.

4'11"

7½"

2×10's
(will extend below stringer)

8"

**SECTION THROUGH
LOWER PLATFORM**

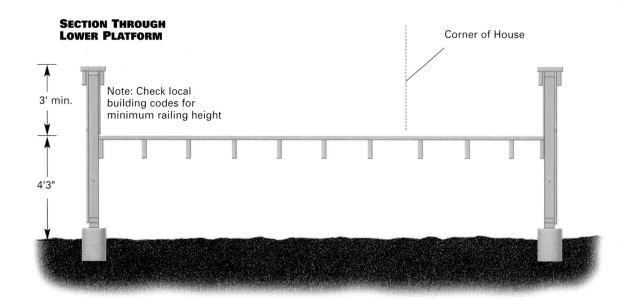

Corner of House

3' min.

Note: Check local
building codes for
minimum railing height

4'3"

**FOOTING AND
FRAMING PLAN**

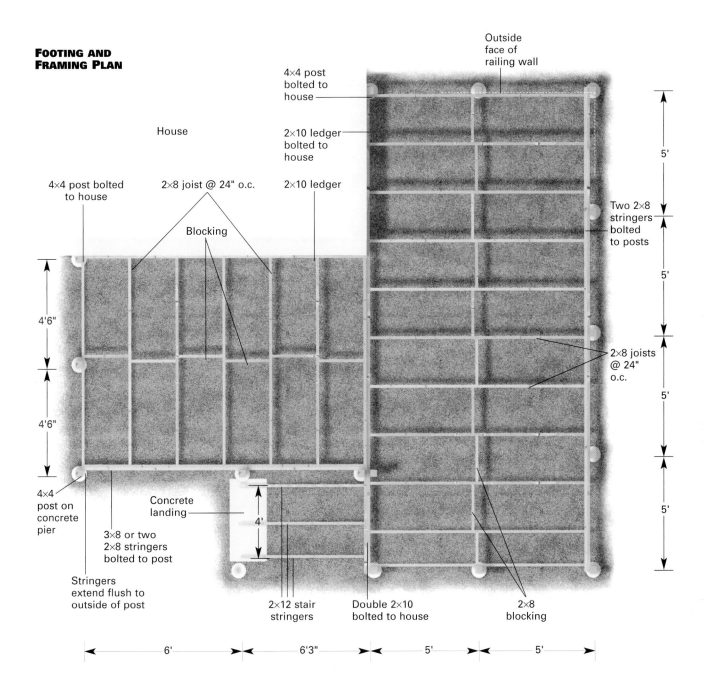

Outside
face of
railing wall

4×4 post
bolted to
house

2×10 ledger
bolted to
house

House

4×4 post bolted
to house

2×8 joist @ 24" o.c.

2×10 ledger

Blocking

Two 2×8
stringers
bolted
to posts

4'6"

2×8 joists
@ 24"
o.c.

4'6"

5'

5'

5'

5'

4×4
post on
concrete
pier

Concrete
landing

4'

3×8 or two
2×8 stringers
bolted to post

Stringers
extend flush to
outside of post

2×12 stair
stringers

Double 2×10
bolted to house

2×8
blocking

6'   6'3'   5'   5'

A WRAPAROUND DECK

continued

FRAMING DETAIL

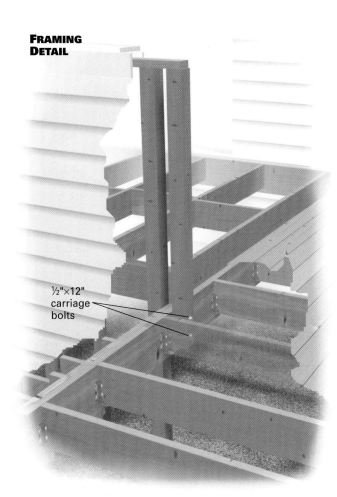

½"×12" carriage bolts

To lay out the stringers, measure the total rise (from the top of the landing to the underside of the decking) and run (from the outside of the stair cleat to a point 7 inches from the edge of the deck). Then use the procedures on pages 130–131 to calculate the number of treads and their depth. Make the stair treads from two 2×6s separated by a 2×2.

■ Lay out and notch the stringers and toenail them in place with 12d nails.

■ Attach the stringers to the double 2×10 beam with joist hangers.

■ Cut the tread boards to length, ¼ inch shorter than the width of the stairs. This will allow proper air circulation between the end of the treads and the siding.

■ Test the layout of the treads on the stringers, but do not fasten them. Depending on the tread width, there should be an overhang of about 1½ inches.

■ Set the tread boards aside; you will install them after the siding is up.

RAILINGS

Construction of the railing begins by cutting the posts.

■ Cut the posts to length: 33 inches above the decking for 36-inch railings.

STAIR DETAIL

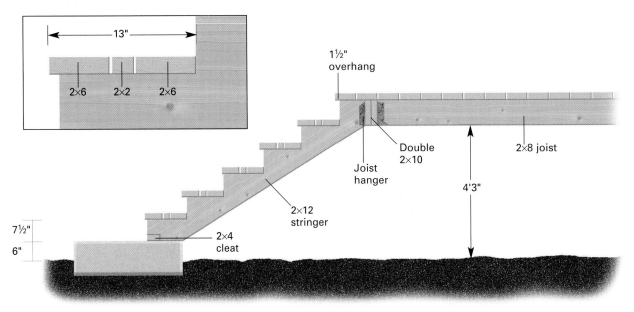

13"

2×6 2×2 2×6

1½" overhang

Double 2×10

Joist hanger

2×8 joist

4'3"

2×12 stringer

7½"

6"

2×4 cleat

■ Nail a 2×4 cap on top of the posts and 2×4 plates between the posts just above the piers. You'll find the plates easier to install if you use framing connectors which will hold the ends of the plates. If you do not use framing clips, toenail the plates to the posts.

■ Measure and cut studs to fit between the bottom plate and the 2×4 cap.

■ Nail the studs in place, 16 inches on center, and toenail them to the beams as well.

SIDING

Fasten sheathing or siding to the framework in the same way you would apply exterior siding (building paper is not necessary).

■ If you use shingles, shakes, or stucco, install CDX plywood sheathing first.

■ Install horizontal wood siding or plywood siding directly to the studs.

■ To prevent moisture from leaking inside the railing, place 15-pound felt or metal flashing over the top plate.

■ Install the 2×8 cap and 1×4 trim.

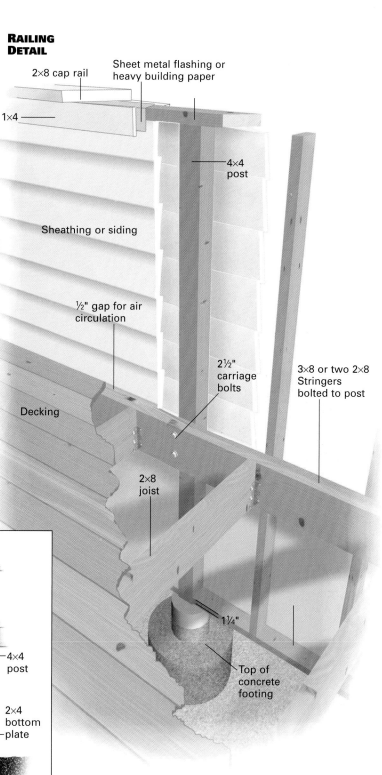

RAILING DETAIL

- 2×8 cap rail
- Sheet metal flashing or heavy building paper
- 1×4
- 4×4 post
- Sheathing or siding
- ½" gap for air circulation
- 2½" carriage bolts
- 3×8 or two 2×8 Stringers bolted to post
- Decking
- 2×8 joist
- 1¼"
- Top of concrete footing

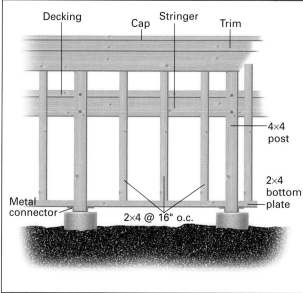

- Decking
- Cap
- Stringer
- Trim
- 4×4 post
- 2×4 bottom plate
- Metal connector
- 2×4 @ 16" o.c.

A MULTILEVEL CASCADE

This seemingly complex deck provides an ideal solution for a steeply-sloping site. Its platforms cascade downhill, providing an outdoor connection between the upper and lower floors of the house.

Built in a series of independent platforms, connected by stairways and steps, this design avoids a problem common to many high decks: it doesn't overshadow and darken the rooms on the lower floor. Downstairs windows of this home still have sunlight and views.

CONSTRUCTION NOTES

The deck system consists of four platforms, two stairways of equal length, and a step between the two lower levels. Two of the platforms are attached to the house with ledgers and two are freestanding.

The freestanding platforms and the outer edges of the attached levels are supported by posts set on concrete piers that extend below the frost line.

The total separation between the highest and lowest platforms will depend on the distance between floor levels in the house and are shown as exactly 10 feet here. This overall separation will of course affect the rise and run of the stairs.

The exact specifications of this project will vary with site conditions and any limitations imposed by local codes, so be sure to either redraw your own plan or change the specifications in the illustrations shown here so your project conforms with the realities of your landscape.

PLAN VIEW INCLUDING POST LOCATION

All dimensions are to post centers or to outside of house.

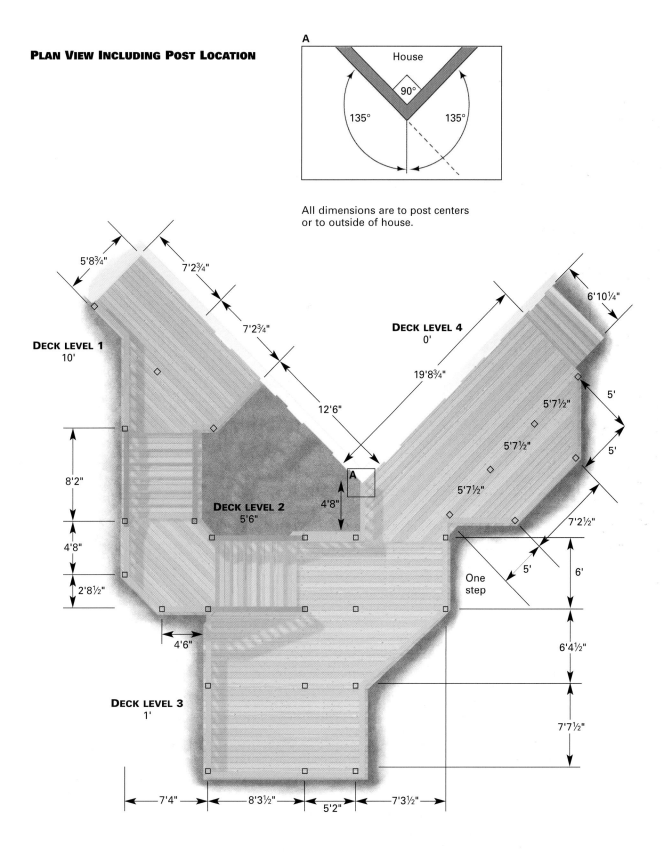

A

House

90°

135°   135°

DECK LEVEL 1
10'

5'8¾"

7'2¾"

7'2¾"

DECK LEVEL 4
0'

6'10¼"

19'8¾"

12'6"

5'7½"

5'

5'7½"

5'

8'2"

DECK LEVEL 2
5'6"

4'8"

5'7½"

A

5'7½"

7'2½"

4'8"

One
step

5'

6'

2'8½"

4'6"

6'4½"

DECK LEVEL 3
1'

7'7½"

7'4"   8'3½"   5'2"   7'3½"

A MULTILEVEL CASCADE
continued

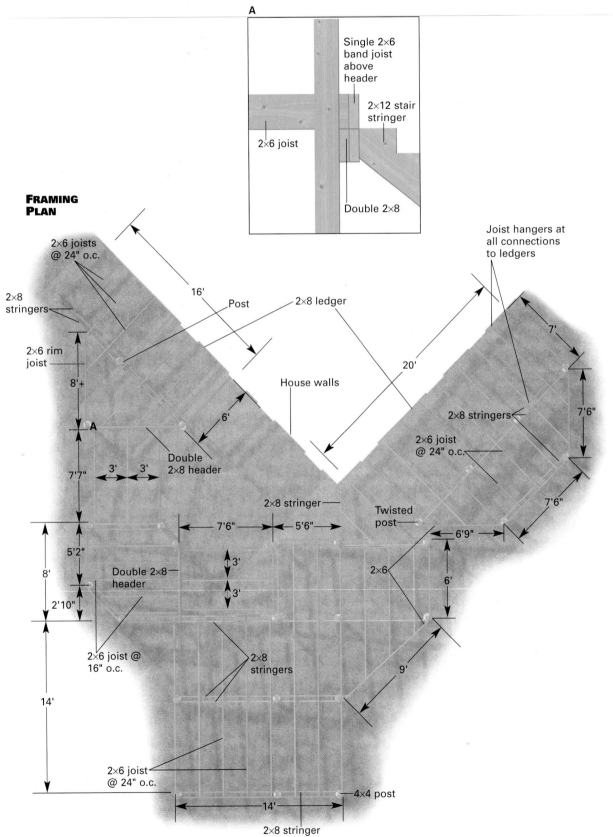

A

Single 2×6 band joist above header

2×12 stair stringer

2×6 joist

Double 2×8

FRAMING PLAN

2×6 joists @ 24" o.c.

2×8 stringers

2×6 rim joist

Post

2×8 ledger

Joist hangers at all connections to ledgers

16'

20'

7'

House walls

8'+

A

Double 2×8 header

6'

2×8 stringers

2×6 joist @ 24" o.c.

7'6"

7'7"

3' 3'

5'2"

7'6"

2×8 stringer

7'6" 5'6"

Twisted post

6'9"

8'

Double 2×8 header

3'

3'

2×6

6'

2'10"

2×6 joist @ 16" o.c.

2×8 stringers

9'

14'

2×6 joist @ 24" o.c.

4×4 post

14'

2×8 stringer

ORGANIZE YOUR WORK

Building this deck may seem like a formidable task, but it will proceed smoothly if you organize your work in sections. Start with the platforms connected to the house first, then proceed to the intermediate platforms.

LAYOUT AND FOOTINGS

Start by laying out the locations of the piers for the uppermost platform, as shown on page 223 in the Plan View Including Post Location and the Framing Plan.

Locate all the piers precisely, because the posts that sit on top of them not only support the floor system, they act as railing posts.
■ Set batter boards, and stretch a length of mason's line parallel to the side of the house along the center of the three main posts.
■ Dig the holes for the footings and piers.
■ Set the forms, and pour the concrete.
■ Insert metal post anchors in the wet concrete, making sure they are in line with one another and facing the right direction.
■ Repeat the process for the lowest platform.

LEDGERS AND POSTS

■ Bolt the 2×8 ledgers to the house, 2½ inches below the floor levels, following the procedures outlined on pages 116–117. Note that the ledger for the lower deck has a 2×8 stringer connected to it near the corner of the house.
■ Bolt the posts to the piers, then plumb and brace them temporarily. Do not cut them to exact length until you've built the deck platform.

STRINGERS AND JOISTS

■ Position the top of the 2×8 stringers 5½ inches below the top of the ledgers, and fasten them to the posts with two ⅜-inch bolts at each post. In most cases, the stringers will extend 1½ inches beyond the posts to carry the outermost joists.
■ Hang double 2×8s at the top of each stairway.
■ Attach the joists to the ledger and rim joist with joist hangers, using 45-degree hangers at 45-degree intersections.
■ Install blocking at the midpoint of any joists longer than 10 feet.

SECTION VIEW

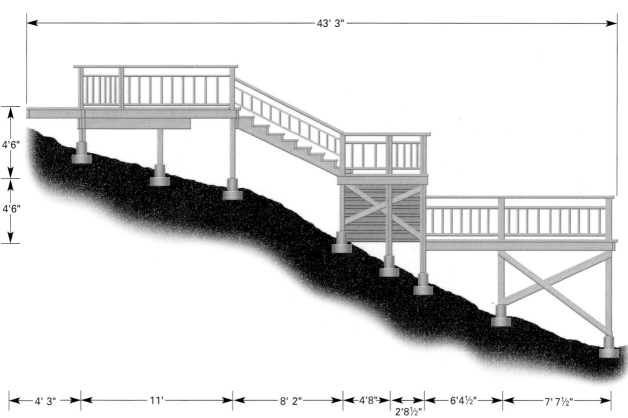

43' 3"

4'6"

4'6"

4' 3" — 11' — 8' 2" — 4'8" — 2'8½" — 6'4½" — 7' 7½"

A MULTILEVEL CASCADE
continued

DECKING

On the small platform between the two stairways, the joists are 16 inches on center, so you can install the decking diagonally to accentuate the deck's direction of flow.

■ Screw the 2×6 decking perpendicular to the joists on the three main platforms.

■ Allow the ends of the decking boards to overhang the band joists 3 or 4 inches.

STAIRS

Each stairway is supported by three 2×12 stringers. The actual dimensions of the stringers will vary depending on the requirements of each site. And, although the exact width of the treads will depend on the run of your stairway, you'll probably be able to use some combination of 2×6s and 2×2s as shown in the *Section Through Upper Platform*.

■ Calculate the rise and run of your stairs.

■ Lay out the stringers and cut them, using the procedures outlined on pages 132–134.

■ Attach the tops of the stringers to the double 2×8s with joist hangers.

■ Fasten the bottoms to the decking boards with wood cleats.

■ Nail the risers to the stringers, and then screw the treads in place.

RAILINGS

The railings in this design are supported by extensions of the 4×4 posts.

■ Measure and cut each post so the top of the cap rail will be 36 inches above the decking (or as local codes require).

■ Attach the framing clips to the posts, then slide the stringers into them.

■ Once the stringers are in place, toenail 2×2 balusters between them, spacing them as required by local codes (usually no more then 4 inches).

■ After the balusters are in place, nail the 2×6 cap rail to the top of the posts.

■ Cut a 2×4 block to fit between the decking and the bottom rail at its midpoint and nail it in place. this will prevent the rail sections from sagging over their 6-foot span.

■ Cut another block to fit between the top rail and the cap rail.

■ Finish the deck with preservative and stain or paint it to match the overall scheme of your landscape design.

MATERIALS LIST

	Quantity	Material	Size
Footings	2.8 cu yd	concrete for 28 piers (8" dia. × 36") and 28 footings (18" dia. × 8")	
	28	metal post anchors	
	56	½"×4½" carriage bolts with nuts and washers	
Framing			
Posts	4	4×4s	4' (approximate heights)
	6	4×4s	6'
	12	4×4s	8'
	6	4×4s	10'
Ledgers	2	2×8s	10'
	1	2×8	16'
Stringers	7	2×8s	8'
	2	2×8s	10'
	3	2×8s	12'
	5	2×8s	14'
	4	2×8s	16'
Band joists	7	2×6s	8'
	3	2×6s	10'
	2	2×6s	12'
	1	2×6	14'
	1	2×6	16'
Joists	10	2×6s	10'
	10	2×6s	12'
	8	2×6s	14'
	4	2×6s	16'
Blocking	6	2×6s	8'
Stair stringers	6	2×12s	10'
Joist hangers	20	2×6s	
	10	2×8s	
	1	45°	
Ledger bolts	60	½"×5" lag bolts and 360 washers	
Stringer bolts	30	⅜"×5½" with nuts and washers	
	28	⅜"×7" with nuts and washers	
	2	⅜"×9" with nuts and washers	
	2	⅜"×12" nuts and washers	
Decking and stair treads	1685 lineal feet	2×6s (700 sq ft of deck + 96 sq ft stairs + 2% waste)	
Railings			
Rails	12	2×4s	10'
	6	2×4s	12'
	6	2×4s	14'
	4	2×4s	16'
Balusters	260 lineal feet	2×2s (cut into 250 2' pieces + waste)	
Cap rail	1	2×6	8'
	5	2×6s	10'
	2	2×6s	12"
Nails	2 lbs	joist hanger nails	
	25 lbs	16d HDG common nails	
	10 lbs	8d HDG finishing nails	
Screws	50 lbs	#8×3½" decking screws	

SECTION THROUGH UPPER PLATFORM

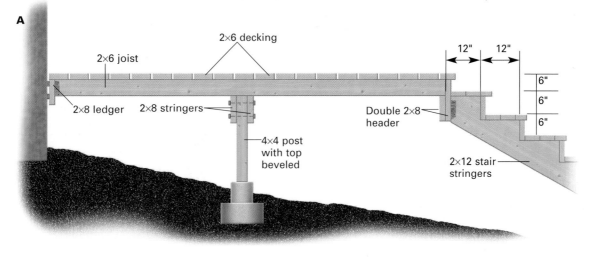

A

2×6 decking

2×6 joist

2×8 ledger

2×8 stringers

4×4 post with top beveled

Double 2×8 header

2×12 stair stringers

12"   12"

6"
6"
6"

SECTION THROUGH LOWER PLATFORM

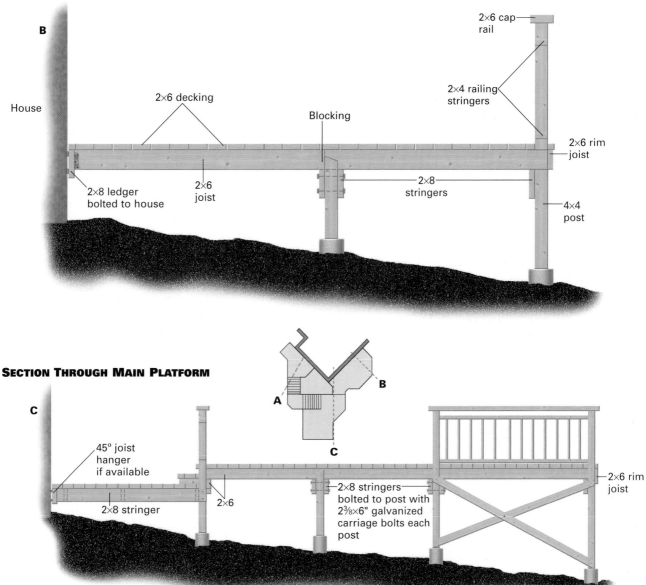

B

2×6 cap rail

2×4 railing stringers

2×6 decking

House

Blocking

2×6 rim joist

2×8 ledger bolted to house

2×6 joist

2×8 stringers

4×4 post

SECTION THROUGH MAIN PLATFORM

C

A

B

C

45° joist hanger if available

2×8 stringer

2×6

2×8 stringers bolted to post with 2⅜×6" galvanized carriage bolts each post

2×6 rim joist

DECK CARE AND REPAIR

A well-built deck will give you years of service and enjoyment, especially with proper maintenance. The outdoor elements, and even normal usage, give wood a tough beating. Rain, wind, snow, and constant exposure to the sun take their toll.

Deck maintenance is a task where little things can go a long way. Simply sweeping and removing debris, for example, minimize the chances of rot causing structural damage. And if you do need to make repairs, doing so quickly will keep a localized problem from becoming a major reconstruction task.

Because you get used to seeing the deck change slowly, you might not remember to clean or refinish it regularly. Make a written calendar to help you stay ahead of the dirt and grime.

Once a year, tighten loose fasteners and check for damaged wood. Most rot occurs in areas that are not easily visible, such as under the decking and at the bottom of posts. To check for rot, poke the lumber with a screwdriver. If it slides in easily, there's a problem. Check joists and beams, too. They're not as likely to rot but are subject to cracking.

Wood that has turned gray can usually be brought back to life by washing with a deck cleaner or a wood bleach. Once you have cleaned it, apply stain or sealer within a few days to prevent the gray from returning.

REFINISHING

Weather takes a toll on all finishes. Even the highest-quality paint needs periodic reapplication. Apply new paint when the old begins to chip or show signs of excessive chalking or wear. Apply a new coat of sealer every two years to protect the wood and to maintain its appearance.

If the surface is dry, it will soak up water like a sponge, promoting not only rot but also cracking when the boards go through a freeze-thaw or wet-dry cycle. Sprinkle a little water on your deck. If it beads up, the boards are protected. If the water soaks in within a minute or two, the wood needs to be sealed.

Before you decide to make extensive—and expensive—changes to your deck, consider the easiest solution. Cleaning and refinishing can give a drab deck a fresh, new look. Many neglected decks mildew, cover with algae, or take on a dingy gray hue. But these conditions are usually only skin deep, and a good cleaning will remedy them.

You'll be surprised how much bigger a clean deck looks—and you may change your mind about making major modifications.

CLEANING YOUR DECK

■ Sweep the surface once a week—more often if the weather requires it.
■ Scrub the deck with warm water and a mild detergent every month.
■ If simple washing does not do the job, or if you want the deck lightened so you can apply an attractive finish, purchase a deck cleaning product.
■ If the wood is in very bad shape, use oxalic acid mixed with water. Scrub the area with a stiff, natural-bristle brush; rinse, allow it to dry, and repeat if necessary. Wear protective clothing; oxalic acid is caustic.
■ To clear away all the dirt at once—along with any debris, dirt stuck in joints, or loose paint—rent a power washer (with 1,200 pounds of pressure). Use a fan tip so you won't tear up the surface, and follow the safety precautions. Used improperly, a power washer can damage the surface of lumber.

REMOVING MOSS AND ALGAE

Mix a solution of 1 ounce laundry soap, 3 ounces trisodium phosphate (TSP) or a nonphosphate TSP substitute, 1 quart chlorine bleach, and 3 quarts water. Brush it on, let it sit for five minutes, and rinse.

HIRING PROFESSIONAL CLEANERS

You can find deck-cleaning companies in the Yellow Pages in many areas. Call around for prices and get a list of references. Visit decks the professionals have cleaned and finished—decks made of the same lumber as yours. If you find just the right finish and color you are looking for, ask the company to do the same for your deck.

TSP is caustic, so wear rubber gloves and eye protection.

REMOVING MILDEW

A slimy black surface indicates mildew, which rarely causes a structural problem but is unsightly and gives off an unpleasant odor. Clean a mildewed area with a bleach solution, and improve the ventilation so the wood can dry out when it gets wet.

Solutions of bleach and water or cleaners with oxalic acid can remove mildew stains and inhibit the growth of new mildew. Apply these products on cloudy days, and rinse thoroughly.

Wood rots when it can't dry out—and rot is usually hidden from view. Check the underside of stair treads, stringers, and decking, and the tops and bottoms of the posts. Poke the wood with a screwdriver. If it feels spongy, rot has begun. A half inch of soft wood may require replacement of the rotted member.

DECK CARE AND REPAIR
continued

WET AND DRY ROT

Sitting moisture is the worst enemy of wood. It's the primary cause of wet or dry rot.
■ Wet rot is black and spongy or has dark brown strands.
■ Dry rot is lighter in color but just as soft; it actually thrives in moist conditions.
   Take steps to ensure that the wood can dry out, or see that it is completely covered with

Stair stringers are especially susceptible to rot. Here, the joint between the stringer and the deck has rotted, causing a hazard. Another area prone to rot is just below the treads, where they rest on a part of the stringer that has been cut.

paint. Cracked paint allows water in and makes it hard for the moisture to evaporate—a dangerous combination. Often, the best prevention is as simple as sweeping away collected leaves so that air and sunlight can get to the wood.
   Rot weakens the wood and is a structural problem that requires immediate attention. If a rotted section is small and not weakening a structural member, you might be able to get by with an application of epoxy hardener. Most rotted boards, however—especially beams, joists, and posts—need replacement. When replacing rotted wood, use pressure-treated lumber.

WOOD-EATING INSECTS

Thin channels drilled along grain lines indicate the presence of wood-eating insects, such as termites or carpenter ants. Because they like to eat in darkness, most of the damage is usually done by the time it's visible. Check for insect damage by rapping on lumber and listening for a hollow sound or by sticking an awl in suspected boards. Inspect

any lumber near or touching the ground, especially pieces that are attached to the foundation. Repair a damaged section as discussed below. Then call an exterminator.

PATCHING SURFACE DAMAGE

You may be able to repair small areas of surface damage (no more than about 3/8 inch thick) by cleaning them out and patching the area with an exterior-grade wood putty or an epoxy patching compound (it's actually harder than the wood).
   Fill holes with exterior wood putty. Vinyl spackling compound and ready-mixed wood filler won't stand up to outdoor stresses or exposed standing water. "Plastic" fillers may not bond well with the surrounding wood. Use only filler designed for outdoor use.
   Push the filler into the hole with a putty knife, leaving a little excess. When it's dry, sand it smooth and apply a finish.

Rotting wood may not look different than preserved wood, but it is very soft. Check for rot with a screwdriver, and apply hardener to softened sections—or replace them.

Termites and carpenter ants can cause severe damage. The best remedy for infestation is prevention, so make sure your deck is sealed against insects, or use a preservative that repels them.

REPLACING DAMAGED DECKING

Damaged decking can be dangerous.
To replace it, locate the joists on each side of the damaged area. Drill a starter hole and use a keyhole saw or saber saw to cut out the damage flush with the joists. Fasten a cleat to the side of the joist, flush with the bottom edge of the decking. Cut a new piece of decking, scrub it with a solution of 1 cup baking soda and 1 gallon water to give it a weathered look, and fasten it to the cleats.

REPLACING BEAMS AND JOISTS

This is a job you can tackle yourself.
■ First tack a piece of 2×6 scrap under the damaged section.
■ Set a screw jack (preferred to a hydraulic jack) under the 2x6, and support it on a concrete block. Set the jack on another 2×6 on the block.

■ Raise the jack until it touches the 2×6.
■ Cut 2× braces to span 3 feet beyond the damaged section on each side, and fasten the braces to both sides of the beam or joist with lag screws.

Wood that weathers poorly can separate, creating splits and splinters. Fill and sand minor splits, and sand off splinters. Seriously damaged boards should be replaced.

Nail heads that rise above the decking surface should be driven back in. If they won't stay down, replace them with decking screws.

Damaged electrical wiring, especially for line-voltage systems, is dangerous. Disconnect power at the service panel and replace any frayed or nicked wires. Take the same precautions with low-voltage systems.

Over time, joints between framing members can work loose. Most can be held in place and reinforced with additional fasteners or new hardware. Pay extra attention to stair stringers.

Railings can separate from their supports. If a railing feels loose or weak, replace the fasteners.

REPAIRING RAILINGS AND STAIRS

Deck railings and stairs can prove challenging to repair because their fasteners are often hidden. Because they receive almost constant use, they are often the first part of a deck that needs attention.

REPAIRING RAILINGS

Loose posts and balusters might crack or come out altogether, so solve the problem while it is a quick fix.

POSTS: Railing posts handle a lot of abuse, and they often come loose because they are anchored only at the bottom.

Some railing posts are anchored to an end joist or header; stair posts are often tied only to the stringer and stair tread. Here's what you do to repair a post:

First try tightening the existing fastener. If that doesn't work, you'll have to employ more extreme measures.
- Drill pilot holes in the base of the post and countersink or counterbore the holes.
- Drive hefty screws into the stringer and tread.

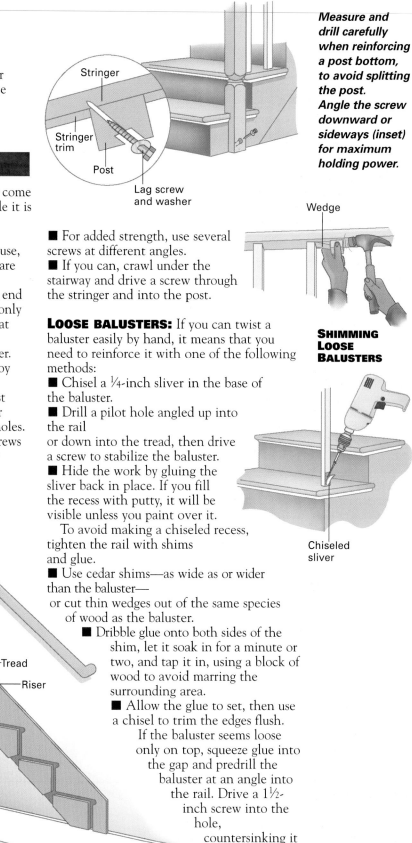

Measure and drill carefully when reinforcing a post bottom, to avoid splitting the post. Angle the screw downward or sideways (inset) for maximum holding power.

SHIMMING LOOSE BALUSTERS

Chiseled sliver

- For added strength, use several screws at different angles.
- If you can, crawl under the stairway and drive a screw through the stringer and into the post.

LOOSE BALUSTERS: If you can twist a baluster easily by hand, it means that you need to reinforce it with one of the following methods:
- Chisel a ¼-inch sliver in the base of the baluster.
- Drill a pilot hole angled up into the rail or down into the tread, then drive a screw to stabilize the baluster.
- Hide the work by gluing the sliver back in place. If you fill the recess with putty, it will be visible unless you paint over it.

To avoid making a chiseled recess, tighten the rail with shims and glue.
- Use cedar shims—as wide as or wider than the baluster— or cut thin wedges out of the same species of wood as the baluster.
- Dribble glue onto both sides of the shim, let it soak in for a minute or two, and tap it in, using a block of wood to avoid marring the surrounding area.
- Allow the glue to set, then use a chisel to trim the edges flush. If the baluster seems loose only on top, squeeze glue into the gap and predrill the baluster at an angle into the rail. Drive a 1½-inch screw into the hole, countersinking it

slightly.

REPLACING A BALUSTER: Remove a damaged baluster by sawing it in half, then twisting it loose with a pipe wrench.

Getting a baluster to match can be difficult. You may find a matching baluster at a good lumberyard. If not, call around to find a woodworker who can duplicate balusters.

Wedge

Underside of stairs

TREADS AND RISERS

Evaluate the condition of your stairs by having someone walk on them while you watch closely. You may be surprised to find that some of the treads flex noticeably. If so, you should solve the problem right away.

SQUEAKS: You may be able to live with squeaking deck stairs, but a loose step is potentially dangerous. If there is no major flexing but a step makes an annoying squeak, you can usually solve the problem quickly.
■ If the squeak comes from the front of the tread, drill pilot holes and drive screws down through the tread and into the riser.
■ If the rear of the tread squeaks, work from underneath the stairway and drive screws up through the tread and into the riser.
■ To fix from above, tap glue-coated shims into the joint between the tread and riser, and trim them flush when the glue has set.

LOOSE TREADS: If the treads are very loose, a stringer may be damaged, or it may have moved outward so it no longer supports the tread adequately. You have to get under the stairs to fix this. If the area beneath the stairs is covered, remove two or more treads and risers to get under it. For extensive repairs, it may be less trouble in the long run to cut out any sheathing or covering to give you access.

A sagging or cracked stringer can be reinforced by attaching 2×4s running vertically up from the decking or by attaching a strip of ¾-inch plywood to the side of the stringer with lots of screws.

Treads on a closed stringer whose treads are set in dadoes are often snugged into the dado with vertical and horizontal wedges. Sometimes just hammering the wedges back into place will do the job.

If the treads and risers are pulling out of the stringer, use pieces of ¾-inch plywood to provide new support. Drill pilot holes for all screws, or you may crack the stringer.

To support sagging treads, install a carriage brace (*at right*). Construct the brace from 2×6s and install it along the length of the

stairway, in the middle.

REPLACING A TREAD OR
RISER: To remove a tread or riser, work carefully to avoid splitting adjoining boards.
■ Remove any trim first.
■ Use a flat pry bar (*above right*) to pry in several directions. If you can get underneath, you may be able to tap the piece loose. You can often pry up the tread, then hammer it back down in order to pop the nails up.
■ If the pieces do not respond to prying, saw a riser in half lengthwise.
■ Replace treads with the same wood. For maximum strength, make sure it's as free of knots and as close-grained as you can find.

Use the old tread or riser as a template for cutting the new one. If the front edge of the tread is beveled,

Pry carefully to remove treads or risers without damaging the adjacent boards.

Carriage braces reinforce sagging stair treads.

Carriage brace

GLOSSARY

3-4-5 method. A technique for checking whether a corner is square. Determined by marking a point 3 feet from the corner along one side, and 4 feet from the corner along the other side. When the diagonal distance between the marks is 5 feet, the corner is square.

Actual dimensions. The actual physical dimension of a board or masonry unit as it is measured. See Nominal dimensions.

Aggregate: Gravel, sand, or crushed rock mixed with portland cement and water to form concrete.

Anchor: A metal device set in concrete for attaching posts to footings or piers.

Awl: A sharp-pointed tool used for starting small holes for screws or for scribing lines.

Baby sledge. A small sledgehammer, usually 2½ pounds, used for a variety of construction tasks and repairs where more weight is needed than can be supplied by a carpenter's hammer.

Backfilling. Replacing earth excavated during the construction process. A material other than the original earth may be used to improve the drainage or structure of the soil.

Baluster: A vertical railing member between the top and bottom rails.

Base: A prepared surface of gravel or sand designed to support bricks, pavers, or concrete.

Batter board: A 2×4 frame supported by stakes set back from the corners of a structure.

Beam: A horizontal timber supported by posts that holds up joists and decking; can be made of a single board or built up from two or more. Also called a girder

Blocking: Short lengths of lumber fitted perpendicularly between joists to stabilize them.

Bracing: Diagonal crosspieces nailed and bolted between tall posts or other structural members.

Building codes: Local rules governing the way structures may be built or modified.

Butt joint: A joint formed by two pieces of material fastened end to end, end to face, or end to edge.

Cantilever: The portion of a joist, or of an entire deck, that extends beyond the beam

Carpenter's level: A tool for establishing level over short distances.

Catch basin: A hole in the ground for collecting water; often connected to a drainpipe.

Cement: A powdered mix of gypsum and other materials that serves as the binding element in concrete and mortar.

Chamfer. To bevel a piece of lumber.

Concrete. A mixture of portland cement, fine aggregate (sand), course aggregate (gravel or crushed stone), and water. Concrete becomes harder and stronger with age.

Curing. The process of aging new concrete with proper moisture to reduce cracking and shrinkage and to develop strength.

Dimension lumber: A piece of lumber that has been dried and cut to modular dimensions. Refers to boards at least 2 inches wide and 2 inches thick.

Drainage trench: A shallow excavation for carrying water away from higher ground.

Dry-stacked wall: A wall of masonry units (stones) laid without mortar.

Dry well: A hole in the ground dug at a level below grade (a patio site, for example) and connected to the site by a drainpipe.

Durable species: Wood species that are naturally resistant to decay and insect damage, such as heart redwood, heart cedar, tidewater cypress, and some locusts.

Earth-wood clearance: The minimum distance required between any wood and the ground; exceptions are made for pressure-treated or durable-species lumber specified for ground contact

Edging: A border used to contain and define a surface; common materials are brick, concrete, plastic, and wood. Also, the rounded edges of a concrete slab that are resistant to cracking.

Elevation: A drawing of a proposed structure as it should look from the side.

Excavation. Earth dug to a level that is hard and uniformly graded.

Fascia: Horizontal trim that covers the ends of decking boards and part or all of the rim joist or header joist.

Finish. A coating, such as stain, water repellent, or paint, applied to a surface to protect it against weathering.

Flagstone: Irregularly shaped flat, natural stone, such as granite, bluestone, redstone, sandstone, limestone, and slate.

Flashing: Aluminum, copper, or galvanized sheet metal used to cover joints where moisture might enter a structure.

Flush: On the same plane as, or level with, the surrounding surface.

Footing. The bottom portion of any foundation or pier. The footing distributes the weight of the structure into the ground. For decks, it often refers to the concrete structure consisting of the pier as well as its footing.

Formwork. The wooden forms used to shape wet concrete.

Frost heave. The movement or upheaval of the ground when there is alternate freezing and thawing of water in the soil. This is one of the reasons why concrete slabs crack, making control joints necessary.

Frost line. The lowest depth at which the ground will freeze. It determines the code-required depth for footings.

Galvanized nails: Nails dipped in zinc rather than electroplated; preferred for outdoor construction.

Grade: The top surface of the ground; also describes the action of removing soil to level the ground surface.

Grout: A thin mortar mixture used to fill the joints between tiles.

Hardscape. Those elements in a landscape that are made of wood, stone, or other hard, permanent materials.

Header joist: The joist attached to the ends of inner joists; the horizontal structural board farthest from the ledger.

Joist: Any 2× lumber, set on edge to support decking and in turn is supported by beams, ledgers, or stringers.

Joist hanger: A metal connector for attaching a joist to a ledger or header joist so the top edges are flush.

KDAT (kiln dried after treatment): Pressure-treated lumber that has been dried after being treated with preservative; more expensive than undried pressure-treated lumber but less likely to warp.

Lag screw or bolt. A heavy-duty screw with a hex head for attaching structural members to a wall or to material too thick for a machine bolt to go through.

Landscape fabric: Tightly woven fabric that allows water to flow through but prevents weeds from growing.

Lap joint: The joint formed when one member overlaps another.

Ledger: A 2× or thicker piece of lumber attached to a house for supporting the ends of joists.

Level: The condition that exists when any type of surface is at true horizontal. Also, a hand tool for determining this condition.

Loads: Weights and forces that a structure is designed to withstand; includes dead load (the structure itself) and live loads (occupants and furnishings, snow, wind uplift, and earthquake forces).

Mason's line. The twine used to lay out posts, patios, footings, and structures. Preferred because it will not stretch and sag, as regular string does.

Masonry cement: A mix of portland cement and hydrated lime for preparing mortar.

Miter joint: The joint formed when two members meet that have been cut at the same angle, usually 45 degrees.

Modular. A term describing a unit of material whose dimensions are proportional to each other.

Mortar. A mixture of cement, fine aggregate, and water used to bond bricks, blocks, or stones.

Mud-jacking. The process by which fallen sections of a concrete slab can be raised to level by injecting a mixture of mud and concrete under them.

Nominal dimensions: The stated dimensions of a masonry unit or board, representing the proportion of one dimension to the other. Often refers to the actual dimension such material occupies, including its mortar or grout. For masonry, it includes the thickness of the mortar joints on one end and at the top or bottom. See Actual dimensions.

Pier. A small concrete or masonry structure that holds a post off the ground. It has its own footing and can be precast or cast in place.

Plan drawing: An overhead view of a structure, that shows locations of footings and framing.

Plumb: The condition that exists when a surface is at true vertical.

Plumb bob: A tool used to align points vertically.

Portland cement. A type (not a brand name) of cement that is a basic ingredient of concrete and mortar.

Post: A vertical framing piece, usually 4×4 or 6×6, used to support a beam or a joist.

GLOSSARY
continued

Premix: Any of several packaged mixtures of ingredients for preparing concrete or mortar.
Pressure-treated wood: Lumber or plywood soaked in a solution to make the wood resistant to water. One commonly used pressure treatment is waterborne chromated copper arsenate (CCA). CCA specified for aboveground use is labeled LP-2 or 0.25. CCA rated for ground contact is labeled LP-22 or 0.40 .

Ready-mix concrete. Wet concrete that is ready to pour, transported in a truck from a concrete supplier.
Reinforcing bar: A steel rod for reinforcing concrete, sometimes called rebar or rerod.
Reinforcing mesh. Steel wires welded into a grid of 6- or 10-inch squares and embedded in concrete. Ties a concrete pad together to minimize cracking.
Retaining wall: A wall constructed to hold soil in place.
Rim joist: A joist at the outer side of a deck; may refer to any joist on the perimeter of the deck.
Riser: The vertical portion of a step.
River rock: Medium-size stones that have been smoothed by river or lake water.
Rubble: Uncut stone, often used for dry-stacked walls.
Scratch coat: The first coat of mortar or plaster, roughened (scratched) so the next coat will stick to it.
Screed: A straightedge used to level concrete as it is poured into a form or to level the sand base in a form.

Screening: The maximum opening allowed between railing members; distances vary by code.
Set: The process during which mortar or concrete hardens.
Setback: The minimum distance between a property line and any structure, as defined by local building codes.

Site plan: A map showing the location of a new building project on a piece of property.
Sleeper: A horizontal wood member laid directly on the ground, patio, or roof for supporting a deck.
Slope: Ground with an inclined surface, usually measured in vertical rise per horizontal distance.
Small sledge. See Baby sledge.
Span: The distance between supports, measured center to center.
Spindle: A small-dimension baluster.
Square: The condition that exists when one surface is at a 90-degree angle to another. Also, the hand tool used to determine this condition.
Stringer: A heavy, inclined member that supports stair treads; can be solid, with treads attached between the stringers, or cut out, with treads resting on top of the sawtooth sections.
Sub-base: Soil or gravel, compacted to hold a base surface of gravel or sand.
Swale. A shallow depression made in a landscape used to collect runoff. See Drainage trench.

Tamper: A tool for compacting soil, sand, or other loose materials.
Trowel: A flat and oblong or flat and pointed metal tool used for handling or finishing concrete and mortar.
Troweling. Giving the concrete a smooth final finish with a steel trowel. This step is for interior applications; it creates an extremely smooth and possibly slippery surface.

Water level: A tool composed of two clear plastic tubes that attach to a hose, used for establishing level over long distances or irregular surfaces.
Weep hole: An opening made in a mortar joint to allow water to drain through.

Yard: A unit of volume by which ready-mix concrete, for example, is sold; equal to a square yard (27 cubic feet).

Zoning requirements: Ordinances that affect deck size or location, such as setback limits (distance from property line to structure), lot coverage (percentage of lot that can be covered by improvements), and deck size and height.

INDEX

METRIC CONVERSIONS

U.S. Units to Metric Equivalents			Metric Units to U.S. Equivalents		
To Convert From	Multiply By	To Get	To Convert From	Multiply By	To Get
Inches	25.4	Millimeters	Millimeters	0.0394	Inches
Inches	2.54	Centimeters	Centimeters	0.3937	Inches
Feet	30.48	Centimeters	Centimeters	0.0328	Feet
Feet	0.3048	Meters	Meters	3.2808	Feet
Yards	0.9144	Meters	Meters	1.0936	Yards
Square inches	6.4516	Square centimeters	Square centimeters	0.1550	Square inches
Square feet	0.0929	Square meters	Square meters	10.764	Square feet
Square yards	0.8361	Square meters	Square meters	1.1960	Square yards
Acres	0.4047	Hectares	Hectares	2.4711	Acres
Cubic inches	16.387	Cubic centimeters	Cubic centimeters	0.0610	Cubic inches
Cubic feet	0.0283	Cubic meters	Cubic meters	35.315	Cubic feet
Cubic feet	28.316	Liters	Liters	0.0353	Cubic feet
Cubic yards	0.7646	Cubic meters	Cubic meters	1.308	Cubic yards
Cubic yards	764.55	Liters	Liters	0.0013	Cubic yards

To convert from degrees Fahrenheit (F) to degrees Celsius (C), first subtract 32, then multiply by $\frac{5}{9}$.

To convert from degrees Celsius to degrees Fahrenheit, multiply by $\frac{9}{5}$, then add 32.